Mockridge,
You're Slipping!

Books by Norton Mockridge

* In collaboration with Robert H. Prall.

Norton Mockridge

Mockridge, You're Slipping!

DRAWINGS BY JERRY SCHLAMP

The John Day Company
New York

FOR VAL

*A peek into a world
she never knew*

Prologue

IT was cold and bleak, that Thanksgiving Day in 1940, and a few flakes of snow were fluttering outside the windows of the city room of the White Plains *Daily Reporter*.

I stood there in that small city room where I'd worked night and day for nearly four and a half years, and realized, with a chill, that it was the last time I'd ever stand there. I had been fired the day before and now the fat, balding little man sitting in front of me was telling me why.

The night before, after I'd received my dismissal slip, he'd told me that my job as a reporter hadn't been filled yet, and that if I'd come in the next day, Thanksgiving, we'd talk it over. So, I had driven the 16 miles from my home to the Daily Reporter Building in White Plains—only to find that the little man had changed his mind. He didn't want to talk it over at all.

He was Walter V. Hogan, editor and half owner of the *Reporter*, and a man who, in my estimation, was on the verge of a nervous breakdown. Hogan, sitting at his desk, pushed his glasses forward on his nose and peered over them, fixing me with a chilling stare.

He mentioned several things I'd done which had displeased him—such as trying to get more pictures into the paper, trying to prevent him from firing seasoned reporters and replacing them with $15-a-week high school kids, and writing what he called a "lousy" review of a theatrical production.

"But," he said, leaning forward and sneering a bit, "none of those is the main reason. The main reason is:

"Mockridge, you're slipping! And you've been slipping for a long time!"

I thought the man was insane. Nobody had worked harder for the *Reporter* than I. Nobody had put in longer hours—without overtime—and nobody, with the exception of the city editor, had done more things to improve the paper and increase its circulation. I began a reply, but Hogan went on:

"I tell you, Mockridge, you're slipping. I don't want any guy on my staff who's slipping. You're through!"

Well, I had quite a temper in those days and my impulse was to lean over, yank Hogan out of the chair and punch him through the window behind him. Somehow I fought down that tiger and contented myself with expressing my opinion of him in a few, well-balanced sentences. Then I left.

But, as I walked out of the building for the last time, I looked back and I had tears in my eyes.

I was slipping. I was out of a job. I was a has-been.

And I was only twenty-five years old.

Chapter One

I STARTED slipping when I was just twenty-two months old. Up until that time I'd been quite a success in life. I was a pretty, rosy-cheeked baby with a few freckles nicely placed here and there. I had tousled, reddish-gold hair and a quick and winning smile. I'd been drooled over by ladies, patted on the head by gentlemen, and adored by my parents and relatives.

Then, one hot July afternoon in 1917, something happened

9

on the beach at Atlantic Highlands, New Jersey, that changed the whole picture. I was sitting in the sun, wearing a blue woolen bathing suit that extended from my neck to just below my knees, and I was loading sand into my blue and yellow pail with my little red shovel. I was having a wonderful time, when along came a motion picture crew.

There was a director attired in riding breeches, puttees, a belted and pleated coat and a wide-brimmed fedora, and carrying a megaphone. There was a cameraman, wearing his cap backwards, and carrying a hand-operated camera on a tripod. And there was a tall, voluptuous, flaming red-haired actress with an enormous bosom. She was wearing something akin to an evening gown and, as she sloshed through the sand in her evening slippers, she kept swearing softly to herself.

Suddenly, she spotted me.

"Look, look, Harry!" she shouted to the director. "We don't have to go any farther. Look at that kid there. The one with the red hair. That's the one I want!"

And so, at the precious age of twenty-two months, my big moment had come. I was about to launch my motion picture career. And I had a big jump on my contemporary, Jackie Coogan. Although he already had toddled onstage and had played a couple of bits in the flicks, he was still nearly four years away from doing *The Kid* with Charlie Chaplin.

Anyway, the actress trudged over to me, cursing the sand that filled her shoes, and said something like, "Hello, nice baby. You wanna be in the picture with me? You're beautiful! You look just like me—and so you be my baby in the picture, huh?"

I, of course, don't remember what she said or did. But my father and mother saw and heard everything, and my father never let me forget one bit of it for the rest of his life. He told the story, I suppose, a thousand times and, curiously enough, with painful fidelity. He never embellished it. He didn't have to. No father, apparently, ever was more shaken by a son's actions.

Accustomed as I was to lots of cooing and chucking under

10

the chin, I smiled at the nice, big-bosomed lady and I gurgled happily and batted my beautiful blue eyes. Encouraged, she bent over and picked me up and held me against her bosom. I imagine that I was quite startled at being picked up by a strange woman, especially one with such flaming red hair, but at first I did nothing.

Crowds, attracted by the camera and the spectacle of the evening-gowned woman on the beach, began to gather and they formed a huge circle around us. The director started to talk to my father to arrange a suitable payment for my forthcoming performance as the redhead's baby, but they never came to terms.

The actress swung around and started to carry me toward the camera which was propped up in the sand, and I got a look at all those hundreds of faces staring at me. I didn't like being carried, either, and so I began to protest.

At first I just yelled a few times. "Hush, nice baby," said the actress. "Be quiet and watch the birdie."

My mother, who had been tagging along, said: "Now be a good boy, Norton. Mind the nice lady."

"Yaaaaaaaaaaaaaaaaah!" I yelled. My father and the director rushed over.

"Nice baby," said the director, chucking me under the chin. I screamed at that, and began to kick. Tears started to flow, and I wriggled around, and opened my mouth as wide as possible and yelled and yelled.

"Jesus, Harry," said the actress, "this kid kicks hard." The director grabbed my feet, but I kicked harder and broke his grip.

Then, with both feet, I kicked the actress in the stomach. She grunted, and I did it again and again. I clutched her hair with both hands and pulled with all my might. She screamed.

"Leggo, you damn kid," she cried. "Harry, for God's sake, get this thing off me!"

The crowd now was roaring with laughter, and the director, the cameraman and my father put out their hands to take hold

11

of me. But I, my eyes wild with terror and my screams hitting C over high C, started to scramble up the actress' imposing façade. I was trying to get away, I guess, but my strategy was poor. And so was my sense of direction.

As I climbed up the actress, my right foot, shod in a wet, sand-covered blue bathing shoe, slipped into her cleavage, and sank a good 12 inches.

The gown she was wearing was extremely low-cut, and it had a bodice that was held together in front by a crisscross lacing of some sort.

And when the poor woman felt that sand-covered foot slash down between her breasts, she shrieked in pain, indignation and anguish and, I do believe, she tried to hit me.

This infuriated me all the more. I clenched my chubby little fists and began to pound her face. Somehow I got twisted around and my foot, deep in the cleavage, twisted too, and it shot out through the lower part of the lacing. And there it stuck.

The actress couldn't pull me out. And she certainly didn't want to push the rest of me through. By now her hair was a mess, lipstick and blue mascara and sweat and tears were smeared all over her face, and she had my foot sticking out of her bosom. Everybody was helpless with laughter, and nobody could tell who was doing the most yelling—she or I.

She, however, was the madder. And she showed it by slapping my sunburned face. I didn't wait a second. I bit her on the nose. Baby teeth are quite sharp, and this had a most painful effect. Agonized, she staggered backward, fell over something, and crashed to the sand.

My father, leaping forward, took advantage of a temporary slack in the bodice to push my foot back through the lacing and to pluck me off the lady.

Well, as it turned out, by the time they picked the actress up, dusted off the sand, washed her face and got her put together again, she no longer desired me as her movie son. In fact, she stamped off the beach in an almost hysterical rage, and

12

I don't know whether she ever returned to make the picture or not.

I do know, however, that the little incident had put quite a damper on my theatrical career, and it had embarrassed my father so much that he packed us up and left the beach within an hour or so. In his bachelor days, he'd spent a couple of summers there as a life guard and, until this unhappy moment, he'd been regarded as a big man on the beach. With his friends' laughter still stinging his ears, he never again returned to the Atlantic Highlands. And he never forgot to remind me every once in a while that I had blown my chance at stardom even before I went before the camera.

Whether by accident, or out of sympathy for my father, I caused no more trouble for quite a time. And my mother often told me later that Dad wasn't really sorry that he'd sired me. "He just SAYS so," my mother explained.

In any case, I didn't slip again until 1919. And that was in the tiny hamlet of Stamford, New York, in the Catskill Mountains. My father had become quite ill in 1918—I think it was due more to overwork during and after the war than to the effect I had on him—and his employers, the New York Telephone Co., had suggested that he take a year or so in the mountains to rest and recover.

He went there for a few months by himself, and then my mother and I, and my newly arrived brother, Roger, joined him. Dad had rented a charming black and white frame house on a hill overlooking a fine, green valley, and we lived there for a year or so, quite happily. Dad raised chickens, more or less for occupational therapy, and I was privileged to collect the eggs every day. I seldom dropped more than one or two.

Our good friends were the Will Canfields who owned the local stable and the filling station. Whenever it snowed, and it seemed to me it snowed nine months a year, Mr. Canfield would get out a spirited horse and a fast cutter, and away we'd go. One afternoon, as we rounded a bend, my baby brother fell

13

out of the cutter and into a bank of snow. I noticed it, but I was afraid that if I told Mr. Canfield about it, he'd stop and the ride would be over. So I said nothing until we returned home.

My father, as I remember it, was not impressed by this expression of my judgment, but I don't think he made his displeasure felt in any physical way. In fact, I think he and Mr. Canfield spent the next two hours digging in each and every snowbank along the way until they found my brother, securely bundled in his blanket, and sound asleep.

Where I fell into extreme disfavor, however, was in the matter of the chickens. In the autumn of 1919, my father, having recovered, notified the telephone company that he was ready to resume work and they directed him to report to the central office in the village of Mount Kisco, in Westchester County, about 35 miles from New York City.

So, Mother and Dad began to close down the Stamford house. They packed everything we owned—clothes, dishes, silverware and such—and stuffed it into or tied it onto our Model T touring car. I might say here that this Model T, and I mean no slight to Henry Ford, was an ornery vehicle to say the least.

One of the few things that people who lived in Stamford could do, of an evening, was to get into their cars and drive 30 miles to Oneonta, a metropolis then of about 5,000 souls which was noted principally for its milk cows and the manufacture of women's silk underwear. People, however, didn't drive there for either milk or underwear; they usually went to Oneonta because it was the only place within 50 miles or more where you could buy ice cream.

My father purely loved ice cream and he was willing to suffer to get it. And suffer he did. The Model T would start off brightly enough, with Mother in back with my brother, and me up front with Dad, but very soon we'd begin to strike big, thick, fat, juicy yellow bugs, and within a short time the windshield would be covered with something like yellow goose grease and you couldn't see the road. There was no sense in trying to wipe

14

this stuff off. It stuck like glue. So, my father, a brave man, would flip open the windshield, fastening it up with the adjustable screws, and we'd career along at 28 miles per hour.

This meant, of course, that the bugs now hit us directly in the face. But Dad tightened his jaw, and drove on. Then—and I believe this happened almost every time we went to Oneonta —the Model T would hit a crater in the road, and the windshield would fly loose from its ratchets, crash on the hood of the car, and shower us all with glass.

My father took this with great patience, but he did lose his temper, now and then, especially when the Model T produced more flat tires than he thought par for the course. One night, my mother told me later, we had no fewer than eight flats on the round trip. There were no service stations along the road in those days, and each driver repaired blowouts and punctures by jacking up the car, removing the wheel, taking off the tire, ripping out the tube, vulcanizing a patch onto the tube, stuffing it back into the tire, remounting the tire (taking extreme care to see that the steel tension ring that held the tire in place didn't fly off and hit you in the mouth), pumping up the tire and then lowering the car and proceeding.

Each time, of course, you had to start the car's engine again. You did this by cranking. And this particular Model T didn't like to be cranked. Once the crank flew out and hit my father on the shin. Another time it sort of kicked backwards and broke his wrist. But no matter how much travail, there is no record of my father's having failed to make it from Stamford to Oneonta and return—or of his missing out on the ice cream.

But, to get back to the chickens. This little matter was the beginning of what became known as my "open-door–closed-door policy," a situation that seemed to plague my father inordinately and even cause him various injuries.

When Mother and Father decided to leave the Stamford house and go back to New York City, from whence we'd come, to spend a few weeks' vacation before reporting to the Mount Kisco office, Dad first thought of selling our chickens. Then he changed his mind. Better, he said, to slaughter them and take them to our relatives and friends as gifts.

Mother agreed, and they made a list of which chicken was going to whom. Then Dad killed all our 24 chickens and he and Mother plucked them, turning the kitchen into something that looked like the aftermath of a pillow fight, and they cleaned and dressed the chickens and put them in the huge icebox that stood in the pantry just outside the kitchen.

On the day that we were to leave, Dad rigged up a sort of insulated box which he put in the back seat of the Model T and half filled with ice. "We'll put the chickens on the ice," he told Mother, "and they should last nicely till we get to New York."

He then opened the door to the pantry and announced to one and all: "Leave this door open so it'll remind me to get the chickens out of the icebox at the last minute."

Well, time moved along and we all helped load the car. On one of my trips, I noticed that the door to the pantry was open and, since I'd always been told to keep it closed, I closed it. Then, happy as larks, everybody bundled into the car and we were ready for the big, 170-mile trip to New York. Dad took a firm grip on the crank and spun it around three or four times. Nothing happened. He muttered a little and gave it a few more twirls. Nothing. Then, snarling a bit, he gave it a vicious going around and all of a sudden the engine caught, kicked the crank backwards and broke Dad's wrist again.

Despite the pain, he drove to the local doctor and had the wrist set in splints. Then, gritting his teeth, he took off for New York. Well, it was a hot day, and the car boiled over four or five times, and there were three or four flats—which were not easy for Dad to repair, what with the broken wrist, and all— but on the whole he wasn't especially unhappy. Not until we reached Kingston, that is.

At Kingston, about halfway to New York, Dad said to Mother, "Look in the box and see how the chickens are doing. Maybe we'll have to stop for more ice."

Mother looked in—and even today, about 45 years later, I can still hear the cry she let out. She didn't have to tell my father. He knew.

"Goddammit," he cried. "Who closed that pantry door?"

Manfully, like George Washington, I said, "I did it, sir."

"WHY!!!" roared my father.

"Because," I said, "everybody always told me to keep it shut, and so I shut it."

I've been close to death quite a few times in my life, but I think that at that moment I was as close as ever. My father's face, soaked with perspiration, lined with the pain from his wrist, and contorted with frustration, was something to see. He just sat there, staring at me. He didn't say anything. And then, suddenly, he turned back to the steering wheel and said, "Aw, the hell with it," and continued on to New York.

We all explained to our relatives and friends in New York that we'd left their chickens in Stamford, and we phoned Stamford and told friends there to help themselves, and after a while the whole thing was a big joke. You could get a huge laugh in our circle just by saying "chickens" and I think the business of the open-door–closed-door policy might have been forgotten except for something I did when we moved to the village of Katonah, near Mount Kisco, in Westchester County.

We rented a big house there to give Dad time to look around before buying, and my brother and I used to ride our tricycles all through the kitchen, dining room and living room. I had a pretty good-sized bike, and Roger had a smaller vehicle, appropriate to his age, a sort of three-wheeled platform with a horse's head.

Well, one Saturday morning when both Mother and Dad were upstairs, Roger and I got to riding around downstairs. Roger tried to propel himself from the dining room into the kitchen, but he struck the swinging door, which was closed, and bumped his head. He screamed bloody murder.

My father angrily stumped downstairs, bathed Roger's head,

17

and gave me what for. "Can't you open the door for him?" he cried. "He's too little to do it himself. Don't let him crash into doors like that."

I said I was sorry I had been so thoughtless and, after my father went upstairs again, I opened the door between the kitchen and the dining room and shoved something under it so it would stay open. I then opened the door between the kitchen and the pantry, I opened the back door leading to the porch, and I even opened the door leading to the cellar stairs.

I was standing there thinking about this, wondering whether it might not be dangerous, when my brother, really pushing his trike, came slashing from the dining room into the kitchen. I stood horrified as he skidded across the linoleum, headed for the cellar door and—plopped right through it and down the stairs into the basement!

That's another scream I can well remember.

And I shall never forget the yells that I myself put out when the hairbrush was applied!

However, I survived it, and late in 1919 we moved to the village of Mount Kisco. Our arrival there was, more or less, without incident, and we rented a large four-story, ten-room house on Moger Avenue, a maple- and elm-shaded street that ran from Main Street in the village out toward the outskirts of the village.

Nothing terrible happened in the next year, that I can recall, but then, one black, ghastly day in September, 1920, disaster struck.

My mother bundled me into the old Maxwell phaeton that we then owned and took me off, about a mile and a half, to the Mount Kisco elementary school and enrolled me in the first grade. I was within a few days of being six at the time, and I resented this change like hell.

There was nothing I could do, however, and Mother, who knew Harold Jennings, the principal, took me to his office. He smiled at me, absently, and patted my head, and I measured the distance from my right foot to his leg.

Before I could kick, Mr. Jennings took Mother and me down the corridor to one of the first grade rooms and introduced us to the teacher, a Miss Cuccia. I took one look at the 32 other kids in the class and decided I wanted no part of them. I didn't like the kids, I didn't like Miss Cuccia, and I didn't like the whole damn school.

The first few grades in the Mount Kisco school at that time were loaded with youngsters of Italian descent whose parents only recently had come to this country and who, for the most part, were laborers, construction workers and demolition experts who'd been shipped into Westchester County to help build roads and construct power lines. Most of the parents couldn't speak English, and the kids couldn't do much better. They were the mangiest, toughest-looking boys I'd ever seen, and I didn't like the situation at all.

I was absolutely horrified when my mother kissed me, shook hands with Miss Cuccia and Mr. Jennings, and walked out of the room, leaving me with this hostile crew.

I took the seat I was assigned to and looked around. I noticed that a few of the girls were fairly prettied up—Eleanor Knapp, Helen Pustina, Sara Marciano and one or two more—but my impression of the boys was uniformly bad. I was the only kid in the class who was wearing a tie—and it was one of those floppy bow ties you wear with a Buster Brown jacket—and George Cohen was the only other boy who looked as though he'd washed in the last three weeks.

And, I must admit, the other students' impression of me wasn't much more flattering.

"Hey, kid," said the boy next to me, a hulking, bruiser-type of seven-year-old named Dominick, "ya wanna fight?"

"Waddya got around ya neck?" demanded a Mussolini-kind of thug named Tony. "Ya mudder's nightgown?"

"You wait," said a third, a bald kid named Rocky. "Right after school. We getcha then!"

Well, none of this set well with me. With all the dignity I could command, I got up from my seat and strolled toward the front of the class. I haven't any idea what the teacher, Miss Cuccia, was doing, but I don't think she saw me.

Then I reached the door and opened it. In a flash, I was out and running down the hall. I didn't even know which way to go. But finally I saw a door to the outside world, and I flung myself against the brass handles that opened the door and fairly leaped into the open air.

I raced for the front of the school and the highway that ran in front of it. Instinctively, I turned left—although I had no idea where I was going—and I ran the length of that street. I tore down the hill that's called Hyatt's Avenue, and at the bottom, I turned left and ran down East Main Street, heading for the center of the village.

I had absolutely no idea which way to head. I'd never been over these streets on foot, but like a lost dog, I somehow smelled my way home. I ran and I ran and I ran, the whole mile and a half, and when I got into the heart of the village, and found Moger Avenue, I turned right on it and ran up the long, long street till I found my house.

I flung open the door, dashed in and collapsed at my mother's feet. My mother, who only a moment or so before had returned and parked the car, was staggered.

"What's the matter?" she asked, picking me up.

"The teacher kicked me!" I gasped.

Never before or since have I ever seen my mother look so astonished. She couldn't believe what I said, but she also knew that *something* had happened to me to make me race like that and now lie palpitating in her arms.

She questioned me gently, but it was 15 minutes or so before I could get my breath and tell my story. Then I said that I'd been sitting at my desk and that Miss Cuccia had called me up to her desk and that when I got there, she suddenly jerked forward her foot and kicked me, and that I had run from the room.

Mother got on the phone right away and called Mr. Jennings. He was appalled, but he said he was sure that Miss Cuccia, under no circumstances, whatsoever, could have kicked me or any other student. "Why, she's one of the sweetest women in the school," he said. My mother, defensive as a lioness with cubs, said he'd better investigate.

That night, of course, she told my father, and my father called Mr. Jennings. Mr. Jennings said he'd talked to Miss Cuccia and that she'd denied the whole thing. She said she had turned to the blackboard, and when she looked back at the class, I was gone. Other than that, she knew nothing.

My father happened to be quite tired that night and, as a result, he got angry. He knew a couple of members of the Board of Education and he phoned them. One of them, I gather, didn't like Mr. Jennings, and so he called the village attorney.

There was a powwow among all these men until the wee hours, and the next day Mr. Jennings was notified that action was going to be taken. Then the village attorney questioned me.

"Are you *absolutely* sure that it was Miss Cuccia who kicked you?" he asked me.

"WELL," I said, rather dramatically, I thought, "it was either Miss Cuccia, or that *other* lady who came into the class."

"What lady came into the class?" the attorney asked.

I said I didn't know who she was. But she had, indeed, come in, and she had kicked me. Yes, it was she who had kicked me. Not Miss Cuccia. And where did they ever get the idea that it had been Miss Cuccia, anyway?

That night I got the second worst spanking of my life.

In addition, in the next few weeks, I had to fight every kid in the class because, sooner or later, they all called me a sissy for running home from school. It cost me eight or nine black eyes, four bloody noses and a number of lip cuts to convince them that it was not fear that had caused me to dash out of the classroom—merely a matter of independence. But in the process, I distributed quite a bit of facial damage too, and after that we all got along just fine.

Chapter Two

MOUNT Kisco, when we arrived in 1919, was a sleepy little hamlet with only about 2,000 people living in and around it (it has only 7,000 today), and nobody we knew had ever heard of it. But it was the telephone company's central office location for the northern part of Westchester County and so my father went to it, as directed.

He had five flats driving up from New York City, and he got lost at least a dozen times. Finally, when he was within a mile or so of the village, he saw a policeman sitting in a car at an intersection and, much as he disliked asking directions, he drove over and asked the cop, "Which way to Crisco?"

"Which way to where?" asked the cop, with a big grin.

This irritated my father and he said angrily, "Crisco. Mount Crisco! Don't you cops know where anything is around here? Crisco. Crisco."

Instead of taking offense, the cop got to laughing, and he laughed so hard and so long that my father got mad and, his hands clenching the wheel, he gunned the motor and took off. He went so fast he failed to notice a sharp rock in the road and —*Bang!*—another blowout!

The cop stood there and laughed and laughed, and my father steamed into such a rage that he started for the cop and probably would have punched him except for the fact that my mother clung to his arm. Dad could hit with the power of a mule's kick and if he'd up-ended that policeman that day— well, I don't know what our future in Mount Kisco would have been.

However, my father took out his frustration by deciding to hate all Mount Kisco cops (which was too bad, because I was to have a rather extensive relationship with them), and by referring ever afterward to Mount Kisco as "Mount Crisco." "I jumped out of the frying pan into the fat," he'd bitterly tell his friends.

However, once we'd settled in our house on Moger Avenue we had no further encounters with the police until one Sunday afternoon when I did an unfortunate thing. My father and mother were visiting the Gorhams about four houses down the street and my brother and I were playing outside. When it began to rain, we went inside our house.

The house, an ancient structure with carved cornices, bay windows on the street level and vaulted windows in the attic, also had a most intriguing thing—a dumbwaiter. This device originally had been used by servants to send food from the kitchen, which was lower than the street level, up to the dining room. We never did use it for that purpose, because we constructed a dining room downstairs at the kitchen level, and my father eventually had the dumbwaiter removed.

That Sunday afternoon, however, it was still there—and in working order. I suggested to my brother that we play elevator —"Like in the New York hotels"—and that he get into the dumbwaiter and ride up and down while I pulled the ropes.

This worked very well for some time, until I decided to make the dumbwaiter go faster. And I gave the rope a mighty yank. It jumped off the pulley and the dumbwaiter stuck between the first and second floor—and my brother, trapped, began to yell.

A family named Wood lived next door at the time, and I ran to enlist Mr. Wood's aid. He, unfortunately, was lying comatose on a sofa, the result of a liquid lunch, but Mrs. Wood, even though she'd had a good bit of the same, was on her feet and active. So active, in fact, that she got hysterical and called the police and told them a little boy was suffocating.

Within a couple of minutes, a police car and a sort of emergency truck loaded with axes, crowbars, acetylene torches and other such rescue equipment roared up Moger Avenue, sirens screaming, and turned into our driveway. Two policemen and five or six men in civilian clothes who'd been hanging around police headquarters leaped out of the vehicles, grabbed the wrecking equipment and rushed into the house.

Within seconds, they made a complete shambles of the dumbwaiter and the walls around it, and they were just dragging my shrieking brother from the interior when my father, who'd been attracted by the sirens, rushed in.

He was, of course, appalled at the damage—and once more he had to be restrained.

The next visitation from the police occurred a few weeks later when my mother had a little accident which, I guess, was partly my fault. It happened one morning when she was preparing to drive me to school.

Our garage, I must explain, was located about 10 feet lower

than street level (our house was built on the side of a small hill), and when you backed the car out of the garage, you had to really give it the gas to shoot it up the driveway and out into the street. If you didn't give it enough gas, it stalled and rolled back down into the garage.

Well, my mother started the car in the garage, pressed down hard on the accelerator and shot backwards up the driveway. I happened to be standing up in the front seat at the time and I fell forward, my head striking and tilting the rearview mirror.

This was disastrous to my mother because she had been looking in it to see where she was going. Instinctively, she thought of jamming on the brakes, but, because she had only just learned to drive, she got excited and kicked down hard on the gas pedal.

The car shot backwards twice as fast—possibly as much as 25 miles per hour—and raced up the driveway, over the sidewalk and out into the street.

But it didn't stop there. It tore right across the highway, mounted the curb on the other side, went over the sidewalk, raced backwards up a slight embankment, plunged through a hedge and onto the Smiths' lawn, knocked over and demolished a concrete birdbath, slashed through a bed of flowers and slammed into the latticework beneath the Smiths' front porch. When the car stopped, it was half under the Smiths' porch. The canvas roof of the touring car had been ripped off and was lying on the hood. And my mother put her head down on the wheel and started to cry.

Mrs. Carpenter, who lived next to the Smiths, heard the crash, and when she saw my mother's head on the wheel, she phoned the police and told them that Mrs. Mockridge had been killed.

Once again a police car and the emergency truck roared up Moger Avenue, but this time it was followed by an ambulance from the Northern Westchester Hospital. All had their sirens going full blast.

Neither Mother nor I had been hurt, and the cops pulled the

car out from under the porch without much trouble. They cleaned up some of the mess and took the car back across the street to our driveway. Then the lieutenant, a big fat man with a huge mustache, gently suggested to my mother that, even though operators' licenses were not required in those days, it would be a good idea if she gave up driving (he'd seen her other times around the village!) and she, tearfully, declared, "Don't worry, I'll NEVER drive again!"

And she didn't. Not for about 20 years, anyway, and so—thereafter, and for the duration of my whole educational career—I walked to and from school.

This incident, of itself, wouldn't be of much import, I imagine, except for the fact that I did something a few months later which brought it vividly to mind.

After Mother had ripped the superstructure off the old Maxwell, my father decided that the cost of repairing it was more than the car was worth. And so, he bought a Chrysler sedan. It was practically new, having been used only as a demonstrator.

The car was my father's great pride, but shortly after he bought it, he found that a number of screws and bolts, both inside and outside, were loose. He couldn't stand anybody who didn't keep machinery and cars right up to scratch and so he took a screwdriver and wrench and began to go over the whole car, tightening everything that needed it. Before he was finished, however, my mother insisted he come in for dinner, and Dad did so, saying he'd "get the rest of it tomorrow night."

Well, I decided to surprise him. And the next afternoon, I took a screwdriver and started in where he'd left off. Eventually, running out of screws to tighten on the chassis, I took a monkey wrench and crawled under the car, which was parked in the garage. There I found an interesting array of nuts and bolts.

Much to my sorrow, all of them were quite tight. And I was about to give up the afternoon as a complete waste of time, when I happened to notice that there were some octagonal bolts projecting from the brake drums. The heads of these bolts seemed a little too far out from the surface of the drums, and I fastened my monkey wrench on one of them and tested it. It turned easily.

"Hah!" I said to myself. "How loose can you get? What sloppy workmanship! Why, these bolts will work themselves loose and get lost!" And so, industriously, I tightened each and every one of them to the nth degree.

I didn't know, of course, that the bolts regulated the braking system and my father certainly wasn't aware that night when he backed the car out of the garage that the bolts had been tampered with. Otherwise, he wouldn't have gunned it so.

Anyhow, giving her plenty of gas to get up the incline—Dad always did have a heavy foot on the accelerator—he got the Chrysler going about 30 miles an hour, and then he stepped on the brake.

The pedal went right down to the floor and my father, not getting the expected resistance, fell forward and cut his lip on the steering wheel. The car shot up the incline, tore across the highway, mounted the curb on the other side, went over the sidewalk, raced backwards up the slight embankment, plunged through the new hedge onto the Smiths' lawn (recently re-planted), knocked over and demolished the new concrete bird-bath, slashed through the bed of flowers (recently replanted), and slammed into the newly rebuilt latticework under the Smiths' porch. The car halted about a quarter of the way under the porch, its roof dented in and its trunk crushed against one of the pillars holding up the porch. My father's temper gave way, and, leaning forward, he doubled his fists and began beating furiously on the steering wheel.

Mrs. Carpenter, having heard the crash, looked out her library window and saw my father punching the steering wheel. She assumed he was in great pain and slashing at the wheel in an attempt to extricate himself, and so she phoned the police and said that Mr. Mockridge was trapped in a wrecked car and was bleeding to death.

Once again . . . the sirens . . . the police car . . . the emergency truck . . . and the ambulance. They raced up

27

Moger Avenue and men with axes, crowbars and acetylene torches swarmed all over. My father, out of the car by then, told them to get themselves hence—but the lieutenant, the one with the great girth and huge mustache, blandly gave my father a ticket for driving with faulty brakes.

Now that I think back over those days, I wonder why it was that the Smiths ever put up with us. Dad, of course, paid for the reconstruction of their lawn and flower beds and for the rebuilding of their porch, but there were many other irritants.

The first irritant came when Mr. Smith, a general contractor and painter, excavated the land and started to build his new house. The site was diagonally across the street from our house and, as you can imagine, it was a wonderful place for youngsters to play. We weren't allowed there during the day when the workmen were busy, but when they left about 4:30 we swarmed in like mad.

We jumped into the soft piles of dirt, we leaped into the excavation for the cellar, and we built castles and forts out of the concrete blocks that were to be used for the foundation. We had a wonderful time and, so far as I know, we caused no trouble. Every kid in the neighborhood, and there must have been 20 or so, played there every night.

Well, in time, the masons got the foundation in, and the carpenters put in the beams for the first floor and began covering them with planks. Then was the most fun.

Late in the afternoon, and sometimes even after dinner, we kids would go down into the cellar, which had a dirt floor, and we'd fix up tables and chairs from the leftover concrete blocks and the planks and boards, and we'd create living rooms and bedrooms and secret dens and heaven only knows what else.

The Smiths had two daughters, Maizie, who was older than most of us and whom we rarely saw, and Chubby, who was about our age but twice as large. She was a lot of fun.

I don't know whether it was Chubby who introduced cigarettes into our street hideaway, or whether it was the beautiful Charlotte Gorham from down the street, or maybe it was the

Carpenter boys—but I do know that it was down there, in the Smiths' freshly built cellar, that I had my first taste of a cigarette. It was a most exhilarating experience. And I coughed and choked and sputtered all the way to the bathroom at home.

Nobody minded our playing in the cellar, so far as I know, until after the night we had the party. I think I was the one who had the idea—maybe it was somebody else; I don't know—but anyway it was arranged that one Friday night, when we all could stay up late, we'd have a big party in the cellar. Right after dinner.

Each boy and girl was delegated to bring some cake, or cookies, or candy, or whatever, and I said that I would bring the fixin's for lemonade. During the afternoon, I got to thinking about how much water I'd have to lug over from my house for that gang of 20 to 30 very thirsty kids and I decided there must be an easier way.

I'd noticed that the men mixing concrete used a hose for water, and I found, with only a minor bit of investigation, that it was connected to an outside faucet on the Sherwoods' house next door to the Smiths'. So, I went and got that hose, dragged it down into the Smiths' cellar, and turned it on. The water came through perfectly, and I was in business.

That night I used the hose to fill the huge pot I'd brought from my house, and I dumped in the lemon juice I'd squeezed, and the sugar, and then I ladled out lemonade by the dipperful. The party was a great success and we were all having the most fun when our mothers began to call us:

"Ohhhhhh, Sallllly," cried Mrs. Gorham. "Ohhhhhh, Chuuuuuuby," cried Mrs. Smith, who was staying nearby with friends. "Georrrrrrge, Loooooooooie," cried Mrs. Carpenter. "Norrrrrrrrton, Raaaaaaaager," cried my mother from across the street. "Bedddddddddtime."

And so, sadly, we picked up the dishes and the napkins and the cups, and started to depart. I dumped what was left of the lemonade into one corner of the dirt-floor cellar, and then I took the hose and washed out the pot. We extinguished the single candle we'd been using to illuminate our party, said good night to each other, and went home.

Next morning, I was surprised to see a lot of men standing around on the Smiths' property and I ran over to see what had happened. It didn't take long. One corner of the concrete block foundation had given way, the dirt wall had caved in, and the wooden first floor, which had been level last night, now was tilting crazily toward the corner without the foundation.

"They'll have to build the damn thing all over again," one man was saying.

"Yeah," said another. "Helluva waste of money."

"What happened?" I asked.

And the men quickly told me. Seems that somebody—some workman, no doubt—had left a hose running all night and the water had washed away the dirt around the footing in that particular corner, the dirt wall had fallen in and the concrete foundation had toppled. Then the floor had dipped.

"Oh, gosh," I said, unable to stop the flow of words, "I must have forgot to turn off the hose last night!"

This, as I was to learn quite swiftly, is an example of saying something when you don't have to. Later I was to learn that saying the wrong thing is even worse.

But in this case, I must say, my father was quite reasonable. He offered to repair the damage himself, promising to rebuild the concrete block wall, dig out all the dirt and shore it up, and to jack up the tilted floor. Mr. Smith, however, wouldn't let him do it.

"Frank," he said, "no great damage has been done. It won't take the men long to fix it all up again, and I'll handle whatever extra expense there is."

My father said he'd handle the expense himself.

"No, Frank," said Mr. Smith, with a twinkle. "After all, my girl, Chubby, drank as much lemonade as anybody."

I was greatly relieved, of course, to see the whole thing end on this happy note—and I was especially glad that the police

30

hadn't been called in. I was sick of seeing blue uniforms. But my peace of mind didn't last long.

One Saturday afternoon, a month or so later, a dozen or more neighborhood boys—including my brother and me—were tossing footballs back and forth in the street in front of our house and generally yelling and whomping it up.

Finally, Mrs. Smith, who'd moved into her new house, came out and asked us to cease and desist. She had a headache, she said, and couldn't we play somewhere else?

So, we moved to the front lawn of the Carpenters' house, a big black and white frame house next to the Smiths' but right on the corner between Moger Avenue and Carpenter Avenue. There we organized a football game, and spent a happy afternoon. After a time, the boys drifted away. Some had chores, others had early suppers and, in time, my brother Roger and I were left alone.

We went to the Carpenters' back door and knocked, planning to ask for a drink of water. Nobody was home and so, as kids were accustomed to do in our neighborhood, we opened the screen door and went into the kitchen. We each got a glass of water and, as I was drinking, I looked through into Mr. Carpenter's study and noticed his shotguns and rifles standing in a rack.

I'd seen them before, of course, but I didn't think my brother had, so I took him into the study and showed him. Well, boys hardly ever can keep their hands off guns, and I was no exception. I picked up two or three of them and displayed them to my brother.

I was about nine at the time and he was seven. There's a vast difference in intelligence at that age. A seven-year-old knows nothing; a nine-year-old knows everything.

And so, I gave Roger a lecture on the care and handling of guns. I explained that a rifle is used for hunting animals and that a shotgun generally is used for birds. I even explained the scatter pattern of a shotgun, and my brother seemed impressed.

"How does it sound when it goes off?" he asked.

31

I was a little irritated with this question, because it didn't seem to be in keeping with the high level of my lecture. On second thought, I realized it was a perfectly reasonable question, and so I decided to demonstrate.

I looked around for some shotgun shells and I found a box in a closet. Then I became a bit apprehensive. Even though I'd never fired a shotgun, even though I'd never even seen one fired, I had a pretty good idea that a shotgun throws a hell of a lot of lead all over the place. And I didn't think that a residential neighborhood was the place for it.

But my eye lighted on a box of blanks for a .22 rifle and I felt that one of those ought to make enough noise for my brother. The box was stamped BLANKS, and when I took one out, I could see that it was indeed a blank. It had no lead in its nose.

So, I selected a .22 from the rack, broke it open, and slid a blank cartridge into the chamber.

"Come," I said conspiratorially to my brother. "Listen to this."

I opened the rear door of the study, a door that overlooked the garden, and I poked the rifle out of the door, pointed it toward the ground, then I pulled the trigger.

CRRRRACK! went the rifle. Both my brother and I were impressed.

But then we heard a scream. And more screams. And a woman crying, "I've been shot! Somebody shot me!"

I don't remember what I said. But I think it was something like, "Let's get out of here!" I stuck the rifle back in the rack, and my brother and I dashed into the kitchen and out the back door on the other side of the house. We picked up our football and raced for home.

Pretty soon we heard the siren, and a police car scooted up the street and stopped in front of Mrs. Smith's house. My brother and I watched from under the shade of the front window. We expected to see Mrs. Smith's body carried out and we were sure the police would be over to get us any minute.

"But," I said, pounding my hands together, "I couldn't have

32

shot her. First, it was a blank. And second, I shot directly into the ground. I didn't shoot anywhere near her house. How could it have happened?"

Well, as we learned later, after the police had gone, the wadding from the blank had hit a flat stone and had ricocheted across the garden and had hit one of the white pillars on Mrs. Smith's back porch. Mrs. Smith had been sitting on the open porch at the time, shelling peas, and she'd been startled to hear the rifle shot. And, almost at the same moment, the blank's wadding plunked against the pillar about four feet from her and made a black mark which she thought was a bullet hole.

It was then she screamed that she'd been shot.

She later realized that nobody had been shooting at her, and that even if she'd been hit by the wadding, she wouldn't have been hurt—the distance was that great. But still, she contended, a murderer was at large, and what were the Mount Kisco police doing about it?

I don't think the Mount Kisco police ever had had a murder on their hands, nor even an attempted murder, but they did have a pretty good idea as to who might be firing blank .22s from the Carpenter house.

And so, naturally, they came to see me.

I do not remember the names of the officers who interrogated me—there were only six or seven on the force at the time, but I never did get to know their names—but I well recall that each of them was nine feet tall. They all had five hundred or a thousand brass buttons on the front of their uniforms, they had voices that thundered and shook the whole house, and they carried revolvers that looked like the pictures of World War I Big Berthas I had seen.

But I stood up to them, stalwartly.

"I have no idea who fired the gun," I said. "None at all."

They turned on my little brother. But he turned and ran and hid in a corner where he sat and cried.

"Well then," said the police, "you know who *did* fire the gun, don't you?"

33

I said that I certainly did not. I had no idea.

But they kept pressing me, and my mother was there and she kept looking at me appealingly. I felt that the police needed my help and that I'd be letting them down unless I gave them some information.

"C'mon, now, sonny," said one officer. "Help us out. Tell us who did it."

"Well, sir," I said, "as much as I wish I could tell you who did it, I cannot." And then I paused for a pregnant moment. The officers could see I was about to come out with an important statement.

"But," I said. And I paused again.

"Yeah, yeah," said one cop.

"But," I said, "right after the shooting—I looked out of the front window there—"

"Yeahhhh," said all of the cops, in unison.

"—and I saw Georgie Carpenter running down the street!"

"Wow! The Carpenter kid," said one officer.

"That's the older one, isn't it?" asked another.

I gravely explained that the Carpenter boys, who were my good friends and who lived across the street, were Georgie and Louie, and that Georgie was the elder.

"And it was Georgie you saw, huh?" asked one policeman.

"It was Georgie," I said, with quiet emphasis.

The officers left then, after thanking me and my mother, and I felt happy that I'd been able to be of assistance to them.

The next two or three days passed uneventfully, and I heard nothing more about the detection phase of the Smith shooting. Everybody in the neighborhood still was talking about it, but most of the men said that the whole thing had been blown up out of proportion and that Mrs. Smith had made a ridiculous fuss and shouldn't have bothered to call the police and get everything stirred up.

"Oh, no," I said, politely interjecting a word when I could. "I think she did the right thing. How does she know that somebody isn't out to get her, and he just used a blank by mistake?"

This brought quite a laugh—an unseemly laugh, I thought —but no one challenged my theory, and so I retired from the discussion. And, as a matter of fact, I thought little or nothing about the whole business for the next few days.

Then, one day when I was in school, a policeman suddenly entered our classroom and whispered to my teacher. I think it was Miss Aikman—a pretty lady with long, blond hair (I was in 3B at the time)—and she crooked her finger, and beckoned to me.

I don't know which emotion affected me more: I never had felt so important in my life—and I never had been so afraid. Somehow, I got to my feet and went up to her desk. The policeman took me by the arm and said something like, "You wanta take a little ride with me?"

I realized that I wasn't in any position to argue, and so I nodded. And together, the cop and I marched stiffly from the classroom.

He said nothing on the ride to headquarters, and I sat shriveled in my little suit.

I knew exactly what the chief was going to say to me when I was placed in front of him, and he said it: "*You* shot at Mrs. Smith, didn't you?"

"No, sir, I did not," I said. And then I added, "Who told you?"

The chief laughed so hard he nearly fell out of his chair. The other cops in the place choked with laughter. I felt mortified.

"We checked out the Carpenter kid," said the chief, wiping his eyes. "And he was working in his father's hardware store at the time of the shooting. He couldn't have been running down the street. And so, we figured it was you."

"Who *told* you?" I asked, coldly. I felt certain these cops were too dumb to solve this mystery without an informer—but I was too polite to say so in so many words. I think, however, that the chief got the message.

"Well . . ." he said, leaning back in his chair, "as a matter

35

of fact, it was your brother who told us. We talked to him this morning, and he said you shot the .22."

Confronted with that, I confessed. But I explained that I'd used a blank, that I'd fired into the ground, and that I certainly hadn't tried or intended to shoot Mrs. Smith.

And I explained that if they hadn't pressed me so hard for information, I wouldn't have thought of saying that George had run down the street. I argued that I was just trying to do my patriotic duty. The cops went into another round of laughter, and then they said I could go home.

I've already told you about the second-worst spanking in my life. Well, that night when my father got home I got the worst. And the next day I had to go and apologize to Mrs. Smith. And to George Carpenter, who seemed pretty annoyed with me. And to Mr. and Mrs. Carpenter. It was most humiliating.

But—I had learned something!

And that was—never commit a crime when your brother is watching. He'll rat on you!

Chapter Three

MY father, as I think I've said, was a very practical man. He had no use for anybody who couldn't work with his hands. He sincerely believed that he could do carpentry better than the carpenter, electrical work better than the electrician, and plumbing better than the plumber. And, in about 90 percent of the cases, I think he was right.

Dad never actually built a whole house with his own hands, but he could have. He did build rooms when we needed additions to our house, he built at least two garages, and he built a huge, glass-enclosed porch across the back of our house. In addition, he was capable of fine cabinetwork and he built and installed quite a few permanent examples in various rooms.

He had nothing but contempt for a man who couldn't use a screwdriver, a saw and a hammer. And he saw to it that I possessed and worked with these tools within a day or two after I started to walk. Fortunately, I inherited some of his practicality and I took to handling tools with considerable enthusiasm and some skill.

My father was proud of me, and he didn't complain when, practicing the use of the crosscut saw, I cut off the legs of the high kitchen stool. And he didn't even kick when I straightened some bent nails by pounding them with a hammer on the leather-covered, mahogany coffee table. Instead of blowing a fit, he went to work immediately and built me my own workbench in the cellar.

For quite a while, I made many of my own toys. The Mockridges were not overburdened with money in those days—in fact, we *never* were—and so my father was enormously pleased when, for a few cents, I made a wooden sword and painted it silver, and a wooden rifle which I painted brown and black.

I made wagons and scooters and simple pinball games and one day I made a magnificent cannon. Some of the kids in Mount Kisco had little steel cannons that fired a small pellet when you touched off the powder in the chamber, but my mother considered those too dangerous for us. However, I got her permission to build a wooden cannon which, I said, would be operated by a spring. I'm pretty sure that what I had in mind, was not what *she* had in mind, but anyway I got the green light.

I spent nearly a month making that cannon—it was a faithful replica of a howitzer—and I was very proud of it. And then when it was done and mounted on wheels, I rigged up the firing mechanism. This was an extremely powerful spring that I found after hours of rummaging around in Elman's junk yard, and I installed it in the barrel of the cannon. I sawed some brass curtain rods about the thickness of a pencil into half-inch slugs and they were my ammunition.

When all was in readiness, I shoved one of the slugs into the barrel of the cannon, aimed it at a big piece of quarter-inch paneling I had in the cellar, pulled back the spring—and let it go. Much to my satisfaction, the slug drilled right through the paneling.

I fired a few more shots and was highly pleased with my handiwork. I could hardly wait to show it to my father, and so I took it to the dining room and waited for him to come home from work. Needless to say, he was most complimentary and together we inspected the little masterpiece.

My father tinkered with this and that, dropped in a slug to see how easily it slid down the barrel, and then toyed with the spring mechanism. Whether he had cocked it, or whether it already had been cocked, I don't know. But suddenly it went off with a loud report, and the brass slug zipped across the room and shattered a large crystal bowl that stood on a shelf above our sideboard.

It went merrily on to shatter the mirror behind the bowl, and parts of the bowl itself dropped to the sideboard where they shattered two Wedgwood plates, a Steuben pitcher and a crystal candy dish. All in all, it was a most shattering experience.

My next big project was a work-saving device—intended to make life easier for me.

We had a maid named Helen who, unfortunately, was unavailable for duty much of the time because of severe cases of pregnancy. When she was missing, it became my duty at dinner each night to carry all the dishes and food from the kitchen to the dining room and, after dinner, to carry all the empty dishes and leftover food from the dining room to the kitchen.

Now, it was 18 good-sized steps from the kitchen table to the dining room table, and I estimated that on an average night I made 11 trips, taking things into the dining room and clearing the table after the meal. That meant 11 round trips of 36 steps each, or a total of 396 steps. In addition, of course, there were the trips necessary to set the table in the first place, the countless but uncounted steps taken in the kitchen picking up the food and the scores of steps walking around the dining table, placing the plates and picking them up. On nights when we had soup *and* desert, of course, the tally was even higher. And then, too, there was the business of being sent to the kitchen two or three times during dinner to get extra bread for my father—he ate at least eight slices during each meal—or to get more coffee for my mother. All in all, I estimate, I took at least 650 steps each night.

This worried me because I had read somewhere that that plodding kind of walking was terribly bad for the leg muscles. I had read, too, that waiters get muscle bound and eventually develop chronic Charley horses and this horrified me, because I had decided at that point to become a great football player and electrify the world.

So, I began to think of ways to handle the whole thing more expeditiously. I at first thought of stringing some cables between the kitchen and dining room, running through the pantry, and placing the food in baskets which would be pulled by string from one room to another. But somehow or other, that didn't seem to be the professional way to do it.

I thought of building chutes, something like playground slides, one of which would be high in the dining room and low in the kitchen, and the other which would be high in the kitchen and low in the dining room. But I couldn't think of any easy method of stopping the plates, without damage, once they reached the bottom of the chute.

It was then, however, that I thought of my electric trains!

Every year since we'd moved to Mount Kisco, it had been my supreme pleasure in the month before Christmas to go to the corner of Moger Avenue and Main Street every single day of the week and peer into the main display window of Abel's Department Store. Abel's Department Store wasn't a heck of a lot bigger than a couple of Nedick's orange juice stands thrown together, but I didn't know that then. To me, it was the biggest store in the world, and its window display was sheer artistry and perfection.

There in Abel's window, for the full month between Thanksgiving and Christmas, ran an electric train. Around and around and around. The electric locomotive drew a coal car, a few freight cars, three or four coaches, and a caboose. Slowly, at a regulated speed, this train snaked its way in a convolution of tracks, all around Abel's window, going over little bridges, where the gates had been let down and a warning light flashed, and disappearing in tunnels in little white, cotton-batting-covered mountains, and stopping at realistic stations with lights flickering in their windows.

I had my own set of Lionel trains, but they never seemed so enchanting as the Abel's display. And, try as I would, I never was able to achieve the dramatic effect that the department store owner created, apparently, almost without effort. That was a long, long time ago, but today, even though far more important things have faded from memory, I can see myself in sharp focus, standing outside Abel's window, and watching the train go by. Nothing in life more beautiful.

Anyway, it was that train that gave me my brilliant idea. Mr. Abel, you see, although he obviously was my idol, was not exactly above crass commercialism. He had the train running there, of course, to attract attention to his window and, hopefully, to sell electric trains and equipment. But—and oh, that Mr. Abel was a sly one—whenever he had a certain piece of merchandise that he wanted to push—like a snow boot, a pair of rabbit-fur-lined gloves or maybe a meerschaum pipe—he'd tie it on top of one of the freight cars and around and around it would go, its price tag fluttering in the breeze.

Once in a while a heavy article like a boot would slip its moorings a bit and, projecting too far from the freight car, would slam into one of the cotton-covered tunnels and tear the whole thing down, derailing all the cars, and the engine, too. This was a thrilling sight, if you happened to be around when it occurred, and I was privileged three times in three years.

And so it was that when I thought of expediting the dishes from the kitchen to the dining room, and back again, I thought of Mr. Abel's merchandising program. Why not rig up an arrangement whereby my own Lionel trains would carry the dishes back and forth?

So, without revealing my plan, I spent all my spare time the next few weeks at my cellar workbench building a trestle of light pine, making it in sections so I could move it easily and link it together when I was ready to put my plan into effect.

Then I made shallow tin boxes, about six inches by six, and bolted them to the tops of six or seven of my Lionel flatcars. The walls of the boxes were only about half an inch tall, but I felt that I could place a dish on these boxes and, no matter how much the flat car jiggled, they couldn't slip out.

Then, one wonderful Saturday, when my father was working overtime and my mother was ill in bed with a quinsy sore throat, I decided to unveil my invention. My brother, happily, was spending the day with a little playmate (he always got in the way because he thought that his system of handling a project was better!) and I dragged my trestles into the kitchen.

I set them up and connected them securely, and they ran from one end of the large kitchen table, right through the pantry (I took the doors off both sides of the pantry) and out into the dining room, and they stopped at the sideboard, which was near my chair at the table.

Then I got my tracks and tacked them to the top of the trestle. There wasn't room to make a turnaround, but I had a reverse on my train, so I figured I could drive it out of the kitchen with the food-filled plates, empty it, and then, reversing the engine, back it into the kitchen, either with empty plates, or just to pick up more food.

I tested it a few times, and it worked perfectly. I was all set for dinner that night.

My father was a bit staggered when he came home and found

a trestle, four feet high, extending from the kitchen, through the pantry, and into the dining room. But he was of an inventive frame of mind himself, and so he said nothing much more than: "Hmmmm, hmmmmm, hmmmmm."

But my mother, when she dragged herself out of bed, with a piece of flannel wrapped around her throat, had some caustic comments. One of them was: "Norton, get that junk out of here!" I explained, however, as quickly as I could, that this was going to be a great labor and time saver, and that it would be of great service to all of us. My father sort of went along with this, and my mother was too sick to argue.

She got dinner that night—and I'll never forget what it was. It was roast lamb, with pan browned potatoes, succotash and mint jelly.

I helped around the kitchen and then, when the great moment came, I showed Mother how my invention would work. I backed my train into the kitchen, right up to the table. I put the four plates, filled with the lamb, the vegetables and the jelly, onto the flatcars and I told her to go inside and sit down. She did, and I followed.

I sat in my chair, near the sideboard. On the sideboard rested my rheostat and my transformer—the controls for the train. I pushed the transformer gently to the No. 1 button, not giving the train too much power, and then, carefully, I began to slide the handle around the rheostat. We couldn't see it, but you could hear the train react out in the kitchen.

The locomotive spun its wheels for quite a while, unaccustomed as it was to pulling such a heavy load. I pushed the transformer to the No. 3 position, and slid the rheostat handle the full way around. Suddenly, the locomotive's wheels gripped the rails and the train began to move. We could see it coming through the darkened pantry, the headlight blinking and the wheels spitting sparks left and right.

I was transfixed with the magic of it all as I watched the train, carrying the four plates of lamb, emerge from the dark pantry and race into the light of the dining room. So transfixed, in fact, that I forgot to ease up on the rheostat, and the train, now running at top speed, raced across the trestle and crashed full tilt into the backstop I had arranged at the end of the line on the sideboard.

It was derailed, of course, and the four plates of lamb, potatoes, succotash and mint jelly were catapulted through the air. They landed on the floor about six feet away.

My mother, weakened by her illness, began to cry. But my father, surprisingly, was quite calm.

"Look, Freddie," he said (my mother's name was Fredricka), "look, it isn't all that bad." And he picked up some of the lamb and began brushing it off with his napkin. He picked up a few of the potatoes and brushed them too, but when he tried scooping up the succotash, my mother really wailed.

"I'm sorry," she sobbed, "but I just can't stand it." And she got up from the table and went upstairs to bed.

My father looked at me, and I sat there, shaken.

"Well," he said, with a smile, "if you don't try something, you never learn. Now let's clean up this mess."

I never loved my father more than at that moment.

My brother and I helped him, and we cleaned up the floor. We salvaged some of the lamb and ate it. And we made a peanut-butter-and-bacon sandwich for my mother, and I took it to her bedroom, along with a glass of milk. She was still crying, but she was grateful for the sandwich, and she kissed me and said she wasn't angry at me at all. And then I started to cry, and I kissed her, and said I was very sorry, and that I would pay for the plates and the food that was spoiled, and she said that there was no need for anything like that, but would I promise, please not to invent anything else for a while—at least not until she got better.

I promised, and when I got downstairs, my father was taking down the last of the trestle.

"I think," he said, "that the old system was better. But, as I said before, there's no harm in trying."

Strangely enough, I was in good favor around the house for

the next couple of weeks. And I might have remained so—except for a small incident that occurred.

It had to do with one of the smokers held at the American Legion hall in the village. The Legionnaires had these smokers once every two or three months, and other men's clubs in the village held smokers now and again at the hall. And whenever we saw the sign put up outside: SMOKER TONIGHT, we kids made careful plans.

Just as soon as it was dark, we'd walk the length of Carpenter Avenue and stand on the top of the small hill at the foot of which nestled the Legion Hall. We'd wait until all the men attending the smoker had arrived and gone inside, and this generally was about 9 o'clock, and then, one at a time, we'd sneak through the bushes and go down the hill to the rear of the building.

Then, crawling on our bellies, we'd snake up to one of four windows, and peek inside. Two of those windows were in the auditorium, at a level we could reach, and two of them were basement windows, set in sort of recessed concrete culverts, and they commanded a fine view of the downstairs dressing room.

And the name of the game was—GIRLS!

It was well known in the village that some of these smokers were pretty racy affairs. One night, bald old Ernest Christie went home from one of them and told his wife he'd been in a church meeting, planning the new parish house. But when he bent over, Mrs. Christie was horrified to find a great imprint of purplish lipstick on his dome where some brazen hussy impishly had kissed him. And Nelson Sanders got into similar trouble when he went home reeking of cheap perfume, unaware that there was a huge greasepaint smear across his blue serge suit, left there by a heavily made up stripper who'd snuggled on his lap.

If you looked into the auditorium windows, there was just enough room under the drawn blinds to give you a partial view of the stage. You could see the performers up to about their waists. But when the girls went down into the audience to min-

45

gle with the gentlemen guests, you could see all of them. And they never had very much on.

But it was even better when you looked down into the basement dressing room. There you often could see the girls with absolutely *nothing* on! We all of us felt that this was most educational, and we might have gone on indefinitely watching the show if I hadn't had a bright idea.

Being terribly interested in the theater, I'd been irked for some time that I never could see the upper half of the stage performance. The bottom half was nice, but I didn't like having to miss the rest.

So, one afternoon when the SMOKER TONIGHT sign was out, I took a couple of the fellows and we went to an area nearby where carpenters were putting up a huge wooden garage. We took two sawhorses—each about five feet high—which the carpenters used to stand on while they nailed up the siding. We also took two long planks.

I arranged these horses under one of the auditorium windows that we couldn't reach from the ground, and then we laid the planks across them. We shinnied up onto this improvised grandstand and peered through the window and under the blinds. I was thrilled to see that I had a full view of the stage.

We hid the planks and horses in the bushes and went home. As soon as it was dark, we returned, set up the grandstand again, and climbed aboard. The girls were cavorting on the stage and I saw, much to my delight, what I'd been missing all along.

There were four of us on the planks when some other kids came along and they too climbed up. Then some more came. And some more. I don't know how many finally were on the two planks, but I'm sure there was one too many. Suddenly, with a frightening sound like a pistol shot, one of the planks cracked and threw half a dozen boys to the ground. It also pitched two or three other kids onto the plank that the rest of us were standing on, and that cracked, too.

Everybody yelled, both from pain and fright, and two policemen, who'd been guarding the front door against invasion by wives, raced around the building with flashlights and drawn revolvers.

I was the only one caught!

Somehow, as I fell, my knickerbockers became impaled on a long, jagged fragment of the plank, and I couldn't tear myself loose.

A few minutes later I was in a police car, riding up Moger Avenue. My mother and father were sitting on the front porch, eating ice cream, when I arrived. They had been led to believe that I was attending a rehearsal for a church play at St. Mark's, and they were surprised to see that the police were furnishing transportation.

The officer, however, quickly explained what I had been doing, and my mother and father were shocked. I stood there with my eyes closed, expecting the ax to fall. But my father took an unexpected tack.

"Look," he said to the policeman angrily, "you must have little to do if you're running around arresting small boys. What you SHOULD be doing is raiding that dirty show down there. And now go back and close it up, or I'll file a complaint with the Mayor in the morning!"

The cop said nothing. He just turned and got in his car and drove away. Whether he closed the show that night or not, I don't know. But I do know there were no more smokers that summer.

Chapter Four

WHEN I was about seven years old, and shortly before I became so embroiled with the Mount Kisco police, I got my second shot at an acting career. And this time I accepted the challenge quite well, I thought. Unfortunately, this was an opinion not shared by the producers.

This second big chance came one afternoon in the autumn of 1922 when I was standing on the sidewalk outside my house on Moger Avenue making a pipe out of a twig and a horse chestnut that had fallen from a big tree beside our driveway. I was so absorbed in my chore that I didn't notice a lady who was watching me.

But, apparently, she stood there fascinated while I hollowed out the horse chestnut, drilled a small hole in its side with my knife, inserted the twig and then put the pipe in my mouth and began to puff—just as though it were a real pipe filled with tobacco.

"Little boy," said the lady, yanking me out of my reverie, "I'm Mrs. Pelton. And would you like to do some acting?"

I didn't like the interruption, but I knew Mrs. Pelton was a neighbor of ours, and I also was mildly intrigued by her question, and so I said what I now like to think was: "Why, of course, Mrs. Pelton, and how very nice of you to ask," but which I think really was only "Yup."

Anyway, she told me that an English lady, a friend of hers and a great director of children's theater, was staying with her and was thinking of putting on some plays with nothing but children in the casts.

At that time, Clare Tree Major's professional children's theater was nationally known, and, I suppose, Mrs. Pelton's friend had visions of competition.

Well, that night when my father got home I told him, rather casually, that I'd just been selected to be the star of a new children's theater and that Mrs. Pelton had asked me to ask him if it was all right.

"No, it is NOT all right," he said, angrily. "You had your chance to be an actor, and you ruined it. What you'd better do now is concentrate on your schoolwork. You got seventy-five in arithmetic, you know."

I don't remember whether I said anything or not, but I do know that my mother cut in with: "Frank, Mrs. Pelton is Mrs. *Frederick* Pelton."

"I know, I know," said my father, testily. "What's that got to do with it?"

"Nothing, I guess," said my mother, "except that *Frederick*

Pelton is the president of the Mount Kisco National Bank, and it's the Mount Kisco National Bank that holds the mortgage on this house, and I think . . ."

"All right!" said my father. "All *right!* Why shouldn't he have a second chance at acting if he wants it? Why should we stop him? Norton, you tell Mrs. Pelton that your mother and father are very happy she picked you." Then he settled down to his evening paper and didn't speak to anyone until bedtime.

Well, I wish I could tell you that this happening turned out to be an auspicious one indeed. But the truth is, it didn't. There were many difficulties, I believe, but the major one, as I understand it, seemed to be that the lady producing and directing the show didn't see eye to eye with me on the way I felt it should be produced and directed.

The play was something along the line of *Sleeping Beauty*, although I think it was called by another name, and in it I played a prince who got to kiss the beautiful sleeping princess. I had two major complaints: 1, the beautiful sleeping princess was a short, fat, ugly girl, whose father was financing the production, and who always sprayed a lot of saliva after I awakened her with a kiss; and 2, the lady directing the show had some way-out ideas about how a prince should look and act. She had me in some kind of fairylike uniform, and she wanted me to dance on tiptoes into the bedchamber.

We got sort of locked in battle on this while we rehearsed for about two months, and finally the lady won. She canceled the production and decided, instead, to do *Midsummer Night's Dream*. I was not invited to join the cast.

Shortly thereafter, however, word of my unique talent got around and an agent got me a role as one of the children in a summer production of *Rip Van Winkle* that Charles Coburn and his wife, Ivah, were staging in amphitheaters in Westchester County and on Long Island.

My role was small, but important. I had only two words to say in the first act, and two words to say in the second, and last, act. In the first, I was to romp onto the stage, approach Rip (then a young man) and say "Fazzer, Fazzer." This was Mr. Coburn's interpretation of the way a young Dutch boy in the Catskill Mountains would greet his father, and, of course, it stamped me as Rip's offspring.

Then, in the second act, when Rip came down from the mountains after his long sleep, tattered, bent and with long white hair and beard, I was to run onto the stage again—now doubling as my own son—and shrill out: "Grandfazzer, Grandfazzer." This was most important because it established Rip's identity to the townsfolk who couldn't believe he was the Rip who had gone away 20 years before.

Well, I worked very hard on those lines, but try as I would, every time I ran onstage in the *first* act, I shouted out: "Grandfazzer, Grandfazzer." And, in the *second* act, my contribution was: "Fazzer, Fazzer."

This irritated Mr. Coburn quite a bit. And once he dropped his monocle and broke it. This irritated him even more, and it made his wife furious. She took a broom and swept me offstage —to uproarious applause.

However, in time, the Coburns forgave me—they even let me perform in their outdoor production of *Lysistrata* many years later. And, in 1934, when I myself was playing Rip in a touring production of *Rip Van Winkle*, Mr. Coburn did something I shall always remember.

We had a pretty nice little production of *Rip* going and, exhilarated by success, I dashed off a wire and sent it to Mr. Coburn in Hollywood where he was making about $5,000 a week.

It read: ROLE I PLAYED YOUR COMPANY RIP VAN WINKLE, NOW OPEN TO YOU, MY COMPANY RIP VAN WINKLE. PLEASE REPLY IMMEDIATELY.

In due time I got his wire. It went: FLATTERED BY OFFER. MUST REFUSE. NEVER COULD PLAY ROLE THE WAY YOU DID. (signed) CHARLES COBURN.

My production, incidentally, had almost as much trouble with the child's role as Mr. Coburn's had had. At first, the role was played by my younger brother. I think he remembered the lines all right, but whenever he walked onto the stage and looked out into the footlights and the spots, he was struck by terrible stage fright—and he couldn't say anything!

I had to pick up the slack in the second act by ad-libbing: "Ahhhh, zzzzzo you know your old grandfazzer, eh?"

This brought a big laugh from the audience, of course, and Martha Hodge (later Mrs. Myron McCormick and now Mrs. Cleveland Amory), who was helping with the production, worked with my brother to try to get a little improvement. Through no fault of her own, however, she failed, and for three nights he never said a word onstage. Finally, we quickly substituted a young actor of Italian descent and, without rehearsing him, told him what to say.

The first night he appeared, he clutched me around the knees in the first act and in an Italian accent, he cried out: "Papa, papa." And in the second act, he delighted the audience with: "Mama mia, mama mia!"

Well, I had other minor setbacks in my early acting days—like the time when I was to appear as Columbus in a pageant. The day before the show, my brother hit me on the head—inadvertently, I like to tell myself—with a heavy iron bar. And on the day of the show I discovered America with surgical gauze around my head, all splotched with red, and with a trickle of blood running down my face.

And, of course, there was the time when I was to appear as Lincoln, with beard, stovepipe hat and cape, and deliver The Gettysburg Address. Well, the day before, a Sunday, Millie Blackeby, Betty Paddock, Jordan Woodcock and I went to Compo Beach in Westport, Connecticut, and relaxed on the beach the entire day, unworried about sunburn because the atmosphere was hazy.

We didn't know that the sun's rays penetrate such a haze with ease, and the next day—redder than the reddest lobster—I did my little stint, sans makeup, which hurt too much to apply; sans beard, which caused sheer agony when I tried to apply it with spirit gum; and sans top hat, which I couldn't bear on my blistered head.

My faux pas, however, were not confined to the stage. Quite often in everyday life I was able to pull bloopers that nearly drove my father to despair. To be truthful, I think that most of the time I was of great help to him in his little projects around the house—things like building a cement retaining wall in the garden, building a heavy wooden platform on which our steel garage was to be placed, and erecting the grape arbor.

But two or three things I did certainly couldn't be classified under "assistance." The worst, I believe, came on the day that my brother fell out of a tree and broke his arm.

He lay there, screaming wildly, and I could see a jagged end of bone projecting through the skin of his forearm. My father ran over and picked him up in his arms and started to run toward the garage.

"I'll take him to the hospital," he called to me. Then he paused a moment, ever the practical man. "Look," he said to me, "I just mixed a new batch of cement. Keep it moist till I come back, so it won't be ruined."

Then he and my mother put my brother in the car and roared off to the hospital. I'd been quite impressed by what had happened to my brother. Never before had I seen a bone sticking through flesh, with such a lot of blood flowing. And never had I heard anybody yell like that.

It reminded me of a play I was appearing in at the time—I played a twelve-year-old boy who falls downstairs and breaks his leg—and I realized for the first time that in rehearsal I hadn't been getting much realism into the role.

Pondering this, I went over to where my father and I were building the retaining wall—a concrete and stone edifice about 2 feet thick, 10 feet high and about 60 feet long—and musing about how I might improve my performance, I got the hose, turned on the water and sprinkled the batch of cement that my father had mixed.

I stood there for a while, alternately thinking about my characterization and wondering whether I was putting too much water on the cement. Finally, I put down the hose, went down to the lower level of the garden where the cement was and covered it with a heavy tarpaulin so the sun wouldn't dry it out.

Then I went into the house and got my "sides" of the play—the pages containing my lines. I read them over very carefully, understanding for the first time that I certainly hadn't been giving the role what it called for. So I sat down and studied the lines over and over.

Then, with the lines fixed in mind, I went to the flight of stairs just off the dining room, and practiced falling down them. As I poised, before my fall, I said the lines, giving them the light, airy touch that a youngster who doesn't expect to fall downstairs would give. And then, as I crashed down the stairs, I let out the kind of yells that I'd heard from my brother. I did this a number of times, and each time I felt my performance was better.

Time fled by, and all of a sudden I heard a cry of rage out in back. It was my father. He'd just returned from the hospital with my brother, whose arm was in a cast and supported by a sling, and he'd gone to the wall to see whether his cement still was moist.

But—and this is something I hadn't realized until then—I hadn't turned off the hose! Just as I hadn't turned it off in the Smiths' cellar!

I ran out of the house, thinking I'd find that the batch of cement had been washed away. But it was worse than that.

I'd left the hose up on the top of the wall, and it had run and run. And it had sluiced away every bit of concrete that we'd laid that day! All the stones we'd put in the wall lay in a jumble at the bottom. Only the crisscrossing of the steel reinforcements remained. Half of the wall itself had disappeared.

Well, not exactly disappeared. There it was—spread out over a quarter of an acre of vegetable garden!

My father took on about that, I must say, and as a result I

54

wasn't permitted to help him much for two or three weeks. Then, one day, he came to me, and there was a sort of pleading note in his voice, and he said:

"Norton, I've got to do a little work up on the roof. Now, do you think you could help me without pulling the house down? Do you think you can keep your mind on what you're doing— and NOT BLOW THE WHOLE PLACE UP?"

I said that I most certainly could, and I was going to ask him what made him even question me, but I decided that that was a question better left unasked. He then explained to me that there was a leak in the roof somewhere near the chimney and Mr. Gorham, the contractor down the street, had lent him a tar boiling apparatus. He said he was going to boil some tar, and take it up on the roof and repair the leak.

He then showed me the thing, which had a fire going in it, and also some tar, cooking in a deep well arrangement.

"I'll fill this tar pot," Dad said, "and I'll go up on the roof. You see, I've already rigged a pulley up there and all I want you to do is pull it up to me when I get there. Once the pot is up there, hold it till I tell you to release it. And if, for any reason, you should have to go away—see that hook on the tar machine?—just hook the rope around that in a clove hitch and it'll stay there, securely, till you get back."

I assured my father that both he and the tar pot were in safe hands and he mounted the ladders to the roof. Then, slowly, I pulled the heavy tar pot up to the peak of the steep slate roof on which he was perched.

"Okay, hold it," he said. And he dipped some tar out and disappeared as he headed for the leaky area.

At this moment, my mother called me. "Telephone, dear," she said. "Somebody wants to talk to you about a play."

A play! Another part! For me! Wow!

I stepped over toward the red-hot tar machine and started to fasten the rope in a clove hitch to the hook. But the wind had changed and it was blowing heavy smoke and intense heat right over where the hook was. I held one hand over my nose and eyes, but still I couldn't stand it. The tears were beginning to pour.

"Come in, dear," called my mother. "They're holding the phone."

I glanced wildly around. The heat was too much near the machine. I saw a heavy stone on the ground and, quickly, I flicked the rope around it two or three times. I tested it, and it held. Then I dashed into the house and took my phone call.

As I started to talk, I heard the crash. My father, thinking the bucket was secured to the machine, had begun dipping more tar out of it. But the pressure of his ladle had disengaged the rope and—*bang*—down shot the nearly full bucket of tar.

It was months before we got all the tar off the white brick and the gray clapboarding of the house. We never did, of course, get it off the flower beds or the wisterias and hydrangeas—we just dug them up and turned them under. And the tar streakings on the concrete driveway embellished it for many years.

Still, not everything I did caused direct anguish to my father. Some of it was indirect.

While we were building the retaining walls, trucks would come every once in a while and dump loads of sand in our driveway, the nearest they could get to the site of construction. Then, each night, we'd all have to shovel the sand into wheelbarrows and trundle it to the rear of the house where it was handy to the wall. And since we couldn't get the car in or out of the garage while the sand was in the driveway, it had to be cleared as speedily as possible.

This seemed to me like a tremendous waste of energy. And I got an idea. I suggested to my father one night that he ask the Muirheads, our next-door neighbors, for permission to have the sand trucks use their driveway which circled behind their house and ran down to the level where we were doing the concrete work.

"Then," I said, "they can back up to our wall and dump the sand right on our property."

There was both pride and pleasure in my father's eyes. "That's using your head," he said, and I was warm with happiness. Dad went right over and got permission from Ernest Muirhead.

"But, Frank," said Mr. Muirhead, a mousy little man with a quiet little voice, "be sure to tell the truck driver there's an old cistern in the yard back there. It's all covered over and you can't see it, but it won't support a heavy truck. He'll have to go to the far side of it."

So, Mr. Muirhead, my father and I went down to his lower-level backyard and he pointed out roughly where the cistern was. It was, he said, close "to there," and he pointed to his house, and some distance away "from there," and he pointed to his barn.

"So," he explained, "the truck should go over there. It shouldn't go anywhere near here."

My father asked me whether I understood this clearly, because, he explained, I'd be there the next day when the truckload of sand arrived, and he'd have the driver ask me for directions.

Well, the next afternoon about four, a huge truck loaded with sand backed into *our* driveway and the driver, getting out, started the machinery which would tilt the box and slide the sand once more into our driveway.

I protested to the driver and at first he didn't want to pay any attention. "This is the way we always done it, kid," he said, "and this is the way I'm gonna do it now."

Well, I yelled so much that finally he became impressed. I said, "You go in and call your office, and you'll find that my father left directions to take it down the Muirheads' driveway and dump it over our wall down there."

Grudgingly, he did phone. He came out of the house in a fine state of temper.

"Look, kid," he snarled at me, "why didn'tcha keep your mouth shut? Now I gotta *back* all the way down that road." And he pointed to the long, circular driveway. "I was 'sposed to be

57

finished a hour ago. Now I'm gettin' stuck. Why don'tcha mind your own business?"

I loathed that driver and for a wild moment I debated whether to forget to tell him about the cistern. But I was afraid not to tell him.

So, as he pulled out of our driveway and backed into the Muirheads', I ran down to the back of our house and perched on the low wall that divided the Mockridge and Muirhead "estates."

Eventually, the truck appeared, grinding backwards slowly, inching around the curve, with the driver half out on the running board, one foot on the brake and one hand on the steering wheel.

It was a massive truck, eight wheels in back and two in front, and it wasn't too easy to handle. The driver was swearing all the way.

As he came down off the driveway and rolled into the Muirheads' yard, preparatory to backing across to our wall, I held up my hand and shouted, "Stop! Stop! There's a cistern!"

The driver jammed on the brakes, pulled the emergency and flung himself out of the cab and onto the ground.

"Waddya mean, a cistern?" he yelled. "I don't see no cistern."

"No," I explained. "It was covered up years ago. But Mr. Muirhead says it won't hold up your truck."

"Oh, *Jesus!*" cried the driver, throwing his hands in the air. "How'inell am I gonna find out where it is?"

I smiled at him smugly.

"I know where it is," I said.

The driver glowered at me for a minute, and then his face relaxed. "Okay, kid," he said, with a grin. "You win. Where the hell is it?"

I leaped off the wall and walked into Mr. Muirhead's yard. I felt much the way MacArthur must have felt when he returned to the Philippines.

"C'mon, kid, I ain't got all day," yelled the driver. "Show me where it is."

58

As I walked along, I clearly recalled the conversation of last night and remembered how Mr. Muirhead had pointed "there" for the truck to go, and not "here." But, for the life of me, I couldn't remember which way he'd pointed.

I'd been standing, I think, on the other side, and now it was hard for me to adjust myself to the position I was in. I absolutely couldn't get it clear in my head whether he had pointed toward the house or the barn when he indicated the safe route.

I was trying to figure this out when the driver exploded. He used a lot of bad language and said that if I didn't get a wiggle on, he was going to clout me and see to it that my father gave me "one hell of a lickin' when he comes home."

It was a hopeless situation, with the driver rattling me like that, and I did what any other field marshal does under such circumstances. I made an instant decision.

I pointed toward the house and said, "Mr. Muirhead says that's the safe way."

"Well, why didn'tcha say so in the first place? Thanks for nothin'," said the driver. He clambered back into the truck, ripped it into gear with a great crashing and gave it the gas. I retreated toward the wall as the truck backed up.

Slowly, to my horror, the ground began to give way. Just a little at first, then more, and more and MORE. Suddenly the driver felt it, and he kicked the brake.

But it was too late. The rear wheels of the truck were sinking into the ground, the front wheels slowly lifting off the ground. Then there were loud reports as the old, rotting timbers that formed the roof of the cistern began to snap. And a sickening crunch as the thin concrete cover cracked to pieces.

And the truck, lifting its nose high in the air, like a horse, slithered backwards into the cistern. The sand poured out at an alarming rate, cushioning the truck's drop into the eight-foot hole. The whole thing made hardly a sound, but the driver, upended in his cab, was screaming like a maniac.

I would have covered my ears with my hands, but I thought it better to scale the wall and take off. I did just that, and I ran like mad into my house, slammed the door and locked it. Then I told my mother to call the police.

"For protection," I said, "and for a man who is stuck in a hole."

And do you know, to this day, I'm not sure whether I got those directions mixed up on purpose, or not.

Chapter Five

NO matter how many painful and embarrassing experiences
I had, I always consecrated myself to a search for the easier
and better way to do things. If told that the only way to shingle
a barn roof is to start at the bottom of the roof and work up
to the peak, I, of course, would figure that it was easier and
quicker to start at the top, slip the shingles under each other
and work down. And when told to rake some damp leaves
and carry them away in baskets, I decided to sprinkle them

with kerosene and burn them where they lay. They burned all right—but so did our neighbor's chicken coop.

I became fairly famous for instituting services that proved to be something less than perfect. One of these involved a Mr. and Mrs. James Scott who purchased the house about 50 feet to the north of us and hired some carpenters to make extensive repairs. Several days before they were to move in, it became apparent that the carpenters would not have things finished in time and, inasmuch as the Scotts had to leave the rented house they were living in, my mother and father gave them the use of three rooms and bath on the top floor of our house. The Scotts moved in—along with countless cartons of dishes, glasses, silverware and other precious possessions that they didn't want to trust to the moving company.

When the day came for the Scotts to move into their new house, Mr. Scott asked me if I'd help him carry some of those cartons. We made a few trips, struggling down the stairs in our house, walking out to the sidewalk, and along the sidewalk to his house, and then upstairs to his second floor. This seemed to me like a lot of unnecessary work.

I suggested that we rig a sort of rope trolley, with pulleys, from our third-floor window to his second-floor window and then transport his possessions in some big canvas sacks like mailbags that my father had. Mr. Scott thought this sounded like a fine idea, and in no time we installed huge pulleys in the window frames and, because knots wouldn't go through the pulleys, I spliced a good strong manila rope. I was in a bit of a hurry, and I realized that I wasn't making as long a splice as I perhaps should, but I reasoned that none of the bags would be too heavy, and besides, I put friction tape over the splice for extra strength.

Mr. Scott put some china in one of the bags, stacking it carefully between layers of newspapers, and we fastened it to the rope with horse blanket pins and then, gingerly, he operated the pulley system and sent the bag across from our house to the second-floor window where Mrs. Scott disengaged it.

We did this two or three times, and Mr. Scott became so elated at the ease with which everything was being shipped that he began to tell me what a fine system it was and how he'd used something like it during the first World War when he had to move things for the Army, and how he was glad, mighty glad indeed, that he'd happened to think of it in connection with this move.

"A great time saver, and a great effort saver," he told me. "You know, if I hadn't thought of this, we'd be lugging that stuff on our backs, back and forth, back and forth. Yessir, a wonderful system. This is really using your head instead of your back."

Mr. Scott was so overjoyed that I didn't have the heart to try to remind him that it was *my* idea. But I did remonstrate a bit when he began putting about twice as much in each bag as I thought he should.

"Look, boy," he said, "this is *my* system. I know stresses and strains like the back of my hand. Why, I moved hundreds of tons for the Army and they gave me a medal for it. In fact, we've been wasting time. I'm going to send *two* bags at once. Saves pulling the line, y'know."

Mr. Scott pinned two heavy bags to the trolley and started them across. The rope sagged alarmingly but Mr. Scott pulled it taut. It was then that the splice gave way. And as we watched, horror-stricken, the two heavy bags swung in a great sweeping arc and smashed against the side of our house. Even muffled as it was by the bags, the sound of breaking glass and china was a terrible thing to hear.

Mrs. Scott, across the way, shrieked as though she'd been stabbed. And she called Mr. Scott some bad names.

It was then that he turned on me. "Goddammit!" he cried. "I told you that fool system wouldn't work. Now look what you've done! Well, all I can tell you is—your father's gonna pay for this!"

But my father didn't pay for it. He told Mr. Scott that if he were fool enough to try to move things on a piece of string, it

63

was his own damn fault. This, unfortunately, brought about a very strained relationship between the Mockridges and the Scotts and for about a year or so no friendly words flowed across the dividing lines of our properties.

Mr. Scott complained when my brother and I and our friends raced up and down the sidewalk on our wagons in front of his house. And Mrs. Scott phoned my mother and said we were making too much noise, even when we were just standing out in the road and talking. Once when I dumped the ashes from our coal furnace, I spilled some close to, or possibly over the property line, and Mr. Scott, red in the face, came out and took a shovel and dug into the ashes and threw them a good 15 feet into our garden. And he warned me that if I did it again, he'd get the police after me for trespassing.

Well, some days later our radio aerial, which ran from our roof to a pole that had been erected about 100 feet to the rear of the house, broke loose from the pole and fell to the ground. Knowing that my father would be disappointed when he came home from work if he couldn't hear Lowell Thomas and the news, and Amos and Andy, I tried to rig up the wire again. But I couldn't shinny far enough up the pole to reach the point of connection.

So, I looked around and decided, temporarily, to fasten the wire to a branch of a huge tree that stood on Mr. Scott's property, but which had branches extending over our property. I climbed up the tree—all the time expecting to be shot—and wrapped the wire around one of the branches that hung over our land. Then I went into the house and tested the radio. It worked just fine.

That night after dinner, my father settled down to listen to Amos and Andy, but Mr. Scott suddenly appeared at the door. "That kid of yours has put up a wire in *my* tree," he said, "and I want it taken down immediately." My father tried to reason with him. He explained that the Kingfish was right in the middle of talking Andy out of some money, and that he wanted to see how it was coming out, and couldn't the whole business wait till after the show?

"No," shouted Mr. Scott. "I want that wire down right now!"

My father, who well knew that the wire was in Mr. Scott's tree, tried once more to placate him, but it was no use. This made my father wild with rage, but there was nothing he could do. He directed me to climb the tree and remove the wire. Then, acting hastily so as not to miss any more of Amos and Andy than he could help, Dad took the wire and tossed it over the limb of a tree much nearer to the house.

"That's my tree too!" screamed Mr. Scott.

"It is not!" shouted my father. "It's right on the line, and besides, most of the branches are over here."

Mr. Scott then called to his wife: "Mrs. Scott" (he always addressed her that way), "Mrs. Scott, telephone for the police."

"Go ahead and call the cops," yelled my father. "And when they get here, there won't be any tree!"

And with that, he dashed into the cellar, got an ax and started to chop down the tree. The tree, about 40 feet tall, was slender and it shuddered with every blow. Mr. Scott was appalled. He danced around in a rage, his face wildly red and his white hair tossing in the breeze.

"Mrs. Scott," he screamed, "call for more police! It's an emergency! We're being attacked! Our very lives are being threatened!"

"Oh, shut up," said my father. "And get back on your own property or I'll cut you down before I finish this tree." And he hacked away at the tree in a fine fury. Chips flew all over the place and my father, a wiry 190-pounder, was soaked with perspiration as he struck blow after blow. And then, as he saw the tree was about to topple, he stopped cutting and stood up and pushed it over to the Scotts' side—right on top of Mr. Scott, who had tried to skip out of danger but who'd tripped over a small bush and fallen on his face.

"There," said my father. "Now it *is* your tree."

65

He rushed into the house to catch whatever was left of Amos and Andy, but the program was over. He had just picked up the newspaper radio program to see what else was on, when the phone rang. It was the chief of police.

"Look, Frank," said the chief, "I'd appreciate it if you'd leave Jim Scott alone tonight. The only two guys on duty are busy, and I can't reach anybody else to send."

"Sure," said my father, grinning. "But there's no trouble. We're good friends. In fact, I just gave him a tree."

My father, incidentally, was not a pugnacious man. A good many times I saw him walk away from an unpleasantness, rather than fight. But when he lost his temper, his rage became almost unbridled and the punishment he dealt out was severe.

Once, according to some men who saw the whole thing, one of my father's assistants in the telephone company, a rough, tough installer who had fought professionally, gave him a bit of lip.

"That," said my father, "will be enough of that. Don't ever say anything like that to me again."

"Yeah," said the installer. "Sez who?" And he said the same thing again.

My father hit him with a right cross that was so fast hardly anybody saw it. The man fell in the dirt, but my father picked him up with his left hand and hit him two or three more times with his right. Then, as the man staggered backwards, Dad hit him with a terrific right overhand and, somehow or other, this drove the man between the rear wheel and the undercarriage of the huge installation truck that was standing there.

The truck had no covering fender, and the installer's body became wedged in such a way that he couldn't be pulled out without ripping his skin. He was out cold, so he had no choice in the matter, but finally the other men jacked up the truck and took off the wheel in order to get him out.

There was only one time when I saw my father settle a difference of opinion with his fists, but I shall never forget it. I

66

was about nine or ten years old and one Saturday my father took me with him in the car when he went to see a man on business. My Uncle Albert was manufacturing portable steel garages at that time, and once in a while my father, if he heard of a prospect, would spend part of a day off making the sale.

The prospect in this case lived about 20 miles from Mount Kisco, and I can't remember the village, but I do know that after Dad made the sale he took me to a little restaurant for a bite to eat.

"I've heard of this place, but I've never been here," said Dad. "It's owned by a man who used to be a professional wrestler and they say the steaks are very good." If there was anything that Dad loved, it was a fine sirloin steak.

Well, we went in about noon and there was nobody in the place. There were five or six tables and we sat down at one. After a while, a giant of a man pushed through a swinging door at the back and walked up to us. He was a sort of Tony Galento type, only bigger, and he had the meanest face I'd ever seen. And it seemed to me that he was a little drunk.

"Waddya want?" he said.

My father said he'd heard there were good steaks to be had, and we'd each like one.

"Not durin' the day," said the man. "We don't waste time with crap like that. Maybe at night, if you're a good customer —if ya know what I mean." And the man leered at Dad. "So, c'mon in the back room—and get to be a good customer."

It was then it dawned on my father that he was in a speakeasy. I didn't know what we were in, but I didn't like it.

"No thanks," said Dad, "we just wanted something to eat." He started to get up.

"Look," said the man, shoving Dad back into his chair, "nobody gives me that stuff. You come in here, you go in the back room! What's the matter, I ain't good enough for ya?"

"No," said my father. "It's just that I don't drink. And besides, I have my son with me."

"You don't drink!" roared the man. And he bent forward

and put his two huge hands on my father's shoulders and shoved his massive face close to my father's, and then he said something snarly into my father's ear—something that I didn't get but which, apparently, my father did.

From a sitting position, Dad punched the man in the stomach, and as the man grunted and his head came down, Dad's head snapped forward and upward and smashed against his nose. The man fell backward a bit and Dad was out of the chair in a split second. His two hands pumped to the man's face and the man fell across a table and it splintered and crashed to the floor.

The man rolled over, got up and grabbed a chair, but before he could really swing it, Dad closed in and hit him two or three times just under the ear. He fell against the wall and then he started staggering toward the swinging door which led to the kitchen. Dad hit him again, but he got through the door and grabbed a knife.

At this, my father's foot flew out and caught the man on the knee. He yowled and bent forward—and right into one of the best timed uppercuts I've ever seen. The man flipped over backwards and crashed, striking his head on the floor. He lay there, quite still.

A huge, black-haired woman, obviously the owner's wife, then rushed up to Dad from the other end of the kitchen.

"Look," she said, "do what you want with him. But don't do it in here. We don't want no trouble with the cops."

We left after that, and we went to a drugstore where Dad got some surgical gauze and some adhesive tape and bandaged his cut knuckles. And then we went to a little lunch wagon across the street and had some hamburgers.

Dad looked at me and asked, "The hamburger all right?" I said it was. "Well," he said, with a wink, "the steaks would have been better."

As I said, my father wasn't pugnacious. And neither am I. I have run from a good many fights in my life. And I hope to run from many more. But when I get cornered, I suddenly do things that surprise me.

My first years in elementary school were filled with fights—mainly because many of my fellow students were of Italian parentage, only recently arrived in this country and imbued with an overpowering feeling of hostility because they didn't understand the people or the customs. And to many of these boys, I represented all the things that irritated them. They were a tough bunch, and many of the modern Mafia leaders look like sissies compared to the kids I knew.

But, all in all, I held my own, and I didn't worry much about combative activities one way or other. There was one kid, however, who really bugged me. And even to this day, I can't exactly tell why.

His name was David Niss and he wasn't Italian—he was Jewish—and he wasn't anywhere near as rough or tough as the other little mobsters, but he had the whammy on me. I was scared of this David Niss, who was known as Nissy, and I did everything I could to avoid him. Since we always were in the same classes, this wasn't easy.

He'd meet me on the way to school, and one word would lead to another, and he'd push me into the brook. And I'd have to stand in the boiler room at school to get dry. He'd meet me at lunchtime and he'd put a chip on his shoulder and say, "Knock that off, and I'll beat you up. Don't knock it off, and I'll beat you up."

I found this disconcerting. And, more often than not, I ran away, followed by the laughter of Nissy and his friends. Once in a while, I'd stand up to him a bit, and toss a feeble punch. And, with a swift jab, he'd blacken my eye, or cut my lip. His hands were very fast and his mind was even faster. Not like the slow-moving, but stronger, Italian boys who could be forced to fight the kind of fight I wanted.

I fretted about this a lot, and I didn't know what to do. Looking back on it, I'm inclined to think that where the other kids who heckled me made me mad, and thus eager to fight, Nissy never really made me mad. And I didn't have the same compulsion to fight.

Basically, I think I liked him and respected him, and wanted his friendship. How can you fight a guy when you feel like that?

Anyway, there came a day when my temper prevailed. It was a cold winter's day, and there was a lot of snow and ice on the ground. I left school rather late that afternoon—maybe kept after; maybe just waiting till I thought Nissy had gone—and I walked the few hundred yards from the school building to the top of the hill on Hyatt Avenue that led down to East Main Street.

And there stood Nissy! And several of his friends!

For the life of me, I cannot remember just what indignity he visited upon me that afternoon, nor exactly what happened. All I remember is that suddenly I tossed my briefcase aside and plunged into this vicious dragon. I smacked and smacked and smacked, and all of a sudden one of my punches caught Nissy just right and he toppled over backwards, slipped and fell on the ice and then began sliding, helplessly, down the hill. He clawed at the ice to try to stop himself, but he couldn't.

I stood at the top of the hill and laughed and laughed, and Nissy's friends joined me, and we all stood there laughing. At the bottom of the hill this fiend picked himself up and glared up at us, and then his face slid into a grin, and he snorted, and he started to laugh, and he laughed and laughed and laughed.

From that day on, Nissy and I were the best of friends— through all sorts of travail and through all sorts of pleasure— and today, probably 40 years later, we're still the best of friends. He's the owner and president of the Stonington Paper Tube Co., in Holyoke, Massachusetts, and the only thing that I don't like about him is that he thinks his business is more important than spending unlimited time with me in New York.

Only one of my many fights, as I remember it, cost my father any money but this one was quite expensive. It came about as a result of a lack of compatibility between me and a 15- or 16-year-old grocery clerk named Louie.

Louie, who was about three or four years older than I, and much taller and heavier, was one of the nastiest bullies ever and he gave me a rough time whenever I patronized the James Butler grocery store in which he worked. Louie, I think, was the original school dropout—how he managed to stay out of school before he was seventeen and also avoid the truant officer, I don't know—and he had about as much intelligence as a cow. But he was as mean as a goaded bull and my first encounter with him was most painful.

It was the custom in those days for youngsters who were sent to the grocery store to open one of the many glass-topped boxes racked up in a case and help themselves to a cookie or two.

I was reaching for a coconut-covered, creamy marshmallow delight one Saturday morning when Louie sneaked up behind me and suddenly smashed the steel-rimmed cover down on my little finger. I screamed in very real agony, but I had to kick him in the shins before he'd take his hand off the cover and release me. I complained to the manager and he reprimanded Louie with something mild like "Don't do that anymore, Louie," which I didn't think was sufficient punishment.

Our relationship worsened after that and there seldom was a day when I didn't have trouble at that store. Louie would be hiding behind a shelf when I went to get something and he'd grab me and twist my arm behind my back. Or he'd take the long, pincerlike stick and reach 'way up and topple a box of flour on my head. And once he gave me a push and I fell into a pile of rotting cabbages and other garbage that he'd swept up.

During all this, I hardly ever retaliated. First of all, he was too big for me to handle, and secondly, I found that whenever I swung at him or pushed him back, he redoubled his efforts to torture me. Better, I thought, to take my daily allotment of fundamental punishment, and get out as quickly as possible.

71

One day, however, Louie went too far. I had been pleased when I entered the store to see that Louie was up on a tall stepladder, stacking tins of something on the highest shelves in the store. There, I thought to myself, he wasn't likely to bother me.

I hastily got all the items I needed and put them in a huge paper bag. I paid the manager, who then went into the little office in the rear to answer the phone, and I started to walk out of the store. But Louie took the long pincer stick and hit me on the head. I turned, angrily, and he jabbed the stick and knocked the bag out of my hands—and everything I had, including a dozen eggs, fell to the floor.

There were tears of rage in my eyes, and, not even planning anything in particular, I rushed forward, grabbed one side of the stepladder and gave a mighty yank. Much to my surprise, the ladder easily toppled—pitching Louie 10 or 15 feet right into the fruit rack which collapsed under his weight. It cascaded oranges, lemons, grapefruit, apples, tangerines, pears and heaven only knows what else all over the floor.

Louie, unhurt, but purple with anger, rose up out of this mess and threw the first thing he could put his hand on. It was a big, ripe peach and it splattered all over my face.

I grabbed a good-sized can of stewed tomatoes and heaved it at him. It caught him on the chest, and it must have hurt, because he grunted, clapped his hands to his chest and looked down to see what damage had been done. I took advantage of this to shy two more cans at him. One hit him on the ear and lacerated it badly, and when Louie saw blood he yelled in terror, and promptly slipped on the fruit and fell down.

The other can sailed over his head and crashed into the rather elaborate display in the store's show window. Everything, I think, tumbled down.

The manager came racing out of his office, and I started for the front door. But I slipped and crashed into a 4- or 5-foot-high display of canned goods that stood in the center of the floor. Everything went helter-skelter and the manager couldn't pick his way through the rolling cans fast enough to follow me, so I reached the front door.

I could have escaped, but I was so mad at Louie, and at the manager, too, for not having protected me, that I stood there and threw cans at them with every bit of power I could muster. The two retreated and I don't remember whether I hit them, but I can well recall the damage those cans did throughout the store.

They smashed the glass tops on the cookie boxes, they knocked down just about every display in the store, they went through the glass in the window between the store and the office, they knocked down and smashed four or five large bottles of ammonia and within a few seconds the fumes were so bad nobody could stay in the store.

Louie and the manager went out the back, and I raced out the front door, ran across the street into the stationery store, tore right clean through it and out the back door and down into the cellar where I hid for at least an hour. Eventually, I peeked out and when I found nobody watching, I sneaked down behind the whole row of stores on Main Street until I came to the railroad tracks, and then, hugging the fence until I got out of the business section of the village, I walked home on the rails.

And when I got home, I found my mother and father both waiting for me. Their grim faces told me that through the electronic marvel of the telephone, they had been given a pretty good idea of what had happened.

That little episode cost my father something close to $40, and I got a bit of backside chastisement. But victory really was mine. My father insisted that Louie be fired, and after that, Louie went away and I never saw him again.

Chapter Six

WHEN I was in the sixth grade, I fell in love with a beautiful, curly-haired little girl named Bubbles Glou. Her first name really was Miriam, but she was called Bubbles because she bubbled and effervesced with good nature and spread happiness and sunshine all around.

She was something of a cross between Shirley Temple and Rebecca of Sunnybrook Farm and, except for my teachers in the second, third, fourth and fifth grades whom I adored (you remember why I couldn't love the teacher in the first grade!), Bubbles was the loveliest thing I'd ever seen. She had everything that Doris Kenyon, Pola Negri and Mae West had, and she displayed a lot of the "It" that Clara Bow came to use so advantageously.

Now obviously, a girl with all those qualities wasn't going to be much impressed by plain old Norton Mockridge, the kid with the unruly red hair, freckles all over his face and well-bitten nails who sat at the desk across the aisle from hers. A kid of ten, going on eleven, with knickerbockers and long stockings, and shoes that laced up over the ankles.

Oh, Bubbles was friendly enough—borrowed my eraser occasionally, and once in a while asked me a question about a rule in English or a date in history, but she reserved her most enchanting smiles for fellows like Bill Banks, who later went into the FBI; Manson Jennings, the son of our principal; Alexander Baskind; and my old nemesis, Nissy.

Obviously, the courtship of Bubbles required that little extra touch, and it was here that my smoldering talent for instant imagination, creativeness and showmanship had to be brought into play.

I dipped into a good many old pulp magazines devoted to detective, western and ghost stories and found a number that had been written by a certain Capt. Buck Sadler.

They were written simply enough, hardly any polysyllabic words, but they brimmed with action and excitement, and they informed the reader that Capt. Buck Sadler was a devilish fellow, indeed, good-looking, dashing, debonair, sophisticated and God's gift to the ladies—the man, apparently, after whom James Bond eventually was sculptured.

I presented Bubbles with some of these stories, underscoring the more significant and amatory parts, and, after she'd expressed approval, I lowered my voice, looked around to see whether anyone else was listening, and conspiratorially confided that Capt. Buck Sadler was—I. Well, you could see that she was impressed!

75

She did have some reservations about whether I alone was responsible for some of the more lurid details of the plots, but she really wasn't in any position to argue that I was not the writer because, after all, I regularly got between 95 and 100 in my English tests and had a 98 average for the year, the highest, I think, in the class. Several times the teacher had said that my compositions were excellent, my imagination untrammeled, and that I might well have had a 100 in all tests, except for the fact that here and there she couldn't read my handwriting.

That was a good year for me, academically, by the way. I got averages of 92 in arithmetic, 88 in geography, 97 in spelling, 98 in history, 94 in reading, and 96 in nature study. And I might have continued in this rarefied atmosphere if I hadn't pushed my luck a bit too far.

Bubbles, sharing the secret that I was Capt. Buck Sadler, was intrigued by me to quite an extent and, as we walked home from school, I often outlined plots of stories I intended to write, and once in a while I would let her peek at several handwritten sheets of manuscript—which I'd laboriously copied from Sadler's already published stories. But as time went on, it seemed to me, some of the shine wore off and she became less and less interested in Sadler—and me.

Whenever a bunch of us played hide-and-seek near Bubbles' house on Grove Street, she no longer seemed eager to sneak into the cellar with me and, hiding in a darkened corner, hold hands and discuss my literary exploits. Once I saw her holding hands with Stanley Eccles, and another time I caught her twinkling her eyes at Otto Hagen.

It was then that I decided to tell her my most important secret: I was not only Capt. Buck Sadler, devil-may-care author, but I also was a private detective!

One momentous day when we were alone, sitting on the front steps of her porch, I grandly drew from my pocket a shiny, silver-plated shield, bearing the state seal, an eagle with extended wings, and the words: PRIVATE DETECTIVE.

Oh, I tell you, that was a time to cherish! The look on Bubbles' face was ecstatic. Her eyes widened with surprise, excitement, and, I like to think, pure adoration. But then, woman-like, she sputtered, "But, Norton . . . how could you be a detective? . . . You're not old enough."

"Oh, no?" I said. "That's what *you* think. That's not what the International Association of Youth Against Crime thinks." And then I told her, rather witheringly, that here and there throughout the country, in cities where crime was getting out of hand, highly intelligent and extremely resourceful "younger people" had been picked to aid the FBI in its fight against lawlessness.

"You see, Bubbles," I explained, "my greatest power as a detective in this massive national war against the underworld is that nobody, not even you, as well as you know me, would think that I'm a detective."

Well, this made pretty good sense to Bubbles, and, after pledging most solemnly never to tell *anyone*, she kissed me lightly on the cheek and went in to have her supper. I walked home happy—my feet never touching the pavement.

This lovely euphoric state lasted for several weeks. Once again, Bubbles and I hid in the dark cellar during hide-and-seek and we held hands while I told her how I was helping trap bootleggers, rumrunners and counterfeiters. I read crime reports in the newspapers every day and, whenever there was the slightest Westchester County connection, I'd smile enigmatically, describe it to her, and say something like:

"And how do you suppose the police discovered that connection?" Or "And where do you think the tip came from that led to that highly important arrest?" And this, I might point out, was in the days long before such things as Junior G-men ever had been thought of!

Unfortunately, however, disaster was approaching, and it came one day where I'd never suspected it might occur—in my sixth grade classroom.

We had a very fine teacher by the name of Helen W. Burden who only recently had married Clifford (Doc) Burden, the high school athletic coach. Mrs. Burden was love-smitten beyond belief, and she sat mooning at her desk for long periods at a time, almost entirely oblivious to what was going on in the classroom.

Doc Burden used to drop into the classroom two or three times a day to look adoringly at his pretty wife and sometimes, after he'd been in the manual training shop, he'd bring her little love tokens—long, spiraled wood shavings from the edges of planks, and Mrs. Burden, thanking him gaily, would push back her long hair and hang these shavings from her ears like earrings.

Then, after Doc Burden departed, she'd prop her chin on her hands, rest her elbows on the desk, finger the "earrings" and let her mind soar right out of the classroom. It was then that all 34 of us would indulge in extracurricular activity. I don't remember what the rest of them did, but Bubbles and I used to whisper and exchange notes. In this way, I kept her informed of the progress in the fight against crime.

One ghastly day, however, Mrs. Burden came out of her trance more quickly than usual and surveyed what was going on in the class. Expertly, she leaped from her desk, stalked over to me and neatly intercepted a note in which I had detailed rather fully, and perhaps a little immodestly, the role I had played in the capture of four men who'd been counterfeiting $5 and $10 bills in the city of White Plains.

Mrs. Burden read the note and then began to laugh. She laughed so hard that her wooden earrings fell off, but she didn't seem to notice.

"This, class," she said, "is too good not to share with you." And then, to my red-faced horror, she read the entire thing to the other students. They roared, and I was terribly distressed. I buried my face in my hands.

At this, Bubbles, pained by what I was enduring, stood up and cried out, "But that's true, Mrs. Burden. He *did* do that. He's a *private detective*. And he has a badge to prove it."

Well, what happened after that was so dreadful I haven't the heart to relate it, even after 40 years. But, in capsule form, I can tell you that Mrs. Burden made me produce my precious shield and show it to the class, and then she told me that if there were to be any secret agents in the class, they would have to register with the school, and she sent me down to the principal's office for that purpose.

I'll never forget the look on Mr. Jennings' face when I walked in and told him I wanted to register as a secret agent. It was he, by the way, who confiscated my shield, my fingerprinting outfit that I'd just ordered from a mail order house and was carrying in my briefcase, and my "persuaders"—a heavy metal bracelet with steel handles which police use to wrap around the wrists of criminal and persuade them to submit quietly.

I got them all back in time, but I couldn't look at them without getting the shudders. So I put them in a trunk in the attic and I never saw them or thought of them again until 1951 when, after my mother died, we were cleaning out the attic. Then I tried to give them to a little boy who lived near me, but he turned them down. He said he had a two-way wrist radio, a lie detector, a ray gun and a Junior G-man certificate and that was enough for him.

But that experience in the sixth grade pointed me toward believing two things: that love isn't worth the effort or the hell you'll catch in the long run, and that the best way to get even with a teacher for turning you in to the principal is to quit studying.

Unfortunately, I couldn't quite even the score with Mrs. Burden because it was too close to the end of the year to do much but bring my average down a few points, but I applied that principle to the rather startled teacher in the seventh grade and successfully kept my average down to about 80. She never understood why I was reluctant to study, and I never told her. Instead, I turned my fertile imagination and love for the unusual to other fields. And one of the finest outlets was the telling of ghost stories to other kids in my neighborhood.

Night after night, during the warm weather, as soon as it got dark a group of us would troop into the woods near my house and we'd find a clearing, build a small campfire and sit around it. Then an older boy, Dick Hart, and I would start the spooky tales. Nothing was too bloody, too eerie, too outlandish or fiendish for us to tell. (Why I didn't become a TV writer I'll never know!)

We made up the stories as we went along, never knowing how they were going to come out. But many times we didn't even have to finish the stories. This was because, as darkness really set in, and as the fire died down and the wind rustled through the branches and small animals scurried in the blackness, our listeners got gooseflesh, and saying they thought they heard their mothers calling, they fled out of the woods and straight to their houses.

During the day, Dick and I would hunt around through the woods to find even spookier places to hold our storytelling séances. For a time we used an abandoned two-hole privy but we gave it up after a while because one night a rotting plank broke and two of the kids fell through.

The best place of all was the old Kensing mansion at the end of Moger Avenue. This house, which once had been a showplace in Mount Kisco, was a gabled four-story building that sat well back from the street and stood in the middle of three or four acres, surrounded by extremely tall trees.

When the Kensings moved out, the place, for some reason or other, was abandoned. And it stood that way for years. The windows and doors originally had been boarded up, but now and then a hobo or some other homeless soul would rip off some boards, break a windowpane and go into the house for a night's sleep.

All of the rooms still were carpeted from wall to wall, and many of them had draperies hanging like shrouds from sagging poles. A few old chairs and tables had been left behind and there were chandeliers and sconces, although, of course, the electric current long since had been shut off. There was a heavy layer of dust over everything, and there were incredibly large spider webs in almost every room, webs liberally sprinkled with dead flies, and presided over by fat, black spiders the size of half dollars.

I had been in the house several times before the Kensings left it, and I clearly remembered the stateliness of it, and the cheerfulness of the blazing logs in the downstairs fireplaces.

It was hard for me, at first, to understand why anybody would leave so attractive a house, but in time I convinced myself that the Kensings had abandoned it because a member of the family had been brutally murdered in it. This, of course, never happened, but it was a nice thought, it added interest to the house, and it was a wonderful thing to tell friends when you took them in on an inspection tour.

After the hoboes had opened the way, we kids got to removing a board or two at a time—often for use in our campfires in the nearby woods—and then, as we got braver, we made both daylight and nocturnal forays.

At first, we were a little too timid to sit inside one of the gloomy rooms at night for our ghost-story sessions, but we loved to go up on the roof, which had a spiky iron fence around it, and lie there, gazing at the stars and listening to the creak of branches against the gutters and chimneys, while the ghosts came and went and entertained or scared us.

One night, after we'd been telling stories there off and on for several weeks, Dick and I got our small audience so chilled by a ghost story featuring a kind of ectoplasm that radiated from its original spiritual manifestation and attached itself to mortals, burrowing under their skin, eating into their bloodstream and changing them from humans to misty wraiths which had to live in dank swamps to survive, that we soon found ourselves without listeners.

Having nothing else to do, and possessing a flashlight (which we used to hold under our chins and shine upwards on our faces to create monstrous visual effects at proper moments in our stories), we decided to explore the house more thoroughly than ever before. We went from room to room, finding traces here and there of where the hoboes had bedded down after dining on tins of sardines and bread, and finally we came upon a closet which was locked.

Dick, whose father, among other things, was custodian of the Mount Kisco National Bank, had some master keys for various kinds of locks because he often helped or substituted for his father at the bank and needed a quick and easy way to get into the offices. He tried two or three of them on the closet door lock and suddenly the door squeaked open.

There was a radio program at the time called *The Shadow*, which featured a creaking door accompanied by a chilling voice, laughing maniacally and deeply intoning: "The Shadow knowwwwwwws . . . ha, ha, ha, hah!"

And that closet door sounded just like the door on *The Shadow*. Both Dick and I expected to hear the scary laughter and we turned, ready to light out of there any second. But then, of course, we got control of ourselves, and we flashed the light into the closet.

There on the floor lay the skeletons of two birds which, presumably, had been trapped when the closet was closed or the door blew shut (quite a few birds had taken to living in the house, and we always told people they were bats!) and there, hanging from a rod, were five or six musty, dust-covered men's suits and two or three dresses or housecoats.

Almost instantly, the same idea popped into our minds. Why not rig up a dummy with these clothes? A life-sized, male-type dummy that maybe could be suspended by the neck from a chandelier in one of the bedrooms to add a little extra excitement to the trip the next time we conducted anybody through the house.

We took out a suit and stuffed it with cushions from the chairs downstairs and tied it together with some ties we found. We pushed a cushion out the neck of the tightly buttoned coat and placed an old fedora on top of it. Then we lifted it up to see where we could suspend it from the chandelier. But it fell apart.

I ran home and got some large safety pins, as well as an old pair of my father's high-top work shoes, and we pinned the dummy together securely, stuck the tops of the shoes up under the pant legs and pinned them in, too. The effect was most realistic. We were extremely pleased with our work, and we locked the dummy in the closet and went home to think about what we could do with it.

In the next days, Dick and I discussed that dummy quite a bit. Dick had a flair for the theatrical and, of course, so did I, so we felt that the dummy deserved a majestic premiere. Finally, we decided to unveil him to some of our friends—at a specially contrived showing.

"This," said Dick, "will be more fun than just *telling* ghost stories. We'll *give* 'em a real ghost."

Dick, on one of his visits to New York City, went to a novelty store where he bought a Halloween kind of mask of an Italian fruit peddler, a mask with staring reddish-black eyes and a heavy black mustache. I borrowed one of my father's extra large hunting knives, and I also got a pair of old chamois dress gloves that at a hasty glance gave the impression of being made of human skin.

We stuffed the gloves with cotton, and Dick painted nails on the fingers, and even inked in heavy black hair on the backs of the gloves. We pinned them inside the sleeves of the dummy and, in the dim light, they looked exactly like hands.

We laid the dummy on its back on the floor in a bedroom on the third floor, about eight feet in from the door, and we fastened the face mask to the pillow protruding from the coat.

We pulled the old fedora down over the brow and stepped back to inspect our handiwork. The effect was electric. Dick knotted a tie around the dummy's neck and, in his outstretched hand, he placed a large cap pistol that looked exactly like a nickel-plated revolver.

83

I then added my masterpiece. I plunged the hunting knife into the dummy's chest and, taking a bottle of catsup, I smeared a huge, seemingly spreading, red stain all around the wound. The dummy lying there on his back, revolver in hand and knife in chest, was so realistic it caught our breath.

We did all of this late in the afternoon. Then, after dinner that night, Dick and I met at Main Street and Moger Avenue and we began to round up the gang—for some ghost stories.

We told two or three of our confidants what we'd done, but we didn't tell everybody. To this day, I cannot remember just how many fellows we took to the old Kensing house—Tony Castronova, Stanley Eccles, Harry Busby and some others— but I well recall one of them. He was Eddie Laregena, a good runner and football player, who was as brave as the next guy but whose skin itched more than most when he heard a ghost story.

We didn't tell *him* about the man in the upstairs bedroom. In fact, we had a hard time talking him into coming with us to hear the ghost stories. He always claimed that ghost stories right after dinner made it hard for him to digest his food.

However, faced with the prospect of being left alone that night, he walked up Moger Avenue with us, went through the big stone and concrete pillars guarding the unkempt driveway and clambered up the steps at the back of the porch.

It was just getting dark, and Dick asked me whether I'd brought a flashlight.

I said yes, and produced a small, two-cell torch in which I'd put some run-down batteries—just enough to illuminate our little production, but not enough to light it sharply.

In single file, we went through the broken window, across the dining room into the library and up the stairs to the second floor.

"I think I hear something," Dick hissed, holding up his hand.

"Let's get out of here," said Eddie.

"Shhhh," cried all the others. Eddie shushed, but he flicked his head from side to side and shifted from foot to foot.

"Must've been my imagination," said Dick, quietly. "C'mon, let's go."

And we started up the second flight of stairs to the third-floor bedrooms. Eddie went along.

The stairs creaked alarmingly and we could have been heard half a block away. But nobody spoke out loud. And when we whispered, it was very softly. Dick reached the third floor first and I brought up the rear. Eddie was just ahead of me.

We walked slowly along the hall to the staircase leading to the fourth floor and the roof. Suddenly, Dick held up his hand and stopped. I played my dim light on his hand.

"Listen," he whispered.

We all listened and heard nothing, except Eddie's heavy breathing.

Slowly, cautiously, Dick opened the door to the bedroom. He looked in and then turned and said, "Nothin' here. Let's not go up to the roof. Let's tell our stories in here."

Eddie started to say something, but we all moved ahead and I pushed him from the rear.

As soon as we all were in the room, Dick cried out, "Oh, my God! Look at that!"

I then turned my light full on the "body."

The effect was even more gruesome than I had imagined it would be and I felt chilled. But I had no time to admire our work.

Suddenly, I was hurled backwards against the wall, banged against it with the force of a bull, and I crashed to the floor. It took only an instant to realize I'd been hit by Eddie as he whirled and rushed for the door. He hurdled my fallen body, skidded into the hall, raced for the stairs and began leaping down them four and five at a time. He couldn't see in the darkness but that wasn't bothering him a bit.

I jumped up and ran after him. All the others followed me. Together we pounded down the stairs after Eddie. But Eddie, a fine 440-yard-dash man, was going faster than he'd ever gone in his life. As we went down one flight of stairs, we could hear him pounding down the one below.

And as we reached the bottom floor, we heard him going out through the back window—literally through it! He didn't slide through the broken pane. His body ripped out the crossbars and the other panes, too.

We got to the porch just in time to see him vaulting the railing as though it were only an inch high, and he streaked across the front lawn so fast he seemed to be nothing more than a flitting shadow. As we watched, he flung himself right through the high, bushy hedge, landed on the grass on the other side, picked himself up and raced down Moger Avenue so swiftly he disappeared into the darkness in a second or two.

Well—we all of us were so caught up with the speed of the whole thing that we just stood there for a moment, gazing after the far gone Eddie and not knowing what to think. But then we started to laugh, and with this release we really turned it on and we laughed and laughed till we cried, and we howled and screamed and fell down on the porch and rolled around.

We were lying there, hurting from laughter, when, off in the distance, we heard it.

Yes, it was the sirens again. Eddie had told the cops that a man had been murdered in the Kensing house and two patrol cars were streaking up Moger Avenue.

We didn't have time, of course, to dismember or hide our dummy, but Dick and I sped up and down those stairs in record time—salvaging our hunting knife and cap pistol, the only things that could be traced to us.

We went out the back window and off the porch just as the cops were braking in the driveway in front. We fled into the deep grass behind the house, crawled into the woods as the other kids had done, and took off. We made so much noise I thought they'd be after us any minute, but I suppose we were out of earshot before the officers got around to the back of the house.

We took the long way around—couple of miles through the

woods and along the railroad tracks back into the village. And it was a long time before I got to sleep that night.

I'm sure the cops found out who'd pulled the whole thing, but they never approached us or did anything about it. My guess is that they didn't want the "murder" hoax to get into the local newspapers.

But they did order another boarding-up of all the doors and windows at the Kensing house and from then on we never went back there to tell ghost stories. In fact, we never again got together anywhere to tell ghost stories. Dick and I felt we couldn't top our last performance.

Chapter Seven

MUCH of what I am today I owe to my maiden aunt, Lavinia. Or, to put it more accurately, it's largely due to her patience, her guidance and her determination that I'm no worse than I am.

Aunt Lavinia, or Aunty Vene as she was known to the family, took me in hand when I was only about six and tried to mold me and give me culture. I'm afraid that she was not wholly successful.

She did, I believe, give me my love for the theater and for literature in general. But she failed miserably when she tried to get me to understand and appreciate opera, classical music and art. I've squirmed through virtually every opera from *Aida* (which I saw, rather than heard, at least eight times) to *Wozzeck*, which is a dog of an opera if ever there was one.

I've slept through countless philharmonic performances and chamber music recitals. And, with Aunty Vene, I've tramped through the Metropolitan Museum of Art, the Whitney Museum of American Art, the Frick Museum, the Museum of Natural History, the Brooklyn Museum, the Riverside Museum, the Museum of Contemporary Crafts, the Jacques Marchais Center of Tibetan Art, The Cloisters, Asia House, the Jewish Museum, the Schomburg Collection of Negro-American literature and history in the public library, the Jumel Mansion, the Museum of the City of New York, the American Indian Museum and scores of others. And I still don't understand or care much about opera, classical music or art.

At my aunt's urging, I took piano lessons for two years and got to the point where I could plunk out an almost recognizable rendition of "Traumerei," but I junked the whole business because the necessary hour's practice every day got in the way of my football engagements.

I spent many of my summer vacations with Aunty Vene, who lived in an apartment in New York, and our schedule, seven days a week, was as rigorous as the human body could endure.

A typical day went something like this:

Up 8 A.M. Setting-up exercises for 15 minutes. Breakfast. Half an hour on the piano, accompanied by sharp knocking on the ceiling of the apartment below. Out into the great city by 9 A.M. Visits to two or three museums, and possibly a sail to the Statue of Liberty. A trip to the bank to clip a coupon or two and get enough cash for the day's excursions. (It was during a visit to one of my aunt's several banks that she showed me a $1,000 bill. I had never seen one before—and I haven't seen one since.)

Then, lunch at the Automat. My aunt ate at the Automat whenever she could because the food was good, the silver was unusually clean, you could eat and get out in record time and —most important—you served yourself and thus there was no tipping. If there was one thing my aunt hated, it was tipping. She nearly died when she first visited France and found every single servitor with outstretched hands, crying *"Pourboire, pourboire."*

After lunch, and before the price went up at 1 P.M., we'd see a movie in Times Square. And after that, even though the price had gone from 35 cents to 50 cents, we'd see another movie in Times Square. Then we'd go to a branch library to get a book on the history touched on in one of the movies, and maybe visit another museum, or take a stroll through Chinatown.

Dinner at the Automat. Then, possibly, an inspection of an art gallery such as Parke-Bernet. And then, the pièce de résistance—a Broadway play! I liked the movies all right, but it was the plays that really got me. And I couldn't see enough of them. On Wednesdays and Saturdays, matinee days, we saw two plays—eliminating a visit to a museum, which, I must say, set very well with me.

Then, after the show, we'd walk wearily home to sit and talk, study the programs, read some of the book and drop off to the soundest sleep possible.

No boy could have been more grateful or indebted to an adult than I was to Aunty Vene. And the night before she died a few years ago at the age of eighty-five, I kissed her warmly and thanked her again—for the thousandth time, I suppose—for all the wonderful things she had done for me.

But there's a special thing she did for me that I want to tell you about. She taught me how to walk in New York City.

Now, you might think that walking in New York is no different than in any other city, and that nobody has to be taught, but you'd be wrong. In New York, as I learned from Aunty Vene, it's survival of the fittest, devil take the hindmost, and keep it tight on the corners. And, I might explain, Aunty Vene had nothing but scorn for people who refused to listen to her advice.

I should point out, of course, that, actually, there's no need to learn to walk in New York if you're not going anywhere. If you're willing to ride with the tide, well, you've got no problem. But if you've got two or three places to go within an hour or so (or if you're trying to maintain the kind of schedule that my aunt and I set for ourselves), you'd better learn the Aunty Vene Valse.

"The best offense," Aunty used to tell me, "is a *very sharp* offense." And to this end she had trained herself well.

On foot, in wild, whirling pedestrian traffic in Times Square, my aunt, a tall, strong woman who wore Queen Mary hats and carried herself as erect as a Buckingham Palace guard, would set off with me in tow.

She carried a sort of portmanteau in one hand, a set of rolled-up magazines in the other, and she took long, powerful strides.

First she would knife into the backs of the massed pedestrians ahead of her, jabbing deftly with the rolled-up magazines. Then, as the pedestrians separated a bit, Aunty would plunge through the hole.

Smartly and with considerable force, she'd bring up the portmanteau so that the stroller on the right would fall forward, his body striking and blocking out at least two pedestrians ahead of him and thus opening yet another hole.

Then the magazines would come into play again on the left, and so she'd go, jabbing and blocking, jabbing and plunging, until, in triumph, she'd reach the corner ahead of everybody else on the block.

There was only one trouble with this system. It worked perfectly for Aunty Vene—but I wasn't swift or courageous enough to plunge into the holes that Aunty made, and often I was stranded halfway back in the block when she reached the corner. So she'd have to come back for me, or stand on the corner and wait.

Aunty, incidentally, kept close to the buildings, no matter in which direction she was going. She said you could make better time there than in the middle of the sidewalk. Every once in a while, a pedestrian observing the rule of keeping to the right would contest Aunty Vene, who might be keeping to the left. But she'd dispatch him with the magazines, and we'd roll on without missing a step.

People who knew my aunt quite well and who'd walked with her in the heavy Times Square traffic often described her prowess with awe and, noting her effectiveness with the magazines and the portmanteau, they dubbed her Aunty Maim.

But, whatever its merits or demerits, Aunty's system almost always got us to the movie or the theater on time. And, in fact, in plenty of time for the long climb up flights of stairs to the balcony.

My aunt, who was a librarian, never had a great deal of money. She made enough to live comfortably and her wise investment policy brought her enough additional income to indulge her love of travel and to sate her desire for entertainment. But she did everything as cheaply as possible.

"That way, my dear Norton," she told me, "we can see two or three times as many things."

So, we went to the cut-rate ticket offices, like LeBlang's and Gray's, and bought the cheapest balcony tickets available. These seats were, of course, always in the last one or two rows of the balcony, sometimes the second balcony, and sometimes the THIRD balcony, and, believe me, it was quite a climb to what many people described as the peanut gallery.

And, in keeping with her policy of economy and getting as much out of every experience as possible, my aunt always reminded me, as we climbed, to rub the tops and sides of my shoes against the stair carpeting and get a good shine. The movie houses, incidentally, were better for this because they had thicker and newer carpeting. And I quickly learned that the Shubert theaters were a total loss for this purpose because, more often than not, their carpets were so threadbare that you scratched the tops of your shoes.

Our seats, having cost only 50 or 55 cents, were so high that it sometimes was impossible to hear the actors. But that didn't bother us because we'd read the reviews and knew what the shows were about.

But I did, I must admit, get a rather strange conception of

actors. Looking down upon them from such great height, I got the impression that actors, as a group, were short, squat and large-headed. I remember, for instance, seeing Eddie Dowling in *Honeymoon Lane*, and, until I met him in person 20 years later, I always thought he was a midget.

Some of the shows we saw and enjoyed in those days were *The Student Prince* at the old Jolson Theater, *The Desert Song*, with Robert Halliday; *New Moon, Connie's Hot Chocolates, Show Boat* at the Ziegfeld, with Helen Morgan, Paul Robeson, Charles Winninger and Howard Marsh; *The Bachelor Father, Barrets of Wimpole Street, Broadway, A Connecticut Yankee* and *The Front Page*.

My mother and father, as I remember it, were a bit surprised when I came home after some of these vacation trips and proudly recited that I'd seen such shows as *George White's Scandals, Fifty Million Frenchmen, Strictly Dishonourable, Ziegfeld Follies, Skidding* and *Sex*. They discussed this with Aunty Vene and she stoutly defended me. "He's behaved at these shows like the perfect gentleman he is," she said. This didn't exactly satisfy my mother and father, but they didn't have any answer to it.

Only once, as I recall, did I do anything that caused my aunt embarrassment at a show. And, for that matter, it wasn't at a show at all—it was at a movie.

We were sitting in the balcony (where else?) at a showing of *The King of Kings* and the scene in which Mary Magdalene catches it from the crowd was being unreeled. It was a silent picture and the dialogue, of course, was being flashed on the screen.

As some bearded character walked up to Mary, shook his finger in her face and, I think, spat upon her, his words were shown:

"You have committed adultery!"

Instantly, I piped up, much louder than I'd anticipated, with, "Aunty, what's adultery?"

This caused the kind of laughter that I'd never heard before in a theater, and, for that matter, haven't heard since. It was fully five minutes before the last titter died out.

In the confusion, my aunt, a wee bit unstrung, leaned over and whispered in my ear. She explained that to adulterate means to weaken or make something impure, by adding another ingredient. "Like milk, for instance," she said. "You adulterate it when you add water."

And so, for many years, whenever I heard about men and women committing adultery, I figured they'd been caught watering some milk.

However, my aunt and I didn't always confine our fun and games to the opera, museums and the theater. Every so often we would spend a day at an amusement park.

Our favorite was a vast amusement park called Steeplechase, located on Coney Island, right next to another amusement layout called Luna Park, which was pretty good, too. Steeplechase was bigger and had more crazy things in it, and, I think, it was a little cheaper—so we went there more than anywhere else.

Aunty Vene, as I've indicated, was a stately, middle-aged lady then, and she dressed in a most conservative and sedate manner. She wore a pince-nez and she had her blond hair braided and wound around her head, tucked up under that Queen Mary hat. She wore a fine cameo ring on the little finger of her left hand and, usually, she had a massive cameo pin fastened to her bodice. Her bodice, by the way, was rather overwhelming because, as she sometimes said, the good Lord had seen fit "to endow me amply."

I loved to go swimming, but Aunty Vene, whose skin was extremely fair, was afraid of the sun and she absolutely abhorred the seashore. Once in a great while, I could talk her into going to the beach at Coney Island or Brighton, but while I swam she sat on a rented chair which she planted firmly in the sand, and protected herself from the elements with a heavy topcoat, a scarf, which she drew up around her face, an oversized kind of rain hat, and a parasol—all under a huge beach umbrella which she rented and paid a man to stick into the sand. Our beach sessions were few and far between and, I can assure you, of the briefest duration.

However, Aunty Vene didn't mind going to Coney Island in order to visit Steeplechase Park. If we walked the boardwalk, she averted her face from the ocean and shielded herself from the ocean breeze with her parasol. You'd have thought her a frail flower indeed, but once inside the park she revealed that she really had a tiger in the tank.

She absolutely adored all kinds of amusements, the more dangerous the better—but the amusements, it seemed to me, were out to get her. During the course of a normal day at the park, Aunty Vene got so buffeted that I often wondered whether she'd escape alive.

She was well aware of what was going to happen to her, but that didn't keep her away from such spectacular and frightening things as the Blowhole Theater (also called the Insanitarium), the Whip, the Cyclone, the Tornado, the Caterpillar, the Tunnel of Love, the Barrel of Fun and the Dodgem and Scooter cars. And let's not forget the Steeplechase Ride, which featured races involving iron horses, ridden by terrified humans, over a mile or so of the most rickety trestles imaginable.

Sometimes we'd go from Manhattan to the park by subway, but this always got us into trouble. Aunty had a penetrating fear of subways, and she either paused, or scurried—always at the wrong time. Once she scurried into a subway car and left me standing on the platform as the train roared out of the station.

Another time she paused, and I scurried. *She* was left standing on the platform. And once, miraculously, we both got into the same car at the same time, but Aunty's portmanteau, containing our lunch and her purse, remained outside the door when it suddenly closed. As the train went into the tunnel, the bag struck a steel pillar and was gone forever.

But, I'm sorry to say, it was just about as bad when we went to Coney on an excursion boat. Aunty, so deft and decisive in

95

Times Square traffic, was completely bewildered by boat schedules, pier designations and which gangplanks led where.

Once we clambered aboard a fine big excursion boat at the Battery, on the tip of Manhattan Island, and settled ourselves comfortably on the afterdeck. We were enjoying the breeze as the boat swung out from the pier, but in time it dawned on us that we were going north instead of south.

"Where is this boat going, young man?" my aunt asked of a deckhand.

"To Albany, ma'am," said the sailor. "And I'm sure you'll enjoy the trip."

Another time, we got on the Coney Island boat all right, but my aunt slipped as she reached the top step of a companionway and bounced on her you-know-what all the way to the lower deck where she slithered like an eel and crashed, feet first, into the rail with such force that her pince-nez flipped from her nose and plopped into the ocean.

Still another time, she got her shoe caught in some chewing gum and, while I was leaning over the rail to clean it with a wooden ice cream spoon, somebody bumped into me and I dropped the shoe to the pier. A man standing on the pier saw our predicament. He picked up the shoe and hurled it back. It struck a lady on the back of the head, glanced off and fell into the Hudson River.

But it was at Steeplechase that my aunt had her greatest grief. She always started the day in great good humor, with high hopes of having a wonderful time. But the moment after she bought our tickets and entered the main gate, she always stepped into the huge, revolving Barrel of Fun, through which you had to go to get into the main section of the park, and fell flat on her face.

There she'd lie, helplessly turning and rolling, entangled with three or four other equally lost and twisted souls, until I was able to reach her. Clutching her arm or leg, I usually managed to drag her to solid ground. She'd get up then, brush herself off, adjust her dress and her hat, and smile at me. "Well," she'd say, "we're *here* and we're going to have a lot of fun."

Although she loved each and every amusement in the park, they were her natural enemies. Everybody else who sat down and rode on the highly polished mahogany deck that spun around and around, eventually skidded off gently onto the main floor and came to a nice, slow stop. Not Aunty Vene.

She grimly held on as though her life depended on it. She flattened her moist hands against the mahogany and dug in her heels as she whirled. Eventually, of course, she lost her grip and the spinning platform, now at its highest speed, shot her off and across the floor with tremendous force. Once she flew so fast her feet became imbedded in the grillwork of the iron fence surrounding the amusement and workmen with acetylene torches had to be called to cut her out.

She's the only person I know who habitually got caught half in and half out when the heavy hood closed down on our car in the Caterpillar ride. In time, the park operators stopped closing the cover on the Caterpillar and the press said it was because young lovers were using that period of darkness and seclusion for activities incompatible with the current interpretation of morality. But I believed then, and I still do believe, that they stopped closing the cover so they wouldn't cut Aunty Vene in half.

Even in the Tunnel of Love she got into trouble. Once her dress somehow fluttered out of the boat and caught on a nail, pulling her half out of the boat and shredding the dress in a most alarming way. Another time she stood up, for some reason, and was bowled over when her head grazed a beam. Although she was upended, she fell not into the water, but directly onto a loving couple in the boat behind us, a fall which caused cries of pain, indignation and invasion of privacy.

But her first experience at the Blowhole Theater was the one that I shall remember after all the other indignities have faded. The Blowhole Theater was a sort of crazy house which

97

had rooms with tilting floors, steps that disappeared when you reached them, mirrors that distorted your image, doors that rolled away when you tried to go through them, and skeletons and bats and pirates that popped out at you from closets.

The main feature of the Blowhole Theater was the trick from which it got its name. As ladies emerged from this harrowing experience and walked out onto a stage, in front of which sat hundreds of spectators, 99 percent men, a ghastly thing was likely to happen.

A clown, standing near the exit, would gauge the speed with which a lady was walking and then signal a man seated at a control panel not far away. This man would press a button, a jet of compressed air would shoot up through a hole in the floor, right under the lady, and her skirts would be sent flying up over her head.

The first time this happened to Aunty Vene—and it happened only once!—she became wild with resentment. And the howls of the crowd didn't appease her. She turned on the little clown and snatched away his slapstick. Swinging it in a wide arc, she fetched him one on the nose. He fell over backwards.

Aunty was about to let him have another whack, but a second employee, dressed like a cowboy, rushed to his aid and grabbed hold of the slapstick. Aunty instantly let it go. But she wrenched the cowboy's electric stinger (like a cattle prod) out of his hand and bent it over his head.

Both he and the clown took off. However, a third employee, a fellow garbed like a farmer, stood there, somewhat bewildered. Aunty, seeing no one else to strike, advanced upon him, swinging the electric stinger above her head. The farmer scuttled across the stage and, hand over hand, climbed up a rope to an overhead cable. There he stayed, refusing to come down as long as Aunty remained in the Blowhole Theater.

Aunty and I returned to the Blowhole Theater many times —Aunty, I think, wanted to finish the job—but the three employees never again shot any compressed air at her and they stayed respectfully well out of her way.

None of this kind of combat seemed to bother Aunty at all—and even when she hobbled home, bleeding and bruised from falling off the Steeplechase horse, from slithering to the floor of the car when jerked about by the Whip or from crashing head-on into two or three other Dodgem cars, she had a happy, satisfied smile on her face, and, in her heart, a desire to get back to Steeplechase just as soon as possible.

The only time that my dear Aunty Vene seemed to be more than a little troubled was one hot July night in 1927. And it was all my fault.

That was the year when a young lady named Uldine Utley was making a great name for herself as an evangelist. She had none of the rip-roarin', hellfire and slam-bang technique of such spiritual leaders as Billy Sunday and Homer Rodeheaver and she had only a little of the cloying quality manifested by Aimee Semple McPherson, who then was at the peak of her power. But she had unique appeal.

Although Uldine was just a child, she had sweetness, sincerity, beauty, and a magnetic power that's hard to put into words. She had been touring the country, converting thousands of people and drawing much bigger crowds than Aimee. I had read about her in the newspapers and heard about her on radio. And I was pleased that a young lady of about my age could do such a thing.

As I say, she made the New York scene in 1927. She was fifteen, and I was eleven, going on twelve. And I wanted to see her more than anything else in the world.

She had yellow hair, squarely cut in the fashion of a medieval page, a lovely round face with wide, appealing eyes, and a heartwarming, sunny smile. And when she opened two weeks of revival meetings in Carnegie Hall in New York, I longed to go, much as some of our modern youngsters yearn to fling themselves at the feet of the Beatles.

My mother, however, argued that school was more important, and, since she seemed considerably annoyed by the whole idea, I bided my time. Uldine finished her engagement at Carnegie Hall, and got wonderful notices in the newspapers, and then went on tour again, but she said, in a parting statement, that she'd return to New York in the summer—because there were so many sinners there.

I waited and waited for the summer to come, and I read and reread all the clippings about Uldine. And then, one July day when I was with my aunt in New York, I saw in the paper that she had returned!

The paper said that Uldine was going to preach in a huge tent set up next to Yankee Stadium, and I begged my aunt to take me. Aunty Vene was a free spirit and she'd go anywhere, but she was somewhat surprised at my ardor.

"It'll mean missing a play," she said.

"That's all right with me," I replied. "I'm very interested in theology, as you know, and I want to hear Uldine Utley preach."

My aunt swallowed at that, but she promised to take me. I scarcely could wait for the great night, and I'll never forget the thrilling tingle of expectancy as we approached the vast tent and saw the people filing in. Three or four thousand men and women had been attracted by the little evangelist and there was a tension in the air that you could almost touch.

Aunty and I went inside, found a couple of vacant folding chairs somewhere about the middle of the enormous tent and sat down. So far as I could see, there were no other youngsters in the audience.

There was a platform at one end of the tent and somebody was playing a rather squeaky portable organ. Bare electric light bulbs blazed from wires strung above our heads, and flies and moths droned through the hot night air.

I hardly could wait for Uldine's appearance, but I listened politely to a couple of hymns sung by a choir which straggled out on the platform from somewhere in back. And then, at last, the great moment came—Uldine herself walked out onto the platform!

She was lovelier than I had imagined! Spotlights were turned on her, and they gave her hair a golden glow. Divine radiance reflected from her shining, smiling face, and her white linen dress, white stockings, white buckskin shoes and white serge cloak were royal raiment, indeed. I was enchanted!

Then she began to speak, and her thin, girlish little voice shrilled through the cavernous tent.

"Wake up, wake up, you people of New York!" she cried. "Wake up before it is too late! Wake up! God is calling you!"

Well, I'd never been more eager to wake up. I raised my hands in the air and then I pounded them in applause. People all around me began to applaud and soon everybody in the tent was clapping and shouting.

"God has sent me to you," cried Uldine. "I am here as His messenger. I am here to save your souls."

The applause was deafening. People shouted "Yes, yes," and "Praise the Lord," and "Uldine forever."

Uldine raised her thin little arms and motioned for silence. She told them then how she'd started out in life, planning to be an actress, but that God had changed her plans. She said that one day when she went to rehearsal for a play, she'd found the door locked.

"God had locked that door so I couldn't get in," she said, tears glistening in her eyes. "God, you see, told me not to be an actress. So, I went across the street and there was a revival meeting, and it was like a wave of glory breaking over me. God scourged my soul, and he can do it for you, too."

She talked on and on, and I was enraptured. She told about her early life, about the love and guidance her mother had given her, and how God's word had erased all pain for her and for her mother, and how she had been directed by God to move all over the country, all over the world, in time, to deliver His word and spread His love.

Then, reaching the peak of her talk, she invited "all sinners" to stand up for her blessing.

I was the first one up.

Then, here and there, others began to stand. And soon there were about 100 on their feet. Uldine blessed us—"Blessings on

101

thee, my dear brothers and sisters"—and the choir sang a hymn for us, and then Uldine, smiling sweetly and, it seemed, glancing directly at me, said, "All ye who want to be saved and cleansed of your sin, come to me. Come right down the aisle."

I was first out into the aisle, and I looked at Uldine standing there on the platform, a beautiful vision in white, holding out her arms—TO ME. I marched straight down the aisle. And, as I marched, I was joined by dozens of drunks, derelicts, prostitutes, ex-convicts, thieves, con men and, I suppose, a sprinkling of religious-minded men and women.

As we approached the platform, we saw a rail in front of it, with a little kneeling board on the ground. One by one we knelt at the rail and Uldine, starting at the extreme right end of the line, began to bless us. As she moved before each person she asked each of us what our sin was.

Quite clearly I could hear people confessing to crimes, alcoholism, prostitution, sadism, treason and worse. "Oh, I'm a sinner," cried a woman, a few feet from me. "I have sinned from childhood. I have lived a carnal life. I have stolen. God has turned his back on me. There is no hope."

"There is hope, dear sister," shrilled Uldine. "God forgives. You have only to ask him."

Others cried out in similar agony, all admitting their sins and praying for forgiveness. And, as Uldine moved toward my end of the line, I began desperately to search for some worthy sin to offer her. For the life of me, I couldn't think of anything bad enough to sound important in this supremely sinful company. The little errors I'd made in school and at home seemed like so much trivia, and I felt that Uldine would be angry at me because I was too pure.

And then, suddenly, as I still struggled to think of something, *anything* that was terrible enough, she came and stood in front of me. And, in that glorious moment, she put her fragile little hand on my cheek and asked, "Oh, little brother, what sin have you committed?"

102

I lost my head and cried out: "I want to be with *you*, Uldine. I want to be your *slave!*"

Uldine smiled at that. She seemed very pleased, and she patted my cheek.

"Ah, come with me, little brother," she said, gently lifting me to my feet. "Come, and we shall pray together."

I followed her blindly. But soon I became aware, with no little annoyance, that she apparently also had invited about two dozen other sinners to the sanctuary behind the platform.

It was just a small room, partitioned by tarpaulins and with sawdust on the dirt. But it seemed like heaven to me, with God's angel, in shimmering white, standing there. She asked us to kneel in the sawdust, and when we did, forming a rough circle around her, she began to preach, touching our heads with her hands.

I was absolutely carried away—but suddenly, I felt myself being yanked to my feet. I turned and saw the angry face of Aunty Vene.

She, apparently, had got over the shock of seeing me stand in the tent, and then march down the aisle to be converted. But when she'd seen me being taken into the room behind the platform, she'd been shocked all over again.

She had rushed down the aisle, she told me later, shouldered aside some attendants outside our special room, and burst into the circle to rescue me.

And, as she pulled me out of the tent, I looked back and saw Uldine still standing there, still preaching:

" . . . and God will grant you peace, now and forever," she was saying. "Place yourselves in His hands, and He will give you peace. . . ."

I looked at her as I was being hurried along, and there were tears in my eyes. But Uldine didn't seem to notice that I was being taken away. At least, she said nothing—and she did nothing to prevent it.

I was terribly hurt, and I was very angry at Aunty Vene who

told me in what was, for her, harsh language, that I'd made a fool of myself, and of her, too. I was very sad that night, and Aunty's recital later on of the schedule for the next day—two movies, two museums, a boat ride around Manhattan and a play—didn't move me at all.

I vowed to myself, as I lay in bed, that one day, no matter what Aunty or anybody else said, I'd track Uldine down and deliver myself to her once more.

And I might well have done it, too, except for the fact that one day I picked up the paper and read that Uldine had given up being an evangelist, had got married, and had gone out West to live.

It was a sorry end to a noble passion, but, inasmuch as I was studying French at the time, I decided to capitalize on my suffering and to improve my grasp of the language at the same time.

Holding the newspaper clipping and a tiny, frayed rotogravure picture of her in my hand, I assumed my most melancholy mien and went around to all my friends, softly saying, *"C'est la vie."*

I'm not sure they got the point, but one and all, they certainly seemed impressed.

Chapter Eight

I'VE been working for as long as I can remember—in fact, I don't believe I've been out of work a day in my life since I attained the ripe old age of sixteen—but I'm one of, if not THE, worst businessmen in the world.

My father's father, Frank Norton Mockridge, once made a fortune in Philadelphia, building hundreds of those terribly depressing look-alike houses that line street after street; serviceable, but totally without beauty or charm, without individuality or pride of existence. My grandfather was very good about that kind of cookie-cutter construction, which was brand-new in those days, and he really raked in the dough by practically pasting houses together and using only 11 sidewalls for 10 houses instead of the customary 20, and by using communal sewer systems and things like that.

But he didn't know anything about investing in Mexican oil! Within two years after he made his first fortune, he lost it all. Undaunted, he went back to messing up Philadelphia's architecture, and even extended his talents to several other cities. Soon he was rich again.

This time he decided he was an expert on Canadian mines, and he speculated heavily in copper, gold, silver, zinc and cobalt. It was an unfortunate decision. Grandfather did, I'll admit, get thousands of large, heavy, crinkly, parchmentlike stock certificates out of these transactions and they were very impressive, indeed.

In fact, soon after we moved to Mount Kisco, and before we had the house insulated, my father used three or four thousand of them, which he'd found in an old trunk, to place under the carpeting on the ground floor and help keep out the cold.

I still have a hundred or so of these impressive-looking certificates and sometimes I place them alongside a little rubber-stamped business card I had made up when I was about ten years old and which reads:

NORTON MOCKRIDGE

BICYCLE REPAIR SHOP

90 MOGER AVE., MT. KISCO

Cheapest Work—Your Credit Is Good

And when I look at those certificates and at that card, I am forcibly reminded that I inherited a lot of my grandfather's talent for losing money.

I had a very brisk business soon after I opened my bicycle repair shop. So much, in fact, that I even got another boy in to help me. I worked nights after I returned from school, repairing brakes, straightening wheels, fixing flats, installing or repairing chains and so on, and I devoted most of my Saturdays and Sundays to much the same thing.

And I took in a lot of money. The only trouble was that at the end of the second month I found I had spent as much for new parts as I'd taken in for all my labor. I had sort of guessed what the parts would cost and had underestimated when I submitted my bill. But worse than that, I'd made two other grievous errors:

I'd felt sorry for kids who didn't have quite enough money to pay for a required job, and so I'd take just what they had and tell them to forget the rest. And, secondly, I was foolish enough to believe the statement on my business card: "Your Credit Is Good."

Their credit was *not* good.

Well, after a while, I rearranged things a bit and I continued my bicycle repair work, but on a cash-first basis. This, however, cut down the volume of incoming jobs and I made only $5 or $10 a week.

So, I started a car-polishing and Simonizing business. I had done my father's car, which really sparkled, and I quickly got orders from five or six neighbors. I charged them, depending upon the size of the car and the condition of its finish, anywhere from $5 to $15, and all of the owners seemed quite happy.

After this first rush, however, my business fell off to nothing because most middle-income people at that time either didn't care what their cars looked like or preferred to do the work themselves. It was then that I hit upon a marvelous scheme.

Mount Kisco in those days was surrounded by many huge estates and on these estates lived scads of enormously wealthy people. Some of them had as many as five cars and, it seemed to me, all but the limousines in each garage were pretty shabby-looking.

I wrote letters to about 50 of these estate owners and, noting that commercial garages were charging $20 or more for a Simonizing, offered to do the job for from $10 to $15. The only condition I made was that the car had to be delivered to my house and picked up because I was too young to get a license to drive.

It was surprising, I thought, how eagerly these people who were worth a million or so snatched up my offer. I hardly could believe that they were that eager to save $5 or $10, but the cars began arriving faster than I could handle them.

However, whenever the chauffeur, the butler or the handyman came to pick up the car, he didn't have the money to pay for it. "Just give me a bill and you'll be sent a check," he'd say. I'd make out a bill, all right, but weeks would go by and I'd get nothing. Not even a thank-you letter.

I sent out letters, politely requesting payment. But I didn't get more than two or three checks. I took to telephoning the people who owed me, but only once or twice was I able to get through to them directly, and then they said vaguely that they'd thought they'd sent the check and hadn't I received it?

So, I went back to the old cash-on-delivery regulation—and my business fell off 75 percent. I happened to discuss this phenomenon one day with Mr. McCauley, the butcher we patronized and his face screwed up like a prune.

"Git yer money immediately, sonny, or you'll never git it," he said. "I got a little trouble like that myself."

Three years later, Mr. McCauley shut down his store. The estate people had done him in.

In slack periods, I took on all sorts of little jobs, like picking up groceries for neighbors in my wagon or in baskets I fastened to my bicycle, and I made a little money here and there. Once, however, I rode down Main Street to the New York Central Railroad grade crossing and, when the front wheel of the aged bike hit the top of the first rail, the bicycle broke in half—the handlebars and the front wheel and I went sailing through the air, and the rear half of the bike fell to the tracks.

I recovered most of the groceries, but the fall didn't do the four dozen eggs much good. Another time, peddling along

Main Street near the traffic light, I was struck by a car that had slithered through the light and made a sharp turn.

My front wheel was shattered by the impact and my groceries were strewn all over. I ran to pick them up and I half expected the driver of the car to stop and help me. But he didn't. Instead, he shot away.

I caught the license number of the car and wrote it down. Then I picked up my groceries (no eggs this time, but I did have a ruined jar of mayonnaise) and put them back in the baskets and dragged the bike to the sidewalk in front of the Mount Kisco National Bank. Then I went to search for a cop.

I found one sleeping in Manning's taxi shack and together we set off to see if we could find the car. Much to my surprise, we didn't have far to look. There, parked right at the back entrance to the speakeasy that operated at the rear of the old Mount Kisco Hotel, was the car. And red paint from my bicycle was streaked on the black of the right front fender.

The officer and I went into the speakeasy. I saw the man immediately. He was standing at the bar having a drink with the village's police lieutenant.

I was pretty young at the time, but I began to feel old—old enough to get the idea that in this case, at least, justice was *not* going to triumph. But I was wrong. Whether the lieutenant didn't want a kid running around town telling people that he'd been drinking in a speak with a maniac who runs down bicycles, or whether he really was doing his duty, I don't know.

But I well recall that he said to the man, "You busted the bike. So pay the boy." The man pulled out two ten-dollar bills and said, "This oughta take care of it, kid." And I said I thought it would and took the bills. The man then invited the lieutenant and the officer to have a drink with him and they accepted. I thought it would be a good time to leave—and I did.

I was quite elated at getting the $20 because I had estimated that a new wheel and sundry repairs would cost under $10— but my jubilation was dashed somewhat when I got back to the bike and found that somebody had stolen all the groceries!

Oh, I had many other fascinating excursions into the world of big business. One summer, when things were slack, I let a friend talk me into caddying at the old Colonial Hotel in Mount Kisco, which boasted a rather unkempt nine-hole golf course, a couple of rutted tennis courts and a brook-fed, muddy pool.

Despite these obvious lacks, the Colonial almost always was full of New York City people who loved to get out into what they considered rugged country, and really rough it. And they swarmed all over the golf course, smacking balls in all directions, frequently hitting each other, and getting into loud arguments. No really good caddy would work there—and that's how I got the job.

I hate to make this confession now, but I had never played golf in my life, never had swung a golf club, and never even had set foot on a golf course. And so, when I stood beside my first employer on my first day of caddying and he asked me a question about whether he should hit away or play safe, I was a bit shaky.

"What I mean," he said, "is how far out is that brook? Can I clear it from here? Or should I play safe."

I hadn't the faintest idea how far out the brook was. It looked like a mile to me. But I didn't want to discourage the player, so I said, "Oh, not far, sir. I'm sure you can clear it easily."

The player wound up, whapped the ball and it bounced twice and went right into the brook. He played the next hole in grim silence, but on the following tee he twisted and turned and searched the horizon.

"Where's the next green, son?" he asked.

"Right over those trees, sir," I said, pointing, although I hadn't the slightest notion.

The man hauled off and drove right into the trees. He said some bad words and asked me if I'd seen 'er fall.

I nodded and trotted off briskly, heading for the deepest part of the woods. I think I had some idea of throwing myself into the swamp in there, but as we kicked around in the damp underbrush we stirred up so many mosquitoes that I decided against that kind of death. We scrambled around, slipped and fell and got ourselves covered with mud, slime and mosquito bites and the man kept getting madder and madder.

We might have stayed there all day, for all I know, except for the fact that the man's partner, who hadn't entered the woods, suddenly called out, "Hey, Bill. You're playing a Spalding, ain't ya? Here's your ball, right out here on the fairway. Musta bounced out."

Well, the rest of the round was a nightmare—the man never spoke to me, and every time he took a club out of the bag slung over my shoulder he did it so strongly it nearly knocked me down. But the terrible climax came when we got back to the shed that served as the clubhouse and the man counted his clubs. There was one missing!

Simultaneously, he and I remembered that I had taken a club into the woods with me on that hole where I thought the ball had gone into the swamp—and I'd never brought it out!

"Look, kid," said the man, "I ain't got time to wait around. You go back and find that club and give it to me next weekend. Or else you don't get paid." And he stomped off the course.

Well, I trudged back to the swamp and poked around, but all I found was a thousand more mosquitoes. And so, my first day of caddying was a total loss. I improved a bit over the next weeks, but caddying never really was my dish, and I decided to turn to something else.

One day the manager of the local A & P asked my father whether I'd be willing to help out a bit on Friday nights after school and on Saturdays. My father said that since I'd blown my career as an actor, it might be a good idea for me to learn the grocery business, and so I accepted.

The first Friday night was hectic, but not so bad, considering that I didn't know where anything in the store was, that I didn't know the price of anything, and that I couldn't remember more than one item at a time. If a lady asked me to get a jar of mayonnaise, a head of lettuce and a loaf of bread, I'd go off and eventually return with just the bread. This irritated the manager and the customer, but everybody allowed as how I'd catch on in time.

At closing that evening, the manager gave me my $1.50 wages and told me to be at the store at 7 A.M. next day. "Lots of work to do tomorrow," he said. "And for God's sake, try to learn where things are and maybe remember a *couple* of things at the same time."

I reported early, cheered by the fact that on Saturdays I was to get $3. Well, things did go better, and I wasn't such a mess. But I was highly nervous and I worked too swiftly, often upsetting or dropping things. And sometimes when filling phone orders I put an armful of groceries down on a counter and shoved them into the wrong pile, and several customers got more than they bargained for that day, and some got less.

But I staggered through till closing time and then dug into the dull and tiring task of cleaning up. As the manager and the clerks tidied the main floor, I went down into the basement to stack up the bottles of soft drinks and the near beer which was sold during Prohibition. There were hundreds of cases in that basement, and they were all over the place because clerks, in their haste to get this drink or that, pulled out the cases but never put them back.

It was my job to stack them all in orderly fashion. I did all the soft drinks first, putting one case upon another until there were many piles against the walls, some as high as six cases. Then I tackled the near beer. But I found I hadn't left as much space for this as I should have. There was nothing to do but pile the near beer much higher than the soft drinks.

I was doing quite well until I got to the eighth tier, and then tried to put one more case up there—the ninth tier. I was standing on three empty cases I'd piled up as a sort of ladder, and as I lifted that last case and tried to shove it into place on top of the eighth case, I lost my grip a bit and the case fell toward me. I leaped off my boxes to avoid being hit and then, as I stood there in that clammy cellar and watched in fear, one entire pile of near beer cases tilted slowly forward and, like an avalanche picking up speed, crashed to the concrete floor.

The bottles shattered like mad and beer spurted and fizzed all over the place. The noise, of course, attracted the manager and the clerks, and they came rushing down the stairs, slopping right into the beer.

"Oh, my God," cried the manager. "Who's gonna pay for this?"

And then, swinging his eyes on me, he answered his question without saying a word.

We then began emptying out the cases, throwing the broken bottles into a big tin can and putting the good bottles back into the cases and stacking them.

When it was all over, and the last suds had been swept down the drain, the manager said, "Well, that's $4.65 shot to hell. Minus your $3 that's $1.65 you owe me."

I handed over the $1.65, and realized that if I subtracted the $1.50 I'd made the night before, I'd worked the weekend at a loss of only 15 cents.

I was about ready to cry. "Do you . . . do you want me back next weekend?" I asked.

The manager looked at me for a full ten seconds. Then he said, "Yeah, sonny. You're probably gonna be all right."

Well, I worked at the A & P a few more weekends and did nothing outstandingly outrageous, but along about that time I got a temporary acting job and gave up my career as a grocery chain executive. My father pointed out that I now had ruined *two* careers, motion picture acting and business administration, and that there wasn't much more to look forward to.

Meanwhile, I was having a bit of trouble in high school. I had entered high school feeling that I was something of a big wheel, having served as president of my eighth grade, and I was reluctant to let some of those obviously inept first year high school teachers try out their crackbrained schemes on me. Often I paid little attention to them in class, preferring to use the time to memorize the lines in a play, and I seldom did much homework.

As a result, I squeaked through English, algebra, and biology, but I got only a conditional passing mark in Latin I—and that was on the promise that I would do special work in the subject during the summer. This annoying arrangement was proposed by the teacher, Miss Mildred Brown, a lady whom I loathed. I had punished her all year by paying scarcely any attention to her course and now, I felt, she was punishing me by loading me with Latin assignments during the summer when I was working in plays.

Well, there was nothing I could do, and I completed the assignments. Next year, however, I got even with her by hardly ever cracking a book in her Latin II course. As a result, I passed all my other subjects well enough, but got a 36 in the Latin II regents—a record low for the school which, I believe, holds to this day.

This miserable state of affairs—which meant that I'd be left back and unable to progress with my classmates unless I went to summer school and passed the Latin regents—I blamed on Miss Brown. I think I felt she'd flunked me so I'd have to go to summer school and thus miss out on any acting that might have come my way.

Anyway, I went to summer school, really studied the hated Latin II, and passed it easily, getting, I believe, an 82. Then, in the fall, when I returned to Mount Kisco High School, I stalked into Miss Brown's classroom, eager to show her my passing mark and to tell her that thereafter I'd never have to see her or her lousy Latin again.

I'd rehearsed a scathing little speech I'd written and I was about to launch it when Miss Brown stood up behind her desk, held out her hand and said, "Congratulations. I hear you passed. I knew you could do it if you'd study—and I hope you've learned *that* lesson once and for all. I'm very happy for you."

Well, that sort of deflated my indignation and made my "Triumph" meaningless. So, I took her hand and mumbled a sort of apology and she patted me on the back and said there was no need for that, and I said yes there was because I'd acted like a spoiled brat, and she said oh, no, it wasn't as bad as that —and do you know, in the next two years Miss Brown became one of my best friends! In fact, we got so chummy that whenever I had trouble with my faulty car, which was often, she always lent me hers. It just shows how you can win over a Latin teacher if you try!

I had a little trouble in chemistry, also mainly because of the teacher—Miss Cameron. Miss Cameron cautioned all of us, of course, that certain acids, when combined, could become most explosive. She especially cautioned against adding sulphuric acid to *anything* without first studying how the combination might react.

I felt that this was an example of being overcautious and one day when we'd finished an experiment in the lab, I began emptying the contents of all of the test tubes, beakers and other jars we'd used into one huge beaker. Each time as I added another solution I expected to see my mixture turn into a bubbling, seething, steaming mess. But nothing happened.

Nothing except that the colors kept changing. But there was no violent reaction.

Feeling cheated, and blaming Miss Cameron for having advised us wrongly, I went to a shelf, got a bottle of sulphuric acid and, just to see whether Miss Cameron had been *all* wrong, I poured some into my beaker.

She hadn't been wrong at all! It took just one second for the reaction. The mixture boiled upward like a volcanic geyser, shattering the beaker with a loud report and splashing in every direction. Why it didn't hit me in the face, I'll never know— but it did splash all over my black wool sweater and my yellow corduroy trousers, eating huge holes within two or three minutes. And it flowed joyously over my chemistry notebook, destroying half of the work I had done all year.

I mention little incidents like these merely to show that I was of an experimental nature then and somewhat less the conformist than I am today. When I became editor of the high school paper, *The Lantern*, I instantly wrote editorials condemning things that had been done by the principal, Mr. Haddow, and the superintendent of schools, Mr. Jennings. There was quite a furor and in the confusion we missed getting out a couple of issues.

When I was named chief of the school's student police force I arbitrarily took the list of "crimes" and other violations, such as walking on the grass, sitting on the pipe fence and breaking down the hedge under and behind it, and climbing the wire fences to take shortcuts, and cut the list in half.

I told my patrolmen to give out tickets only for jaywalking, running or fighting in the corridors, smoking in the toilets and other major offenses like those. For this I was suspended for a couple of weeks or so till we worked out a compromise.

One day one of our colleagues, Ed Fish—he was called "Citizen Fish" because he was twenty-one years old—brought a pair of real police handcuffs to school. My old buddy, David Niss, and I inspected them carefully in English class and, when it came time to get up and leave the classroom, I discovered that Nissy had handcuffed me quite securely to my seat which was bolted to the floor.

He fled the school with the key and so I sat there all afternoon, listening to freshmen, sophomores and juniors recite their English lessons. Occasionally, I tossed in an observation or two to help Miss Stevens, who, incidentally, was the most beloved English teacher I've ever seen, and twice she permitted me to correct some of the papers handed in. It was a rewarding day and I was sorry when Nissy returned at 3:30 and unlocked me.

We then, however, handcuffed Mildred Blackeby and Rose Huelle to a heavy table in the library and left them there. We returned the key to Ed Fish and told him we'd left his handcuffs in the library. The "Citizen" went there, but he never got over the reception he received from the two enraged females.

Then, after I had been elected president of the school, or

more properly of the student organization that thought it governed the school, I got into quite a flap when I advised the senior class, of which I was a member, to secede from the school because of a battle it was having with its faculty adviser, Miss Margaret Fraser, the French teacher.

Some of the details of this imbroglio are a bit hazy (I had a lot of things on my mind in those days and this senior class thing was just another irritating little incident!) so I asked Nissy, who was president of the senior class and thus more directly involved, to give me a report on it. This is what he wrote:

The Great Senior Class Uprising happened like this: We were putting on the Senior Play "The New Poor," by Cosmo Hamilton, to raise money for our class trip to Washington and the question came up at a class meeting, full of Roberts' Rules of Order, etc., about whether to present the play one night or two. Miss Fraser was for one, so the class vote was unanimous for two.

Miss Fraser got mad and said that we never took her advice, and after all she was the faculty adviser. I said the class took *my* advice, and after all I was the president. This got Miss Fraser really sore and she flounced out of the meeting, and we never saw her again except in French class where she murdered us more than she had done before, if that was possible. You became class adviser, and we didn't do what you wanted either.

You had the lead in the play, the Grand Duke. I had a nice part—Prince Vladimir, a great lover. We used sexy Russian accents. And it was lucky that we did the show two nights because I left out three pages of my lines the first night, but put them in twice the second night. We marked up the backstage walls with cues, lines and an assortment of messages. And, as president of the Senior Class, you all let me paint the goddam walls all by myself.

Well, after a time, we got to thinking we'd been unfair to Miss Fraser, so a group of us went to her house and told her how much we'd missed her and how we'd like to have her back, and so she relented and she returned, just in time to tell us that we shouldn't wear cap and gown for graduation. Ours was the first class in the history of the school to graduate in cap and gown!

Well, you see how things went. As a matter of fact, I'm amazed that the Board of Education, Mr. Jennings, Mr. Haddow and the faculty tolerated us at all. But they not only tolerated us, they did some wonderful things for us. And I want to tell you about just one wonderful thing that was done for me.

Money was pretty tight in those Depression days, and most of the 41 members of our class were short of funds all the time. A number of parents were out of work and others were working only part time.

So, we did all sorts of things to raise money to finance our much-planned and eagerly awaited trip to Washington for a week of sight-seeing, and hell-raising in the hotel. We had class projects, selling magazine subscriptions, tickets to shows and concerts, gym exhibits, polo matches and things like that. We made money out of the Senior Play and we sponsored a couple of other events.

And each student's share was in direct proportion to the amount of time and/or effort he put into each project. Well, as I've told you, I was pretty busy in those days trying to make the adult heads of the school run it the way I thought it should be run and I had little or no time for fund-raising.

Consequently, when the deadline for signing up for the trip came upon us, I had credited to me less than one quarter of the amount I needed. I didn't have a dime of my own to throw into the breach, and I was too proud to ask my father. So, martyr-like, I announced, with a tear in my eye, that I had too many problems at home to be able to take off a week for nothing but sheer entertainment in Washington.

Nobody was fooled by this eloquent address—least of all Mr. Jennings. He summoned me to his office one afternoon and asked me the real reason why I was staying home.

I started reciting something that sounded like the Declaration of Independence, but Mr. Jennings, a gentle, kindly man with a razor-sharp mind, cut in with, "It's money, isn't it?"

I said, yes, it was, and he told me he'd suspected it all along. He said he'd mentioned it to some friends of his the night before.

"And they, Norton, would like to give you as much money as you need to make the trip," he said.

I asked why, and Mr. Jennings said, rather dryly, that his friends had heard I'd been so busy running the school that I hadn't had time to work, and that they didn't think that one so civic- and school-minded should be penalized. I had the feeling that Mr. Jennings was on the verge of laughing, but I couldn't be sure.

Finally, I said that I'd be glad to accept the money but only on the basis of a loan, and on condition that I could work it out after I returned from Washington. I told Mr. Jennings that if he'd give me my benefactors' names, I'd Simonize their cars, wash their windows, trim their lawns and so on.

He promised to give me the names after I returned—and so I went to Washington with the class and had one of the most marvelous times of my life. I'm everlastingly grateful to Mr. Jennings and to my sponsors because that school trip to Washington is something no high school boy or girl should miss.

Well, when I returned, Mr. Jennings identified my benefactors—and it turned out they were a couple who lived near him. And for three or four weeks I worked out the loan, doing the car and the lawn, washing windows, painting a bit, raking the drive and cleaning the gutters.

And I was happy to do it—with one exception. These dear, kind people had a small boy of about five or six, and although I'm sure he's grown up to be a fine American, he was a little, no-neck monster at the time.

Whenever he could—and he could very often—he'd dash out of some bushes, or sneak around a door, and stick me in the fanny with a pin. And if I made a move toward him, he'd start to yell and cry, and his mother would appear.

I didn't have the heart to embarrass her by telling her that her little darling was trying to stab me to death, so I'd smile and say that we'd been having fun and that the little tyke just had got frightened and that I'd be more careful in the future.

In no time at all, this kid knew I was his pigeon. He used to shower me with gravel, dump over my bucket of water, throw my rake into the high grass and even pinch me when he could get close enough. Then came the worst. In the final week I was there, the dear little fellow brought out a rubber-band slingshot and from then on, whenever I bent over he'd pepper me in the rear with a staple.

But I never hit him with a baseball bat or pushed him under a passing car. Because of the fun I'd had in Washington, I kept my sunny disposition and never let my temper sour. Whenever that kid hit me in the rear with a staple, I merely turned the other cheek.

Chapter Nine

THE first time I ever got drunk was in church. And I was only eleven years old.

They found me lying there, face down on the cold flagstone floor of the sacristy, and at first, I guess, they thought I was dead. But when they bent over to see whether I was breathing, they got such whiffs of alcohol that, as Father Brinkerhoff later expressed it: "I began to feel a little dizzy myself."

I fell into this intoxicated state in rather an innocent way.

I was, at the time, an acolyte at St. Mark's Episcopal Church in Mount Kisco and as such, my duties included lighting and snuffing out the tall candles on the altar, laying out the minister's vestments before each service, getting out the linen to be used at each communion service, and—here's where the trouble comes in—placing the wafers on a silver dish and filling a crystal decanter with wine so that the minister, at the altar, could replenish the chalice as needed.

Not being twelve years old, I had not as yet been confirmed in the Episcopal Church and so, while I was allowed to assist at the service, I could not take communion. Up until that time, I had never tasted wine—I'd had sips of beer once in a while (illegal beer, at that!) but my mother and father never had liquor in the house and so there was virtually no opportunity for me to become acquainted with either *spiritus frumenti* or the fermented juice of the grape.

After I'd poured the sacramental wine—it was a claret, I believe—from a large bottle into the decanter for a period of some weeks, I got to wondering what it tasted like.

I loved its rich, heady bouquet and I delighted in sniffing it. It gave an intriguing fragrance to that otherwise dark, slightly dank, oak-paneled room with its lead-paned windows and cold flagstone floor. And when I held the decanter up to the window, especially when the morning sun was shining through, the claret gave forth the most magnificent ruby glow.

It seemed to me that anything that smelled that good, and looked that good, certainly must taste pretty good. And so one Sunday, shortly before the 6 A.M. communion, I withdrew the funnel from the decanter, after I'd filled it from the large bottle, and permitted a few drops to fall into the palm of my hand.

Tentatively, cautiously, I flicked my tongue into this little red puddle and, to be quite honest, felt rather disappointed. This stuff wasn't anywhere near as good as cream soda! Why, I wondered, did adults set such store by it? Was I doing something wrong? Maybe it spoiled the wine, holding it in the palm of your hand.

I got a water tumbler and splashed in quite a bit from the bottle. I tasted the wine again, and this time it seemed much better. So I had a couple of good swallows. Nothing happened for a moment or so, but then I began to feel all nice and warm and cozy inside. This I rightly attributed to the wine—and so I had some more.

Within five or six minutes, I suppose, I finished the water glass of wine, poured another, and finished that too. Just what happened after that, I haven't the vaguest notion. But when Father Brinkerhoff, who was officiating at that service, and Mr. Varney, the organist, went to the sacristy to see what was holding up their acolyte, they found nothing was holding him up. He was on the floor.

They carried me out of the church, still wearing my black cassock and white surplice, and laid me on the lawn where, in time, I got rid of all that fine red wine. And then, after the service, they drove me home and told my parents that I'd set some kind of church record. No acolyte before or since, so far as I know, ever got himself so slopped in church at 6 o'clock in the morning.

I, by the way, was demoted as a result of this unfortunate incident. No longer was I permitted to enter that little sacristy room and prepare the wafers and the wine. All I was permitted to do was to light the candles before communion, and snuff them out afterward. I felt degraded, but it was interesting to note that the other acolytes regarded me with much more respect than they had before. I, it seemed, had lived.

As I mentioned earlier, no liquor was permitted in the Mockridge household at that time. My mother and father weren't Prohibitionists, teetotalers, temperance workers or even advocates of abstinence. Nothing like that at all. It was simply that my mother had given up drinking one New Year's Day when she woke and found herself lying in the bathtub.

And, in the gentle manner exercised by many wives, she made my father give up drinking, too. It wasn't difficult, I imagine, because he found, later on that New Year's Day, that in parking the car the night before—New Year's Eve—he'd backed over a case of Scotch, smashed nearly every bottle and ruined two tires.

All of that happened in 1918 when I was only three years old, and the no-drinking dictum meant nothing to me because I was on solid foods at the time. However, as I grew older and began to detect evidence of convivial drinking in the homes of my teen-age compatriots, I asked my parents why they persisted in plunging along the road to social oblivion.

My mother explained that when a lady goes to bed in the bathtub wearing only a girdle and an ostrich plume hat (which, incidentally, wasn't hers), it's time to reevaluate. And my father explained that it wasn't the drinking that bothered him; it was the thought of the cost involved in wrecking cases of Scotch, not to mention the wear and tear on the tires.

Anyway, for a good many years there was no drinking in our house in Mount Kisco. No drinking of alcohol, that is. Mother and Dad drank copious amounts of coffee and my brother and I did away with four or five quarts of milk per day.

But Mother was well aware of the value of a festive drink at home, and she saw to it that virtually every kind of nonalcoholic beverage known to man was present in the house: Moxie, Dr. Brown's celery tonic, sarsaparilla, Cliquot Club ginger ale, root beer, cream soda, lemon and lime, Welch's grape juice, sweet cider, orange, grapefruit, flamingo punch, Dr. Pepper, Coca-Cola, lemonade, Tru-Ade and even something made from lilies of the valley called lily liqueur. Everything, I'm sure, but Lydia Pinkham's vegetable compound.

Upon occasion my father became irritated at this vast layout —he was especially mad one night when he carried 12 cases of the stuff to the cellar and strained his back—and he'd say something like, "Why don't we throw out all this junk and maybe get just one bottle of booze?"

But my mother was adamant. She, almost single-handedly, kept Moxie in business in the East for many years. And, to be honest, my father never really objected to the no-liquor rule.

A thrifty man, he once took pencil and paper and, after totting up some figures, informed me with immense satisfaction that by not drinking for 14 years, especially on New Year's Eve, he'd saved about $196 on tires.

When I was seventeen, however, something happened that changed this situation abruptly. It ended the ban on strict abstinence and it brought about an arrangement under which Mother and Dad happily consented to consume about five or six ounces of liquor each per week for the rest of their lives.

I had a friend who was in the publishing business and who, for some years, had been in the habit of buying thick purple grapes from California. And, deep in the bowels of his publishing plant, he annually had whipped up (or dripped up) batches of some of the finest, extremely fortified, grape wine you could imagine. He'd permitted me to sample some of this now and then, but in the year after I turned seventeen I did him a favor and about four days before Christmas he presented me with three bottles of this wonderful wine.

I took the three bottles home and hid them in the closet in my room. On Christmas Day, shortly before the family was about to sit down to dinner, I casually reminded my mother that she'd made some grape juice—squeezing the grapes from our own arbor—and I suggested that we might drink some of this grape juice with our dinner.

"A good idea," said my mother. "I made twenty-four quart Mason jars. They're all up in the attic, sealed with wax. Why don't you get one?"

I raced up to the attic and found the 24 jars. I was appalled at the sight. The sugary purple stuff had worked up through the wax, and each jar was covered with mold. I tasted the grape juice and it was vinegary. It was one of Mother's more spectacular failures.

I took one of the jars to an upstairs bathroom and emptied it into the toilet. I scraped off the wax and mold, thoroughly washed the jar, and then I filled it with a bottle of my friend's highly fortified wine.

Smiling broadly, I took the wine to the dining room, complimented my mother on her handiwork, and filled the glasses on the table. We toasted each other before dinner and my mother, tasting her drink, said, "Isn't this just wonderful! And to think I made it myself! I'll have another one, please."

Well, she had another, and then another. It was the gayest dinner ever.

And somewhere in the middle of it, my dear mother, happy as a little girl with a new doll, picked up her glass, held it aloft, smiled at us all and said, "Wheeeeeeee! Isn't this magnificent? And just think—we have twenty-three *more* bottles of it up in the attic!"

Well—of course, we had to tell her in time, and I had thought she'd be more than a little angry. But Mother was great in the way she frequently surprised you.

"Angry? Oh, no," she said the next day when I told her. "Why should I be angry? I'm just sorry that we *don't* have twenty-three more bottles upstairs. But, since that wine is so good, I see no reason why you shouldn't bring home a bottle or two once in a while. That is—if you can get some more from your friend."

I got some more wine from time to time and we enjoyed it. And this got Mother to thinking.

One night she said to my father, "Frank, you know our own grapes are fine and fat and purple. And we have more grapes every year than we ever can eat, or even give away. Why wouldn't it be a good idea to take some of those grapes—not all, of course—but some of them and maybe make a little grape wine of our own?"

My father, a rather accomplished tease, shook his head and said, "No, my dear. I'm afraid that can't be. It's against the law."

"Oh, nonsense," said my mother. "It's against the law only if you sell it. And if you can make wine as good as this, then we certainly aren't going to sell it!"

And so it was that that summer we all of us watched the little grapes beginning to sprout on the vines, tiny green things that got bigger and bigger as the weeks went by, and finally turned into beautiful, big purple grapes that the starlings and other large birds began to descend upon.

"Those birds have got to go," said my mother, who, as it happens, was secretary of the Westchester County Ornithological Society and an ardent bird watcher and lover of our feathery little friends.

"Oh, no!" said my father, in mock indignation. "Not those dear, sweet, darling little birdies that we all love so much!"

"Well," said my mother, "I don't mean to kill them. Just scare them away."

So, much of that summer, and well into the fall, there always were a couple of BB guns standing by our porch door and my brother and I, and my father and mother, too, would snatch them up and pepper away the moment any starlings, grackles or other grape-snatching birds were dopey enough to attack our arbor. The BBs didn't hurt the birds, but they did frighten them, and by the time the grapes were nice and ripe, the birds had given up trying to steal them.

Just how it was that my father made the wine—what formula he used, or what tricks and secrets he employed—I do not know. He did most of his work at night after I'd gone to bed, but I do recall that we picked countless pounds of grapes and filled five or six washtubs and other huge metal containers.

Then Dad pounded them with a baseball bat or something like that and in time he had everything squished and squashed and then he rigged up a kind of Rube Goldberg apparatus in the cellar to bring about the fermentation of all this mess. What he put in, or didn't put in, I cannot tell you. But in time, he drew from this pulpy, reeking grapy mass many gallons of what he assured me would be very fine wine.

"We'll bottle it and then let it rest," he said. "It'll be wonderful."

Whether there were such things as home bottle-capping devices in those days, I don't remember, but I do know that my father said his wine would be corked, and that the cork would be tied securely.

One night when the wine was ready, Dad got out the 75 or 80 quart bottles he'd bought and, standing them on the kitchen table, filled them all with the wine. He drove fresh corks into each bottle. Then he took slender but stout cord, looped it about the ridged neck of the bottle, tied it back and forth over the top of the cork, and knotted it down below the ridge of the bottle neck.

"Gotta do this very tightly," he told me, "because this wine is effervescent and it builds up quite a head of steam inside the bottle. If you don't tie the cork securely, it'll pop out."

It took us hours, but we tied the whole batch that night. We placed each bottle carefully on the floor of a pantry closet, closed the door and went upstairs to bed. Dad was supremely happy. He'd never done anything like that before, and he was pleased that all had gone so well.

And things did go well for a couple of weeks or so. Then one night when we were all at dinner, we heard what sounded like a shot coming from the kitchen.

"What was that?" my father cried. "Sounded like a shotgun."

We sat there for a moment, not knowing what to do. Then came the sound of another shot!

"Ye gods," shouted my father. He leaped from the table, plunged into the kitchen, rushed to the pantry and opened the closet door. The place smelled like a saloon, and wine was dripping from the bottom of the shelf directly over the wine bottles. Two of the bottles had blown their corks. The wine, apparently, had geysered out of them, and the bottles were just about empty. A trickle of wine was running out the closet door and onto the pantry floor.

"Well," said my father, "I must have tied those corks too loosely. I wonder if any of the others are loose?"

He reached into the closet, took one of the bottles by the neck and started to lift it out. It happened to bang gently against another bottle and suddenly, with a loud pop, it exploded in his hand. He and I were showered with wine and bits of glass and my father was so startled he dropped what was left of the bottle. It struck another bottle and that one exploded too.

My father got a blanket and threw it over the bottles. Then he closed the closet door and we left the pantry. He looked like a man who'd just been told his wife was unfaithful.

"I can't understand it," he said, shaking his head. "I just can't understand it. I must've done something wrong."

He pondered a bit and then he said, "I probably filled those bottles too full. You've got to allow for the effervescence and I guess I didn't leave enough room. I think I'll uncork 'em all and put only about two-thirds as much in each bottle."

As he stood there, debating, we heard another POP from the closet. It wasn't as loud as the others, being muffled by the blanket, but it was a mighty discouraging POP all the same.

"That's what I'll do," said Dad. "Tomorrow I'll get some more bottles and we'll rebottle the batch."

The next night, equipped with more bottles and more cord, we set to work. My father put the bottles on the table and he gave me a Turkish towel and said, "Hold this over the neck of the bottle, just in case the wine starts to shoot out."

I stood there, holding the towel, and my father sat down on a high stool at one end of the table. He took a bottle and, with his knife, cut the cord. The cork shot out instantly, with a loud pop. It bounced against the ceiling, closely followed by a fountain of pinkish wine.

"Throw the towel over it," yelled my father.

"I can't," I said. "It's all on the ceiling."

But it wasn't there for long. It was dribbling down on us like mad. Virtually every drop had shot out of the bottle, spread itself all over the ceiling, and now was dropping down onto the floor, the stove, the table, the chairs.

"Well," said my father. "We let that one get away. Let's clean this up and we'll try again."

We mopped the ceiling, the walls, the stove, the floor and everything else that had been deluged. Then my father took another bottle and said, "This one looks calm inside. But hold the towel over it just in case."

He cut the cord, the cork shot out and right into the towel I was holding and the wine followed it. It didn't go all over, but it quickly inundated the table and flowed off onto the floor.

We mopped that up and wiped the table and then my father got a deep wash boiler and said he thought he'd better open the bottles inside that. The first one he opened sloshed around a bit, but gave up rather easily. The second one, however, must have had atomic action because the wine shot directly up and out of the boiler, sluicing my father's face and chest, and showering the kitchen once more.

In time, Dad got so he could angle the bottle correctly in the boiler and keep it from blasting out. And, I think, he might well have emptied the rest of the bottles without incident if it hadn't been for the bottle that slipped.

He was picking up this bottle, about to point it into the boiler and cut its cord, when it twisted in his wine-soaked fingers and dropped to the edge of the boiler. Dad's reflexes were fine and he made a backhand stab at it, but once again the wetness of the bottle and the wetness of his fingers conspired against him.

The bottle squirted out of his fingers like an earth-to-air missile and crashed right into the middle of the remaining 50 some odd bottles. They, of course, skittered in all directions like bowling pins and, falling over on the table and dropping to the floor, they began exploding.

Pow . . . Pow . . . pow . . . POW . . . Bam . . . pow . . . bloop . . . blam . . . pow . . . pow . . . Zzzzzz . . . pow . . . POW . . . bam, bam . . . zzzzzzzzpy . . . pow . . . POW!!!

My father and I just stood there horrified. There wasn't anything we could do. And besides, by now the two of us were totally soaked by wine. My eyeglasses were so covered with it I hardly could see. There was at least half an inch of wine all over the floor and there was broken glass everywhere. The walls, the ceiling, the stove, the refrigerator, the chairs, the sink —everything was dripping wine.

My father, who had quite a temper, was seething with rage and I fully expected him to lift the boiler and shatter it on the table and then take the table and break it to bits and throw it out of the room. But, as I stood there, with wine running down out of my hair, I began to laugh. And then I laughed harder and louder and all of a sudden my father began to laugh, too.

Soon we were laughing so hard that we couldn't stand up any more and we sat down on the wine-covered chairs and gripped our sides and laughed and laughed and laughed.

After a while, we got hold of ourselves and we swept up all the broken glass and shoved the little lake of wine out the rear door and mopped everything until it was reasonably dry. But no matter what we did, the ceiling, walls and floors remained sticky and the smell of wine just wouldn't go away. And when my mother came home from a two-day visit with her mother in New York, she was simply aghast.

Two weeks later we had to have the kitchen washed down and repainted and after that was done, my father came to realize that what with Prohibition in the process of being repealed, his bottling efforts had been virtually unnecessary. So he went out and bought a case of wine. After that there was a reasonable amount of drinking at Mockridge Manor.

And, while we're on the subject of explosions, it was about that time that I acquired my first car.

Ever since I'd received my driver's license, I'd been in the habit of borrowing my father's Chrysler whenever I wanted to go anywhere. But this was a most unsatisfactory arrangement because he all too often seemed to feel that he needed the car at the precise time that I wanted it.

So, taking all my savings, I went to the Rawlings Ford Agency in Mount Kisco to look things over. I had intended to sort of mouse around, appraise the various models and pick out a secondhand bargain. But when I walked in, I was met by the agency's senior salesman, a dashing, well-dressed man named Mr. Paddock, who happened to be the father of Betty Paddock, a young lady at school of whom I was somewhat enamored at the time.

"Well, well, interested in a nice new car, eh?" said Mr. Paddock, rubbing his hands. "Well, we've got some beauties. Here, let me show you a snappy new roadster."

He showed me quite a few models, mostly in the $2,000–$3,000 range, I think, and I inspected them carefully and asked an intelligent question here and there. Then, after I'd seen everything, I said hesitantly, "Really, Mr. Paddock, I was thinking of something a little cheaper."

He looked a little annoyed, but he handled it professionally. "Ah, something in the secondhand line, what?" he said. "Oh, we have some beauties. Here, I'll show you a wonderful phaeton. Belonged to old Mrs. Wentworth. Chauffeur driven. Hardly ever out of the garage."

I learned that this car was $1,500. And I saw others at about the same figure.

Because Mr. Paddock was Betsy's father, I hated to have to tell him that I couldn't afford those bargains. But, eventually, I did.

"Look, son," said Mr. Paddock, pushing his hat back on his head, "just how much do you intend to spend?"

"Well, sir," I said, digging my hand deep into my pocket and clenching my little bankroll, "I'd say about . . . ah . . . about thirty dollars. That's all I have."

Mr. Paddock took off his hat and struck his head with the palm of his hand. "Good God!" he said.

He looked around as though seeking some way to escape, and as he did he glanced out through the show window. And there in the lot, along with a lot of bright and shiny reconditioned Fords, stood a pretty decrepit Model A touring car with a patched black canvas roof and a well-dented blue and black body.

"Saaaay," said Mr. Paddock. "We got that thing in just last

night and they were going to take her away this morning, but . . . well, I guess I could let you have her for thirty dollars. She's a beauty."

It was pretty clear to me that the "going to take her away" was a reference to the junk yard, but inasmuch as the little car was the only thing around within my budget, I looked at her quite carefully.

"Does she run?" I asked.

"My God, I don't know," said Mr. Paddock. Then he quickly added, "I mean, of course she does. It's just that I haven't driven her."

So, we strolled over and got in, Mr. Paddock sliding under the wheel. He switched on the ignition and stepped on the starter. It sounded like a load of gravel being crushed, but suddenly, the motor sputtered and coughed and came to life. It knocked like mad.

"Probably just needs a little heavy oil," shouted Mr. Paddock above the din. "Let's try her out." He clanked the car into gear, released the clutch and we took off. We drove a mile or so up Bedford Road and then returned, braking noisily to a halt in the dusty lot.

"Has a lot of power on the hills," said Mr. Paddock, rubbing his hands together. "She's a beauty."

Well, I paid Mr. Paddock the $30 and then charged some gas and oil—the mechanic put *three* quarts of heavy oil in the engine—and drove home. I parked the car in the driveway and my mother, who'd come out to see what the racket was, stared at the bright blue body and said, "I've never seen a car painted in delphinium blue."

And that's how my car got her name—Delphinium.

Delphinium gave me no trouble at all—for three days. Then one afternoon as I was driving over the railroad crossing (the same one on which my bicycle had parted) I heard a terrible hissing sound under the hood and soon saw clouds of steam rising above Delphinium's bonnet.

When I opened the hood I found that the radiator had just

about disintegrated and was spurting water all over the hot engine. I got a friend to tow the car home and I went to Elman's junk yard—called "The House of a Million Parts"— and spent two or three hours searching for another radiator for that model. I finally found one, bought it for $2, and then spent a whole day installing it myself.

Delphinium seemed to appreciate the attention and she stayed in reasonably good shape for a few more days, although she drank oil in a frightening way. I finally bought the oil wholesale in two-gallon cans and always carried one with me in the car.

There were no windows, of course, in this touring car, but there were isinglass curtains that could be buttoned between the tops of the doors and the roof in case of rain. These curtains were quite old and the fabric around the snappers was somewhat cracked and rotted. I expected to have some trouble with them in heavy weather, but I wasn't prepared for what happened the first time I took the car out in a gale.

I drove down Moger Avenue all right, bucking right into the wind and the rain, but when I emerged into Main Street the side of the car caught the full force of the wind coming down off Kisco Mountain. Within a matter of seconds, every curtain was blown out or ripped to shreds.

From then on, whenever it rained I simply donned a heavy raincoat and a sou'wester hat and let it rain. This did Delphinium's imitation leather seats no good, but there wasn't anything I could do. One of the seats, by the way, got even with me for this lack of care. One night, attired in a dinner jacket, I slid across the seat to get out and go to a dance. A coiled spring picked that moment to burst through, hook into the seat of my pants and tear a jagged, triangular hole about nine inches long. I never got to the dance.

In the summertime, handling Delphinium wasn't too much of a chore. But in winter she was hell. I couldn't use light oil without having the motor knock itself to pieces, and heavy oil congealed so much it was almost impossible for the starter to turn the motor over on a very cold day. Time and again I had to get a tow truck to get me started.

Also Delphinium wasn't the girl to start easily unless her manifold was warmed up. And so, on many a cold day, I placed towels on the icy manifold and then poured boiling water on them from a steaming kettle. This worked nicely until one morning the boiling water cracked the metal manifold—and then it was back to Elman's junk yard for me. The search was much harder this time because the entire yard was covered by nearly two feet of snow!

In the end, it was cold weather that finally did Delphinium in. One January morning, with the mercury slightly below zero, I set out from Mount Kisco for New York to do an afternoon radio show. I had with me a two-gallon can of oil, a gallon of gas (there was a slow leak in my gas tank), two spare tires, chains, and a magnificent buffalo robe.

That buffalo robe was my pride and joy. I'd bought it for $7 at a church rummage sale and time after time it had saved my life. As I drove in cold weather, I sat huddled inside this huge thing, with only my fur-hatted head sticking out the top, and my heavily gloved hands clutching the wheel through two slits I cut in the hide.

People who saw me pass often did double takes, most of them thinking that some animal was driving the car.

Well, that January day I tootled out of Mount Kisco, got to White Plains 16 miles away, and then drove onto Central Park Avenue to take me into New York City. About three miles south of White Plains, I was zipping along the snow-covered road about 40 miles per hour when suddenly the rhythmic knocking of the motor was disrupted by a loud BOOM—and several large dents rose sharply in the hood of the car. There was an unbelievable clanking under the hood and, as I braked the car to a halt, the motor died.

I disentangled myself from my buffalo robe and got out to survey the damage. It was appalling. When I lifted the hood, I found the engine in ruins. Oil and water and steam were all over the place, and bits of broken metal were scattered around.

What had happened was that one of the connecting rods which drive the pistons had broken loose and, instead of just going up and down in the prescribed manner, it had started to swing around in circles. And as it swung, it smashed up the entire motor.

This, it was apparent, was the end of the road for Delphinium. I felt like crying, and if it hadn't been so bitterly cold, I probably would have. Tenderly, I lowered the dented hood and fastened it. It seemed the decent thing to do, and then I started trudging the highway back to White Plains.

Finally, I came to a garage which had a used car lot, and I found the proprietor.

"I've got an old Model A down the road," I said. "Motor's all busted. Connecting rod went—"

"Yeah, yeah," said the man. "I'll give ya ten bucks."

"Sold," I said, with a catch in my voice. I felt as though I'd just disposed of my firstborn child. The man drove me to the railroad station so I could continue to New York, and I said that I'd return the next day to pick up my buffalo robe and the other things in the car.

The following morning, I borrowed a car from a friend and went to the garage. They had my things all piled in the office and I put them in the trunk of the car. Then I did a stupid thing.

I looked into the garage itself and there stood Delphinium— or rather what was left of her. Mechanics had stripped her of everything worthwhile, and she looked like a skeleton.

"Savin' a few parts," said the garage man. "Junkin' the rest."

I choked up, and I turned quickly and walked out to the car. I didn't want anybody to see me crying.

Chapter Ten

AFTER my ill-fated romance with Bubbles Glou in the sixth grade, and the shattering thing with Uldine Utley, I sort of shied away from amour for quite a while. I didn't blame Bubbles or Uldine for what had happened, of course, but I'd learned that women, even when they're not trying, can get you into a hell of a lot of trouble.

I paid virtually no attention to the femmes fatales in the seventh grade and not much more to the Gloria Swansons and

Pola Negris of the eighth grade. Although I do remember that when I was running for the presidency of the class, my campaign manager, Reuben Smilkstein, insisted that I smile at the girls, shake hands with them and say something polite whenever I met them.

It wasn't until my second year in high school, however, that I fell in love again. And this came about in a rather odd way.

My father and mother, who never had been much interested in religion—Dad had been brought up as a Presbyterian and Mother as a Lutheran, but neither joined a church after they were married—got interested in Christian Science.

Just how that happened, I don't recall, but they began attending services at the nearest Christian Science church, a little place in Katonah, about six miles from Mount Kisco. I, of course, continued going to St. Mark's Episcopal Church where I had been reinstalled as a wine-serving acolyte, and also had become president of the St. Andrew's Brotherhood, a church youth organization, and had conquered all comers to achieve the exalted position of junior Ping-Pong champion.

I was quite happy with my church—especially the extracurricular activities such as plays, Gilbert and Sullivan performances, dances and parties—and had no interest whatsoever in the Christian Science church. I had a feeling that Christian Scientists were a little wacky, especially when I heard that every Wednesday night they had special meetings at which they all stood up and gave testimonials—telling about all the bad things they had done, and describing how Science had helped them overcome these faults.

I certainly had no intention of *telling* anybody about the bad things I'd done. I just prayed that nobody ever would find out. But as Mother and Dad got more and more interested in the church, they kept telling me about it and finally, one Sunday, they prevailed upon me to accompany them to church.

My feeling was that the whole trip was nothing but a waste of time, but I felt that the least I could do was to humor my parents.

When we got there, I was surprised to find that the church wasn't a church at all. Just a small house with a large living room in which everybody sat, with the two readers standing behind little lecterns at one end. A lady played the piano and another sang—one of the worst sopranos I'd ever heard, and at that time I didn't even like good ones—and I sort of scrounged down in my chair and hoped that I might fall asleep.

Then some latecomers were admitted to the room, and I sat bolt upright. Among them was a young lady about fifteen, a year or so older than I. This was a beautiful young doll, with lovely blond hair, sparkling blue eyes, high cheekbones, a turned-up nose and a marvelous complexion. And she was wearing a dazzling leopard skin coat.

"Who's that?" I whispered to my mother.

"That's Mrs. March," said my mother, glancing at the lady with the girl—and missing my point entirely.

"No, no," I said. "Who's that girl?"

"Oh, that's her daughter, Marjory," said my mother. "And the boy is Marjory's brother, Tom."

I cannot tell you one word that was spoken or one note that was sung in the rest of that service, but I *can* tell you that I sat and studied Miss Marjory March most intently throughout the whole thing. And I had a good chance to do it because she was sitting just three rows ahead of me.

When the service was over, I was up and out of my seat within a second or two and I stationed myself right outside the front door so I could extend a brotherly greeting to Miss March the moment she came out. I stood there quite a while, as a stream of worshipers filed out, and after a long time, my mother and father came out. I looked inside and there was no one left.

"What happened to Mrs. March and her children?" I asked.

"Oh," said my mother, "I think they went out the side door. That's where they always park their car."

I brooded about this all week, and on Saturday afternoon I startled my parents by saying, "You know, that Christian Science stuff is sort of interesting. I think I'll go with you again to-morrow."

Well, my luck continued poor. Marjory and her mother didn't show up that Sunday. So I had to go for the third straight time. And the sopranos got worse each time.

But on that third Sunday, as my heart leaped, Marjory and her mother walked in. And Marjory was wearing that fabulous leopard coat.

This time, you can be sure, I maneuvered more carefully, and I was outside the right door when Marjory emerged into the sunlight. She was a radiant girl, and I felt for the first time that I might soon be willing to testify as to what Christian Science had done for me.

Well, as a result of our little talk, I got myself invited to a Saturday night party that Marjory was giving for a few friends the following week and I had an enchanting time. We played, among other things, the game of spin the bottle and, since I had long practiced the art of spinning the bottle and had attained the precision of a 30-30 deer rifle, I got to know Marjory quite well. I always, incidentally, have liked the game of spin the bottle on the ground that it's educational, enlightening and most conducive.

The following Saturday night, I took Marjory to a dance at St. Mark's. I also took her brother Tom and his date because Tom had a car and a license to drive, and I had neither. And from then on, it seemed that whenever I wanted to take Marjory anwhere I always had to ask three people. Not complaining; just stating a fact.

But the night that I took Marjory to our first dance is one I shall never forget. Marjory was radiant as usual, beautifully turned out in her leopard coat, with hat to match, and a gay, filmy scarf about her throat, and we had a perfectly wonderful time. And as we drove home from the dance, Marjory and I snuggled in the back seat. Then as Tom took his date home, Marjory and I stood out on the porch, snuggling some more. And when it came time for Tom to drive me home, Marjory went with us and we sat in the back seat and did a little more snuggling.

It had been a wonderful, wonderful evening, and after I kissed Marjory good night, for the 300th time, I whispered gently in her delicate ear, "Good night, my dear. I'll see you in church."

The next morning I was up not so bright, but early, ready to attend worship. I hadn't been to St. Mark's in weeks—except to go to dances or plays—and I had a little nagging feeling about that, but I squared my shoulders and brushed it aside.

However, that wasn't all I had to brush that morning. I dressed carefully, wearing my best silver tie, and combing my long, blond, wavy hair (I really had blond wavy hair at the time), and I was ready and waiting in the hall when my parents came downstairs.

I helped Mother and Dad into their coats and then I got out my overcoat and threw it on. My mother took one look at me and her hand flew to her face.

"For heaven's sake, Norton," she cried. "Where did you get the fur coat?"

I looked down at my blue cheviot overcoat, noticing it for the first time, and found that every single inch of it was completely covered with yellow and brown fur. About half of Marjory's coat had transferred itself to mine!

It took my father, mother and me a good 20 minutes to make the coat presentable so I could wear it to church. (I had no other.) But it was months before I was able to get the last bit of fur out of it. And to this day, whenever I see a lady wearing a leopard coat, I once again am a teen-ager attending the Christian Science church in Katonah.

Marjory and I had a very pleasant year or so together, but the romance finally came to an end. She was a year ahead of me in school, and, when she was about to go to Washington with her class, I talked to a friend of mine in the senior class, a fellow named Johnny, and I asked him to sort of watch out for Marjory during the trip.

Well, he did. And he did a masterful job. A modern-day Johnny Alden yet!

With that romance out of the way, I turned my attention to a beautiful young red-haired lady of Italian descent and we got along very nicely. I'd heard that her father had a terrible temper and that, like most Italian fathers, he was an especially zealous guardian of his little girl.

He put me through several periods of intensive questioning during the courtship and, even though I think I gave straightforward enough answers, I always got the impression that he was, to say the least, suspicious.

After our fourth or fifth date, I took the young lady home and was met inside the front door by her father. He sent her upstairs to bed and took me into the living room. It was obvious that he'd been drinking, and in my humble estimation he was well on the way to getting loaded.

"Look," he said, grasping my arm. "You like my girl? She's nice girl, yes? You like her?"

I said yes, I certainly did like her.

"Ah, hah!" he cried, and he tightened his grip on my arm. "Then when you gonna marry my girl?"

Quite shocked, and a little scared, I mumbled something about not being out of school yet, and no job, and things like that.

"Well," he shouted, "you hurry up the school. You marry my daughter! You BETTER!"

As best I could, I explained that I surely would take the matter under consideration, and wriggling out of his grasp, I left the house as rapidly as possible. Thus ended the romance with the red-haired Italian.

Things were fairly peaceful for a few months after that, mainly because I was a bit gun-shy. But then at a party in White Plains, I met a beautiful brunette who was just launching a career as a singer and dancer.

The svelte artiste, whom I'll call Molly, was fascinating and we had a lot of fun together. She taught me some dance steps, and even tried to teach me singing, which was a huge mistake, but as I got to know her better I was a little disturbed by some of the things she did.

She was a madcap, a pixie at heart, and a girl who loved to thumb her nose at convention. One hot summer night we were at a party at a country estate and Molly, who'd complained a bit about the heat, suddenly announced that she was going to cool off.

She stood up, stripped off her dress, her shoes and stockings and, attired in just her bra and panties, strolled across the lawn to a rippling brook which ran through the estate. She hopped into it and finding a flat rock, sat there, waist deep, enjoying the refrigeration.

Another time at a party, she climbed a rose trellis to the roof of a porch and then, as the orchestra played below, she stood on the roof and sang: "When We're Out Together, Dancing Cheek to Cheek." She once clambered into an airplane in which I was about to take a lesson at the old Armonk Field in Westchester County, and tried to start it.

"Anybody can fly," she said. "Who needs lessons?" And she got into some difficulty with the police when, after we came out of the movies one night, she spotted a bakery truck standing at the curb, with its motor running.

The driver was inside a restaurant and Molly, with a shriek of glee, leaped into the truck and took off. The driver saw her leave and he phoned the cops. They nabbed her about a mile away, but they let her go after she explained that she wasn't stealing the truck, just obeying an irresistible impulse to drive one.

Because of these assorted episodes, and a couple of others like them, I decided that Molly was not for me. And one evening, driving home from a play we had seen, I told her that we'd just had our last date.

She joked about it for a while, but then, seeing that I was serious, she commanded me to stop the car. "Stop it right here," she yelled. "I want to get out."

143

I pointed out that we were driving along a lonely stretch of road near the Kensico Reservoir and that that certainly was no place to leave a lady at night. She insisted, however, even opening the door while we were moving, and so, reluctantly, I pulled over to the side of the road.

She leaped from the car and started to run through the evergreens between the road and the reservoir. "I'm going to drown myself," she yelled. "Then you'll be sorry."

I scrambled out of the car and dashed after her. I emerged from the evergreens just in time to see her strip off her clothes and plunge into the water. It was dark, but there was enough light for me to make out the splashes as she swam far into the extremely deep reservoir.

I yelled at her to come back, but got no answer. So, I took off my own clothes and waded into the chilly water. I listened and I could hear the splashes ahead of me. I began swimming in the same direction. Then, suddenly, about 50 yards from shore, I came upon her. She was lying there, floating. She seemed quite pleased with herself.

Partly out of breath, and madder than hell, I snarled at her and told her to get out of the water.

She laughed, loud and long, and she said, "You want me out of the water? Okay, I'll get out of the water." Then, with one of the finest crawl strokes I've ever seen, she began to churn her way to shore. I followed, but she easily outdistanced me.

By then, several motorists had stopped on the road, attracted by my car parked with its headlights on and the door open. Two or three men were pushing through the evergreens to the water's edge.

Molly hit the shore, slipped into her dress and yelled at the men, "Quick, there's a man drowning out there." Then she ran through the woods up to the road where, as I learned later, she got one of the motorists to drive her home. I also learned later that Molly was a champion swimmer and that she could have swum across the huge reservoir and back without any trouble.

144

It took an awful lot of explanation to convince the men who'd come to rescue me that I didn't need any rescue, that I hadn't tried to drown myself or the girl, and that I'd merely been the victim of a hoax. Two of my would-be rescuers insisted, however, that I go to the police station to report the whole matter —just in case some bodies turned up in the reservoir in the next few days.

I felt like the damnedest fool, but I had to do it. And I can remember the gray-haired police sergeant taking down my statement and then shaking his head.

"Son," he said with a sigh, "I think the best thing for you is to enter the priesthood."

And for quite a while, I felt the same way.

Then I met an actress I'll call Barbara Black. This was a particularly intriguing redhead, sort of a cross between Susan Hayward and Jane Russell, if you know what I mean, and she wasn't a bad actress, either.

We never played in the same show together, but we met at three different summer theaters that season—she'd be playing in one show at night, for instance, while I'd be rehearsing days for the show that was to take over next week. Although she worked nights and I worked days, we, surprisingly enough, found lots of time to be together. We just didn't sleep.

Or, if we slept at all, it was during rehearsals and two or three of our directors took exception to this and some unkind words were exchanged. But Barbara and I, fairly bursting with youth and energy and stimulated by a combination of summer madness and budding love, really lived it up.

Right after the final curtain and the bows every night, we'd take off in her station wagon and go to a party. Somebody always was giving a party for the actors. We'd eat and drink and dance and tell stories, and then, about 3 A.M., we'd drive to a nearby lake, or, when we were on Cape Cod, we'd drive to the ocean, and swim and lie on the beach.

Often we'd build a driftwood fire, and as the sun rose we'd cook our breakfast. We carried the utensils and the food in an insulated wooden ice chest in the back of the car, a chest which, since we both were working, we could afford to keep well stocked.

Then we'd be back at the theater in time for 9 o'clock rehearsals or run-throughs. All in all, it was a very satisfactory summer and when fall, and the end of our theatrical engagements, suddenly arrived, we were quite distressed. I had another year of high school to serve in Mount Kisco, and Barbara had to go back to her apartment in New York and search for work.

I vowed that I'd visit her the very first weekend I could get away, but she said sadly that she probably would have to spend the next few weekends visiting her parents in Baltimore. I said I'd drive to New York some week night, but she said not to do that either. "After walking from one producer's office to another all day," she said, "I'll be dead tired at night. And besides, I have to read scripts for five or six hours every night."

Then she promised that as soon as she got a part in a Broadway show, or a role in a radio soap opera, she'd phone me and, as she put it, "After that we'll have loads of time to be together."

We solemnly vowed to write and to telephone, but it wasn't until after I'd kissed her good-bye that I realized she'd forgotten to give me either her number or her address. However, a little oversight like that was no deterrent to a man of my resources. Through a friend in Actor's Equity, I quickly learned the number and the address.

I called her night after night, but all I got was her answering service. Miss Black, they said, was out of town. They'd tell her I'd called. She, however, never returned my call. This worried me a lot and one night when a friend of mine was driving to New York, I went with him, determined to find out whether something had happened to Barbara.

I went to the address and found that she lived on the fourth floor of a walkup in East 54th Street. And I surmised that she had a roommate, because the bell had a little card over it reading: B. BLACK and R. ROGERS. I rang the bell and in a few seconds the buzzer sounded, unlocking the front door, and I walked in.

A little breathless, I trudged up the three long flights of stairs, walked down the hall to 4C and knocked lightly. The door was opened instantly—but not by Barbara.

There stood a huge man, fully three inches taller than I and at least 30 pounds heavier. He was wearing a pair of slacks and an undershirt and he was barefoot. He looked tough.

"Yeah?" he said.

"Is . . . ah . . . is Barbara home?" I asked, tentatively.

"Waddya want her for?" he asked. And I detected a note of hostility in his voice.

"Well," I said, standing my ground, "she's a very good friend of mine. We acted together all summer, and I want to see her."

"Oh, ya did, did ya?" the man growled. "You *acted* together all summer while I was out West. Well, buddy, them actin' days is over. I'm Barbara's husband, see? And her actin' career is finished—all washed up, see? And so you can get the hell out of here! There ain't gonna be no more actin'!"

Ah, well, I thought to myself as I walked wearily down all those stairs, you really can't expect much from a summer romance. And actresses are remarkably fickle. So—no more summer romances, and no more actresses.

And I stuck to that credo—until the next summer.

Then I met a ravishing French actress whom we'll call Babette. This jet-black brunette had deep, dark eyes veiled by extraordinarily long lashes, and she had a classic nose that tilted most enticingly, and her figure was splendid. She slurred along engagingly in a mixture of English and French, punctuated with a brisk *"Voilà!"* here, a lively "Ha, Ha!" there, and frequent mentions of *l'amitié* and *l'amour*.

She was starring in a French farce at the Westchester Playhouse in Mount Kisco, where I was rehearsing for the following week's play. And since I then was working as a reporter for the Mount Kisco *Recorder*, I lost no time in presenting myself to her and interviewing her for my paper.

When I finished the interview that afternoon, I felt quite sure I was in love with her and, surprisingly enough, she seemed to feel much the same way. I say, "surprisingly" because at the time, I was seventeen and she was thirty-four.

She'd been married once, to a writer, and had been divorced. But in a way, she explained, she really wasn't divorced.

"You see, *mon cher*," she said, "I 'ave zee deevorce, legal, 'ow you say? 'Owever, I am zee devout Catholic, and so, you see, I 'ave not zee deevorce releegeous. So, mos' unfortunate, anozzer marriage ees not for me."

Well, I sympathized with her, but I thought it was a little early to think of marriage anyway, and I changed the subject. I invited her to a little supper after the performance that night, and she accepted with a very gracious smile and a nice little kiss on my cheek.

The evening turned out perfectly, and I was sure this wasn't just a summer romance. (And it wasn't either. It lasted four years!) But in addition to proving what I'd already decided— that this petite lady was lovely, warm, charming, captivating and extremely feminine—the evening also revealed two other important factors:

1, That she didn't drink. (I'd never met an actress who didn't drink.) and,

2, That she was one of the most dominant, willful, inflexible and opinionated human beings I'd ever encountered.

The no-drinking was easily explained by the fact that she was allergic to alcohol. I didn't fully understand this until months later, at Christmas, I induced her to have a glass of champagne. She knew better, of course, but she was carried away with the spirit of the party, I guess, and she drank about half a glass.

Within minutes, her milk-white skin was a mass of crimson splotches. She had these lobsterlike images all over her face,

148

her neck and what you could see of her bosom. And by the way she scratched, it was apparent they were elsewhere, too. I never asked her to drink again.

But her dominance and inflexibility and the manner in which she handed down opinions were hard to explain—and a little hard to take.

I suggested, as we set out for supper that night in my car (I had acquired, by then, a fairly presentable Plymouth coupe), that we go to a small roadhouse where they had a nice, three-piece orchestra.

But Babette said, "Ah, no! Eet ees eempossible for me to withstand zee museec after I 'ave become fatigued from zee performance. We weel go to a verry good restaurant like, possiblee, the 21 Club, and 'ave a quiet, leetle steak."

I tried to explain that we were 'way up in northern Westchester County, 45 miles from 21, and that you just couldn't find such restaurants in a rural area like that. Especially ones that were open at that time of night.

"Oh, yes, my darleeng," she said, "you weel find eet."

You notice that *"weel"*? Not would you please try to find one, or I would be happy if it were possible for you to locate one. Oh, no. Just—you WEEL find it.

Well, I deedn't find it. There simply wasn't any possibility of finding such a place. But I did remember that on Monday nights (and this was a Monday), the old Motor Inn Lodge in Mount Kisco made it a policy to offer no entertainment whatsoever. Other nights they had things like Silver-Voiced Tenors, and Violin Virtuosos and Banjo Bonanzas. And once in a while a girl like Annette Hanshaw, who used to sing on radio, appeared there.

So we went to the Motor Inn Lodge. Babette was enchanted with its old-world style. (Personally, I thought it was falling down—and a few years later, it did.) But she enthused over the colonnades, the vast veranda, the antique lighting fixtures and so on.

But she just never did adjust to the steaks they brought her.

The first one, she said, was too well done. So, it was sent back to the kitchen. The second one was much too burned. And the third— "Zees ees a mos' inferior steak. 'E 'as too much, 'ow you say?—greestle. Ees not feet for 'uman eating."

The vegetables didn't ring any bells, either. And the coffee was "like eet was made from grounds from seex weeks ago." But she had a piece of Boston cream pie that she thought was "magneefeecent"—just like they make in France.

On that basis, I chalked the evening up as a big success. But as I talked to Babette, it became apparent to me that what I thought about anything was of little moment. It was what *she* thought of it.

I mentioned a play on Broadway, said I'd heard good reports about it and suggested that we might go to see it one night.

"Ah, no, eet steenks," she said. "Eet ees one of the worst. Zey should be prosecuted for putteeng on such a bad theeng."

I asked her whether she'd seen it, and she promptly answered, "Of course not. I wouldn't go to such a ghastly theeng." I then asked her how she knew it was so bad and she replied with considerable vigor, "I know! Zat ees all!"

Despite the fact that I cannot recall having ever had a restaurant meal with Babette which wasn't distinguished by her insistence on returning at least 75 percent of the dishes, and despite the fact that she constantly directed my driving— "Ah, my pet, you mus' nevaire, nevaire go so fas' on zee turns" and "Look out, look out! Ees going to crash eento you!"—and despite the fact that she never agreed with any single opinion I advanced like: "I suppose that President Roosevelt had no choice but to close all the banks," and her response, *"Mon dieu!* 'Ow you talk! Eet was sheer madness to close the banks. Eet nevaire would 'ave 'appened een France"—despite all that, I was genuinely fond of Babette and we did, indeed, have many good times together. Of course, I was better able then, I suppose, to roll with the punches, but she was so entertaining in many ways that she more than made up for her faults.

My mother and father liked her—especially my father!—and we dined together often. My mother was terribly worried, however, that I might marry Babette. She had two major points: one was the difference in our ages, and the other was that Babette was Catholic and that if we married, I'd have to turn Catholic, and all the children would have to be brought up Catholic. Mother thought that would be quite too bad.

I explained that the difference in our ages—17 years—really didn't amount to anything. "I suppose," I said to my mother, "that the fact that she's twice as old as I am seems like a lot right now. But you know, in sixty-six years, when Babette is one hundred, I'll be eighty-three—and how much difference will seventeen years make then?" Mother said she felt she couldn't argue against logic like that, but she was tough on the Catholic issue.

And I, too, began to have grave doubts along that line myself. Not necessarily from my mother's point of view, but because of some of the things that Babette, as devoted a Catholic as I've ever seen, insisted on.

She had to go into retreat every once in a while, and she had to make a novena now and again, and she often had long consultations with various priests and Mother Superiors. I had nothing against that on the religious score—even though some of these withdrawals lasted two weeks—but it sure raised hell with my social activities.

It was almost impossible to plan any theatergoing, any parties or trips to football games, because you never knew when Babette was going to take off for spiritual refreshment. And all too often she made up her mind right after I'd brought $20 worth of tickets, or arranged a dinner party for eight.

I lived in Mount Kisco in that period and Babette lived in a hotel in New York. Consequently, we were together mostly only on weekends, but we talked a lot on the telephone. During these talks, I tried to reason with her and to pin her to some kind of sensible schedule. She got angry now and then and accused me of hating God. And when Babette was angry, especially on that tack, she could spill out two or three million words of denunciation without noticeably drawing a breath.

Even this didn't bother me—I could hold the receiver a good two feet from my ear and soften the impact to a large extent—but it was the telephone bills that hurt. I either called Babette or she phoned me—collect. And one month my phone bill was $68—an incredible amount for me to pay at that time, particularly when most of the conversation was critical of me.

Babette also used to send me religious cards which I thought were something less than soul-satisfying, and she wanted me to carry and wear little religious articles such as a cross, a rosary and a gold-leaf Bible—things with which she provided me in some profusion.

I didn't really want these things, but I didn't kick up a storm until she did something which caused me quite a lot of pain. From the day, or rather the night, that she first set foot in my car, she never failed to mention that I was riding on borrowed time because I didn't have a St. Christopher medal in the car.

"Some day you weel be keeled because you 'ave not place your faith in zee good St. Christopher," she said, "and zen you weel be sorree."

I tried to explain that if I were keeled I wouldn't have any time to be sorree, but that outraged her all the more. One day without my knowing it, she bought a large silver St. Christopher medal with silver wings, suitable for pinning on the visor of the car—and that's where she placed it.

The wingspread of the medal was about six inches and I, who won't even wear a club button or Army decoration in my lapel, didn't like this silver emblem decorating the otherwise insignia-less interior of my car. It wasn't that it was a Catholic medal; it simply was that I didn't like anything pinned up or hung up or pasted inside my car.

Babette and I had some words about this—and I lost. The St. Christopher stayed there. And I endured it without further argument for some weeks. Then one morning, driving from

Mount Kisco to my job in White Plains, I was forced to swerve off the road when some idiot strayed over the center line, and my right wheels were caught in a drainage ditch.

I slapped on the brakes, standing almost upright in my eagerness to stop the car, but before they could halt me entirely, I crashed into a concrete culvert. This stopped the car abruptly, but I kept going. My head whipped forward and my left eye struck the St. Christopher medal.

One of those silver wings drove right through the flesh a quarter of an inch from my eye, and it took some doing on my part to unimpale myself without losing my eye. Then I sank down in the seat—uninjured except for the gash caused by the medal. And blood poured like a freshet all over my new gabardine suit.

That weekend I informed Babette politely that St. Christopher would have to go. I said that when I got the car back from the repair shop, I was going to return to my old practice of driving in an "unprotected" state. I explained that before I'd been given the medal, I never had had an accident and that with the medal, I'd nearly lost an eye.

"Thees," said Babette, "ees zee mos' fooleesh, stupeed, and reedeeculous argument I 'ave evaire 'eard. 'Ow can you blame zee good St. Christopher? Eef you 'ad not 'ad St. Christopher in your car, you would 'ave plunged through zee weendsheeld and been keeled. So, get down on your knees and thank St. Christopher for saving you. And also, put 'eem back in zee car!"

Well, I listened to Babette very carefully—and who can say whether or not she was right? The least I could do, I felt, was to give her the benefit of any doubt, and when I got the car back, I was glad I had resisted the impulse at the time of the accident to rip St. Christopher from the visor and toss him into the culvert.

I did, however, take him down from the visor so that I might never again have to blame him for lacerations in an accident, and I placed him in the glove compartment where both of us would be safe. And that's where he is today.

Babette was pleased about this and we lived happily ever after—for about two more years. Then we parted.

And the reason we parted is, I think, rather unusual. During all our four years together, Babette had maintained that if we ever married and had children, they, of course, would have to be brought up as Catholics. I, on the other hand, maintained that if ever we married and had children, maybe they just would *not* be brought up Catholics, simply on the principle that she, Babette, was not going to tell me, even before we were married and our children were born, what religion they were going to espouse.

"I will not make the children Catholics, or Episcopalians, or Methodists, or Holy Rollers before they're born," I said, stoutly. "I'll let the kids go to half a dozen churches, or maybe fifty churches or more, and then let them pick the one they want. That's the way we're going to do it."

"You," said Babette, heatedly, "are zee mos' sacreeleegious man I evaire saw. You 'ave no respect for releegion. And so, I weel nevaire marry you!"

All of which was rather academic. Because, of course, Babette never would have consented to be married in anything but the Catholic Church. And, having once been married in the Catholic Church, she couldn't have been married in it again while her ex-husband lived.

But none of that logic bothered her a bit. She simply was trying to get her point across. And she did.

Chapter Eleven

ROMANCES, such as the ones I've just described, coupled with my acting, working and occasional studying, chewed up so much of my time that I had little time in high school for athletics. It wasn't until after I'd graduated that I went in heavily for football, sometimes playing as many as four games a week, and for boxing—usually one or two fights a week.

I dearly loved baseball, but I never was much good at it. I tried out for the high school team and asked for the position I'd almost always had in sandlot games. Catcher.

But by the time I was in high school, myopia had really set in and I was forced to wear strong glasses. I hardly could see anything without them, but I tried to on that first day when I reported for baseball practice.

There I was squatting behind the hitter, my cap on backwards, mask securely fastened to my face, and chest protector and shin guards in place. I called for a fast ball right across the plate and the pitcher gave it to me. The ball hit me right smack on the mask. I hadn't even seen it till it got to within a few inches of my face.

I called for a curve, and the ball came in fast and gracefully, and swept right past me into the netting behind. This sort of thing happened a couple more times and Coach Burden relieved me of the job. Next day I reported with a pair of small glasses under the mask and then it was no problem at all to catch the pitches. But whenever anybody hit a pop foul in my territory, I had to pull off the mask in order to look up and sight the ball. And every time I pulled off the mask, the glasses came off too.

Coach Burden tried me out in various other positions, both infield and outfield, and finally it was decided that I could do less damage to the team if I were turned into a third baseman. I rather liked that position and, to tell the truth, I did quite well there—as long as the ball was hit to my left.

I could move quickly and easily to my left to field either a grounder or a line drive, but somehow or other I couldn't go to my right fast enough to catch even a slow dribbler. Any ball hit between me and third base was a home run! It didn't take opposing teams long to find that out and practically every man who came to bat tried to drill the ball between me and the bag. I suffered a constant barrage and time and again somebody aimed right and romped around the bases.

In time, Coach Burden developed a swift young infielder who could go both right and left, and who hit as well or better than I, and I was unburdened of my duties. Then, rather than sit on the bench and waste time, I turned in my uniform and went out for track.

My specialty was the 440-yard run but for some reason I never could discover—perhaps it was the same thing that prevented me from going to my right in baseball—I couldn't get a fast enough start. Once I was away and running, I moved swiftly, but the seconds lost right after the starter's pistol always proved costly. While I could beat anybody in school, with the exception possibly of Eddie Laregena (remember him, the ghost runner?), I never won a race in competition with any other school. Always came in second, third or fourth. So, I abandoned track after one year.

I didn't go out for football until my junior year and then, while I made the team, my other activities made it impossible for me to practice each night and so I played in only a couple of games. And then only for a few minutes each. I played more regularly in my senior year, but most unspectacularly.

As in baseball, I had a tough time trying to find the right position. Because I was quite fast, I started out as a halfback. In those days, however, the halfback who was to carry the ball got it fired to him directly from center. The ball never was taken and handed off by the quarterback as is done today.

Well, the first time the quarterback called a play in which I was to receive the ball, the center drilled it fast and sure back between his legs and it hit me on the chest and bounded into the hands of an opponent who'd surged through the line. I hadn't seen it till it hit me.

It took only a few more incidents like that to convince Burden that I'd be better anywhere else. So, he made me an end. This was fine on defense, because I was able to get in quickly and make tackles or race down the field and grab the man receiving a punt. But it was an impossible situation on offense.

Then I'd scamper downfield to catch a pass, but I couldn't see the ball in the air until it was within a few feet of me and 90 percent of the time I then was in no position to catch it. Once a ball struck me on the helmet without my even seeing it.

In desperation, the coach made me a running guard on the offense, and a tackle on the defense. As a running guard, I had to pull out of the line on most plays, sweep around the end and block the rival quarter- or halfback. This I did fairly well, although I really was much too light for a guard. I weighed about 168 and most of the guards and tackles were 200 or more.

I really enjoyed football and I got just enough of it in school to develop a keen taste for it as well as an appreciation of the game. So after graduation, when time was heavy on my hands between acting jobs, I used to go to White Plains, Yonkers or Mount Vernon to watch some of the semipro games.

I noticed that the teams very seldom had the same players working in every game, and when I found that the average payment per game was $35, I approached the manager of the Westchester All-Stars, a squirrel-faced little man named Charlie Wilson, and volunteered my services. "I'm a good running guard," I said, "and a fine tackle on defense."

He regarded me critically and said, "You ain't heavy enough for guard or tackle, and besides you wear glasses."

I then weighed about 172 whereas most of the guards were 200 to 245, but I explained to Charlie that I was very strong and shifty and that I could run the 100-yard dash in close to 10 seconds. And, I said, good eyesight wasn't vital when you played in the line.

"Well," he said, "we sure could use a little speed. Some of them guards got so much lead in the ass they can't get outa their own way."

So I was permitted to scrimmage with the team in a practice session one night and I showed enough talent to impress Charlie. He told me to report for the Saturday afternoon game.

We played a team from Staten Island that day and I was more than a little apprehensive when I got my first look at the opposition as they trotted onto the field. All of the guards and tackles were over six feet and their average weight was about 235. One massive tackle, six feet five, was 275 pounds. And all of their backs, except the quarterback, weighed at least 10 pounds more than I.

I figured I was going to take quite a beating that day, and I was right. Never before had I been so thoroughly bruised, beaten, mauled, kicked, punched, trampled on, tossed in the air and ground into the dirt. I really didn't know how to handle those big guys and they knew it. They took pure delight in smashing the hell out of me.

When the game was over I had a black eye, a cut over the other one, a split lip, a huge bruise on my right cheekbone, five or six cuts on my legs where I'd been kicked, and a million aches and pains.

"Look, Mockridge," said Charlie, when he paid me the $35, "I don't think you can make it. Hell, they run over you like grass. You tackle okay, but you don't know nothin' about openin' a hole or blockin' or pertectin'."

"Well, I can learn," I mumbled between my sore lips. "Anything those guys can do, I can do too. Have you got some guard who could teach me?"

Charlie thought about it a minute and then told me to report for practice early on Wednesday night and he'd arrange for a lesson. When I got there that night, there stood a hulking, well-scarred veteran guard named Rocco Gugliatta. He was six three and he weighed 260. He beckoned to me and said, "Charlie says to teach you some tricks."

And with that, he moved swiftly, hit me with his shoulder and right arm and knocked me nearly 10 feet away. "Never let yourself get hit like that," he said. "That's lesson number one."

Then, as I staggered to my feet, he showed me how to crouch in such a position that if some Man Mountain Dean were to fling himself at me, I could either sidestep him, parry the blow with my body much like rolling with a punch, or, and even more effective, slide under him, plunging my shoulder against his legs and pitching him up into the air.

We tried these maneuvers over and over, until I thought every bone was broken, but I began to get the knack and two or three times I caught Rocco just right as he came at me, and he went flying into the air. I was quite pleased with myself and as we quit practice, I felt I'd learned all that was necessary. But Rocco had other ideas.

"C'mon back tomorrow night," he said, "and I'll learn ya how to tackle. And then next week I'll learn ya the runnin' block. And after that, I'll learn ya how to smack a guy in the mout' without gettin' caught by the ref."

Well, he did learn me all them things, and within two or three weeks I was putting them into practice in games on Saturday and Sunday and Charlie looked at me approvingly whenever he handed out my money.

"You're holdin' your own, kid," he said. "Now all you gotta learn is how to tear 'em apart."

I don't believe I ever did learn that, but no longer did the rival backs plow through my position with ease. And very seldom did I lose a man I had to block. I found that because I was so light—172 pounds aren't much on a six foot one inch frame —I had to establish a certain rapport right at the start of each game with the gargantuan monsters who crouched opposite me. The very first time one of them tried to rough me up on a play, I'd let him have what we called an "elbow block" which, in simple terms, is nothing but punching him right on the nose with your elbow. If properly delivered, that kind of blow can smash a nose and retire the man from the game.

Another effective move was the "knee block." All you did when the opposing guard or tackle rushed you, was to move back a step, luring him in and getting him off balance, and then, as his body fell forward, you came up quickly and powerfully with your knee, full in his face. Sometimes a player treated that way would get up, fists swinging, but then other players on our team would swarm in and in the melee the poor guy would get so chopped up he often had to leave the field.

Most players who received the elbow or knee treatment, however, decided that it just wasn't worth roughing you up and they played the rest of the game like gentlemen.

Rocco had told me that after you'd felled a player with one of these, or any of a half dozen other tricks he taught me, the best thing to do was to act as though you were falling forward and, in so doing, kick the prostrate player in the head. (This was done to me twice, and I have a one-inch scar on my forehead as a remembrance of one well-aimed kick.)

But I never could bring myself to employ that tactic. Instead, I developed a sort of psychological or gamesmanship approach. Right after belting a player to the ground, I'd lean over, grab his shirt and yank the dazed guy to his feet.

"Sorry, buddy," I'd say. "Was I too rough for ya? I didn't mean to hurt ya."

Then I'd walk away, leaving him standing there, slightly puzzled as to just what had happened. But little things like that, I'm happy to say, often took the steam out of what only a few minutes before had been a growling tiger, eager to devour me.

One of the greatest problems I had, however, had to do with telling which player was which—in fact, which *team* was which. It wasn't too tough a problem on a clear, sunny day when our team wore maroon jerseys, which we usually did, and maroon and white helmets, and the opposing team wore white jerseys and, say, blue and gold helmets. You'd have to be pretty blind to make a mistake there.

But my eyesight, then and now, is such that without my glasses I cannot distinguish the features of a person more than four feet away. And, on rainy or snowy days, when the field got churned into a huge mud puddle, and when it was overcast and gloomy, it was almost impossible for me to tell one player from another. A white jersey, you know, quickly turns brown when the player keeps falling in the mud, and to my failing eyes, that ain't much different from maroon. The helmets always were smeared with mud, and they were no guideposts either.

I couldn't, of course, wear glasses on the field, and contact lenses either hadn't been invented, or at least hadn't been developed enough for use of that kind. And I wouldn't have worn them anyway. I've always been afraid of having something driven into my eyeball upon contact.

So, I did the best I could. Which wasn't very good.

Quite a few times when our team was on the offense, I'd pull out of my guard position at the snap of the ball and, for instance, start racing around the right end, searching out the halfback or fullback I was supposed to crush with a running block, only to throw a mighty block on one of our own ends who'd been spun around after throwing a block himself. To me, I'm sorry to say, he looked like an enemy player advancing on our runner.

This caused some ill feeling, particularly because when I tossed a block, I really tossed it. And my colleague, not expecting me to hit *him,* wasn't braced for it. I knocked out two of my own players that way, and dislocated the shoulder of another. But I must say, I also hit quite a few of the enemy and so good old Charlie put up with me.

I also was unable to tell which end of the field was which. Most of the fields we played on were not much more than open pastures, with goal posts at either end, and rows of parked cars along both sides of the field. Now for people with good eyesight, I suppose it's pretty easy to stand in the middle of the field and distinguish the row of cars on one side from the row on the other. But for me, it was impossible. I hardly could make out the cars themselves, let alone detect any differences!

And so it was one glorious October afternoon that when I somehow or other spotted a deflected ball, tossed by the enemy, floating through the air, I leaped and clutched it, cradled it securely in my left arm, and took off for a touchdown.

Players with blurred faces and indistinguishable uniforms kept racing at me, but I straight-armed them, bludgeoned them with my right arm, twisted out of their grasp. I could hear the crowd screaming and it was tonic to my bloodstream. I must have released quarts of adrenalin because I ran faster and more strongly than I ever had before.

Dimly, in the distance, I could see the goal posts, and I

162

poured on the steam. Lifting my knees high to discourage any tacklers, I zigzagged for the goal line, smashing down the one remaining player who took a dive at my legs. Triumphant, I left him slithering along in the mud and raced over the goal line. Touchdown!

It was only then I learned that my magnificent 92-yard run had been the WRONG WAY. And that I'd crossed my own goal line. And that the players trying to tackle me were not the opponents, but members of my own team!

Fortunately, we won by three touchdowns that day, and so my run hadn't been really disastrous. The only fellow who really seemed sore at me was an end by the name of Wojichowski, who crashed to the ground when I straight-armed him. He ripped a muscle in his neck and was out of action for three weeks.

I made one other spectacular contribution to the annals of semipro football. It was the greatest tackle I ever made and it was, I might say, with all modesty, one of the finest tackles ever made in football.

It happened in a blizzard on a partly snow-covered, muddy field in November. It was one of those days when the temperature was high enough to permit the field to become a soggy, dirty mess, but low enough to permit the snow to swirl around in dense clouds. Visibility was difficult even for those with 20-20 eyesight (mine was 20-800 in one eye, and 20-1,000 in the other) and all of the uniforms, soaked through, looked alike.

We were playing a pretty good team at Harrison, New York, and the score was tied. It had been a fierce battle, and all of us were pooped. Incidentally, in those days you played the full 60 minutes of the game, both on offense and defense, and the only way you got removed from the game was by getting knocked out or seriously injured. We had only one or two substitutes on any given day.

Whenever two, three or four players were knocked out or hurt, we had to play with fewer than eleven men. Often we

163

played with ten, and one game, in which we were tremendously outweighed, we played five minutes of the last quarter with only eight men. It was in that game that Charlie, our manager, took to the field for several plays—in his business suit and hat —merely to divert one of the opposing players. He put himself in as a substitute end and then, as the play was called, he'd race toward the sidelines, yelling for a pass. Naturally, the defending end had to go after him, and that, of course, relieved the pressure on the rest of us. We lost that game 48 to 6, I believe.

Anyway, to get back to my great tackle in the blizzard. The Harrison team, stronger and apparently more rested than we were, was driving down the field toward our goal line. It had made three or four first downs and now, with only four minutes to play, it was on the 21-yard line, third down and eight yards to go. If we could hold them, they'd have to try for a field goal and whether they made it or not, we'd get possession of the ball and have a shot at what might be the winning touchdown.

"They'll pass," said our captain, slapping us on the rumps. "Cover your men and try to grab that pass."

Sure enough, they passed. But it was a tricky one, with the halfback passing laterally to the fullback far out to the left. And then, when half of our team was drawn toward him, expecting a run for the goal, he tossed a forward pass to the other side of the field.

I had anticipated this pass and I already was running toward the enemy's potential receivers. I really couldn't see the ball in the air because of the snow, but I could see that a giant of a man about 15 yards ahead of me *was* seeing it and, indeed, was getting ready to leap into the air and snag it.

Gauging the distance, I realized that if I waited till the man actually caught the ball, he probably would get away and the game would be lost. He was only a few yards from the goal line.

So, running at full speed, I waited till he leaped to get the ball, and then I launched myself in what probably was one of the most perfectly timed flying tackles in American football. I caught the poor guy around the knees just as the ball zipped into his hand. Then I tightened my grasp and, as we hit the dirt, I yanked back sharply. The idea was, of course, to flip him from his vertical position to earth so hard that he'd lose the ball, and possibly one of our players would fall on it.

I couldn't have executed the stratagem any better. He hit the ground as though fired into it from a cannon and was promptly knocked out. The ball squirted from his fingers and about six players fell on it.

Elated beyond description, I bent over to see whether he had been seriously hurt, and was appalled to find myself gazing into the dirt-streaked face of Paul Boscarelli—our own fullback! He had intercepted the pass and, had I not tackled him, might well have got loose for a touchdown. And to make things worse, the Harrison team had recovered the ball, and on the next play they kicked the field goal that won the game.

It was little things like that that made me think seriously of giving up football. Little things like that, and like this: One night when we were at practice, Charlie brought a new guard over to me and asked me to show him the ropes, much as Rocco had shown me.

(Rocco incidentally became lost to the team three or four weeks after he'd given me lessons, when he and his brother, who weighed about 300, got into an argument one day while working on a construction project, their daytime employment. Rocco called his brother a bad name, and the brother bent a crowbar over his head. Rocco never played football again.)

I gave this guard a few lessons that night, and again the next night. We played together that Saturday and, during the game, I handed out a few more pointers. Riding home together in the bus, we sat together and he asked me questions about everything I did—the little tricks like pulling back and clobbering the rusher as he came in, the elbow and knee tricks, the "Box," where three men decide to take some of the temper out of an opponent by letting their own men go for one play and turning on him with the fury of rhinos, roughing him up and smashing him to the ground.

I was pleased to see that he apparently had caught on quickly and I said, "We'll use some of these tricks tomorrow." And we did. Only thing bad about it was—he was on the *opposing* team. Players flitted from one team to another in those days, and it was just my luck to have given my whole bag of tricks to the guy who was going to play opposite me. It was a bad day all around.

In my second year as a semipro player, I was approached by an evil-looking little man who identified himself as Hymie and who suggested to me that maybe I might like to fight. Not with him, but with boxers, and for dough.

"How much?" I asked.

"Well, you fight in the prelims. That ain't much," he said. "But I like you. So, I'll give you seventy-five bucks a fight. Win or lose."

That sounded interesting to me, although I'd never really fought any bouts—just fooling around in the Boy Scouts and in the gymnasium at the church—but I didn't relish the idea of going into the ring with professional prizefighters.

"Nah," said Hymie. "I wouldn't throw you in with no fighters. What I want is you should pick some other guy from the team here, a guy your weight, and then you two guys, you put on a fast four rounds on my card."

He told me that he was promoting fairly big fights, ten-rounders, and that he needed a six-rounder, and maybe three four-rounders to fill out his bill. He explained that he was a club fight promoter, the kind of fellow who stages boxing in American Legion Halls, Veterans of Foreign Wars clubs, small sports arenas and places like that.

"You guys, you nuts playing football, you're all in good shape," he said, "and you can go four rounds fast. Most of the hunkies I get, they're fat and they're dead. They don't move. The fans like action. You don't have to kill nobody. But make it look good. Make it like you hate each other."

Well, I got hold of Ernie Jansen, one of our halfbacks who weighed about 180, and he agreed to take a chance. We went to a gym, put on the heavy gloves and sparred for several hours. We worked out a system under which we could go at each other, throwing lots of leather, striking dozens of blows, fast and furious, but not really hurting each other. Every once in a while, under our arrangement, I'd toss what looked like a terrific punch, and Ernie would go down. And I was happy to do the same for him.

The following Saturday night we got our big chance. We were the first bout on a six-fight card in a decaying old sports club in Yonkers. I think the place once had been a theater because there were some boxes on one wall, and half a dozen mildly inebriated gentlemen sat in them and pelted us with paper cups, ice cubes, pieces of candy and, once in a while, a Coke bottle.

There were only about 200 men and three or four women in the place when the bell rang for us—the other 700 or 800 fans didn't show up until the semi-final went on—but Ernie and I did our best and the crowd seemed to like it.

I got knocked down twice and Ernie got knocked down twice. Twice I caught him in a corner and really pounded him. Twice he caught me in a corner and really pounded me. We didn't clinch much, but when we did, we flailed at each other with our free hands, just like we'd seen in the movies. All of a sudden the bout was over—the time goes fast when you're young and fresh—and the ref grabbed the mike.

"The winnah—by unanimous decision by the three judges —is Norman Moskowitz." He walked over, held up my hand for a second, and then dropped it and walked away.

"Okay, guys, scram," said Hymie, as two more fighters climbed into the ring. "I'll see ya in the dressing room."

We went to the dressing room which, I think, was an abandoned toilet, and took a shower, or what passed for a shower. Only a few drops dribbled down on us. In a little while Hymie came in and counted out $75 each.

"Okay, you guys," he said. "You fight again two weeks from tonight. In Brooklyn. I'll write down the place. But you, Moskowitz, you gotta change your name. I don't want I should be accused of having a stable, nothing but Jewish fighters."

I tried to explain that my name wasn't Moskowitz, but Hymie was too impatient to listen. "Change it," he said. "Make up an Irish-type name."

There was a good fighter around then called Irish Eddie Brink and I admired his style. So, overnight, I became Irish Eddie Mackey. And I fought under that name for my next five or six fights. Then Hymie decided that since the very popular Barney Ross was welterweight champion that year, it might be a good idea for me to fight under the name "Barty Ross." "Maybe draw a few fans," he mused.

All went well for a while, with Ernie winning one week and me the next. We got so that we could stage what looked like a wingding of a fight, and never get hurt. "But there should be blood," said Hymie one night. "Couldn't one of you get a bloody nose?"

We decided against that, but we were thinking of getting up an arrangement where one of us would enter the ring with a little beet juice in his mouth and, after the proper blow, spit it out. But Ernie got flu about that time, and Hymie said he'd pick some other 170-pounder for me to spar around with the next Saturday night.

I thought nothing of this all week, but on Saturday night as I was taping my hands (you did everything yourself; there were no trainers, rubbers or seconds), I began to worry about just who my opponent would be. Hymie had said nothing and he wasn't around. There were quite a few fighters milling around in and just outside the dingy cubicle which had been assigned as the dressing room, but I didn't know any of them and had no way of telling which of them was to be my partner.

When I climbed into the ring, however, I found that the other man already was there, seated in his corner. To me, of course, he was just a blur, but I got the impression he was big and apelike. I began to have misgivings and I longed for nice, friendly old Ernie.

At the clang of the bell, I got off my stool and began to trot out to the center of the ring. But the other fighter, whom I'll call Joey, shot off his stool like a bullet. He was about 30 pounds heavier than I, but very fast. He streaked across the ring and belted me with an overhand shot to the head. Then he really began firing, pounding me with everything he had and backing me into a corner.

I'd been completely caught off balance, and all I could do for the moment was cover up. I was a little dizzy from that first rocket to the head and the 50 or 60 other wallops hadn't helped me much either. Never before had I been subjected to so frenzied and violent an attack.

Joey swarmed all over me, snarling and snorting, his long, hairy arms flailing the air and his heavy fists pounding and pounding and pounding. My ears were ringing and blood was running down the right side of my face. One of his punches had opened the old scar on my forehead.

Finally, I don't know how, I got my bearings a bit and began to punch back. Joey seemed surprised. I guess he'd figured I was half knocked out, and he stepped back. I let him have a straight left jab to the face, and followed it with a strong right cross.

I was about to launch another right when he bent over, slipped under my protecting left arm and then straightened up suddenly under my chin, butting me with his head. I saw stars. Then, as I fell back, he hit two low blows. I turned to the ref but he either hadn't seen them or didn't care. When I turned, Joey clobbered me on the back of the neck.

Joey, it turned out, was the dirtiest fighter I've ever seen, and I've seen a lot of them. He used every illegal device he could think of. He did everything but kick me. But the referee paid no attention. I imagine the crowd was loving the whole thing (although I was so involved with Joey that I don't remember hearing any reaction from the fans) and the ref wasn't going to spoil the fun.

The round finally ended and I all but collapsed on my stool. What I did in that minute of rest, I do not know. But, thanks to youth and my good condition, I was in reasonable shape when the bell clanged for the second round.

This time I was prepared for Joey's rush and I sparred with him, back pedaling steadily and keeping him off me. But, of course, every once in a while one of his barrage of punches would get through my guard and my head was getting snapped back time and again.

Good eyesight is one of the most essential things in boxing. Not only do you have to watch the other fellow's hands, but you have to keep track of his eyes. When a man is about to launch a punch, especially a big one, his eyes glint and they widen and then tighten and this warns you to get up your defense.

But I, of course, not only couldn't see Joey's eyes, I barely could make out his face, and his fists were nothing but fast-moving blurs until they got into focus six or seven inches from my face—and by then, generally, it was too late to block them.

Somehow, I survived that round, but I was beginning to tire badly. I'd been pummeled so much on my arms that it was hard to hold them up. I was dizzy, there was both a ringing and a buzzing in my ears, and my forehead and lower lip were bleeding. I decided that this fight simply had to end in the next round, and that the only way I could get out of it alive was to trick Joey.

So, after we'd been sparring for a minute or so in the third round, and I'd taken quite a few punches, butts and low blows, I began to wobble a little. Joey, sensing victory, turned on the pressure. I backed up toward the ropes and didn't hit back. Then he caught my head in a crossfire, and I staggered back and fell against the top strand, dropping my hands to my sides.

Joey took the bait and he leaped forward for the kill. With his left hand down, he raised his right fist shoulder high and started to launch the knockout blow. But I then suddenly came to life. I bounced off the ropes, ducked under the right and put every bit of strength I had into a right uppercut. With no left hand to block it, it shot straight to his chin and lifted him a couple of inches off the canvas. He was stunned but he didn't fall.

I shot a hard left to the solar plexus and Joey doubled forward. Another uppercut straightened him up once more and he stood there swaying, obviously dizzy and, I guess, just as surprised at my attack as I was at his in the first round. He turned a little to the right, maybe to start getting away, and I tossed a long, overhand right which caught him just under the ear. He crashed to the canvas, and he never moved. The referee and the manager of the arena carried him to the dressing room and laid him under the shower. It was 10 minutes before he came to.

After that terrifying experience, I told Hymie that I didn't want any more "surprise" matches. I was perfectly willing to fight other football players, I said, but I didn't want to get into the ring with professional killers.

I fought a few more bouts and then I began to have trouble with my eyes. Things would blur for a few seconds at a time, and there was an annoying flicking or pulsing in my right eye. I consulted an ophthalmologist and he instantly told me to quit fighting. "Otherwise," he said, "you'll suffer a detached retina."

So, I hung up my gloves and my distinguished boxing career was over. Joe Louis and James J. Braddock no longer were threatened.

I continued playing football for a while, but I began to wonder whether the effort was worth the price. I realized that I was paying dearly for every athletic accomplishment.

During the two and a half football seasons and my year of boxing, I broke both thumbs, one once and the other twice; I sprained both thumbs and my fingers innumerable times and I never played a game without having both thumbs and at least one finger heavily taped; I sprained both wrists and one ankle; I played two games with my chest encased in yards and yards of adhesive tape, the result of two broken ribs from a powerful kick; I lost the nail of my right thumb (it later grew again) ; I got kicked on the shins so many times that the wounds didn't heal from the beginning of the season to the end (and I still have about a dozen scars on both legs); I had my nose broken twice and my face cut at least fifty times; and I even got an Osgood-Schlatter.

An Osgood-Schlatter, as I'm sure you know, is named after the doctors who discovered it. It's described in the medical dictionary as: "Osteochondrosis of the tuberosity of the tibia." Just between you and me, that means inflammation of the cartilage and bone of the lower leg.

I got my Osgood-Schlatter one cold Sunday afternoon when a 285-pound tackle watched me intercept a pass and then tackled me with his head. His helmet hit my right knee with the force of a guided missile and the pain was so—what doctors call "exquisite"—that I fainted.

When I came to, I found I couldn't walk. I couldn't even stand up, and my knee was swelling to alarming proportions. They took me to the hospital where the doctor who examined me got all excited. He'd never seen an Osgood-Schlatter before and he got out a notebook and made all sorts of entries in it, measurements of my left knee, measurements of my right knee, areas of sensitivity, flexibility (or rather the lack of it), and Lord knows what else.

Then he went out into the corridors and summoned about ten other doctors and showed them my knee and delivered a little lecture. All of the doctors touched the swollen knee and two or three of them lifted my leg and moved it around.

I was in absolute agony and if I hadn't hurt so much—I also had a torn ligament in my shoulder—I think I'd have sat up in bed and bopped several of those doctors on the nose. In time, however, they gave me an injection and the pain lessened, and then, after they'd X-rayed the leg from every angle, they put it in a sort of semi-cast and splint and within a couple of days I was able to go home.

I sat around with my leg up on a chair, or small table or hassock, taking heat and light treatments two and three times a day. It was more than two months before I was able to put my full weight on it and walk again.

Then, after the swelling went down, the little Osgood-Schlatter remained, a hard, bony lump which projects from the leg bone just below the kneecap. It doesn't bother me at all anymore unless I forget about it and kneel on a hard surface. Then pain shoots in all directions and I get a very clear picture of a 285-pound tackle smashing himself into my knee.

During the two months I sat around listening to the radio and contemplating my knee, I got to thinking about the money angle in connection with this fine sport. And with pencil and paper I totted up my profits.

Taking $35 a game as a base (once in a while we got a few bucks more), I estimated that I played 20 games a season for an income of $700. I played two seasons and 6 games in the third, and that made my gross income $1,610. From this I deducted the $385 I had to pay the hospital and the two or three doctors in connection with my Osgood-Schlatter. I also deducted the $150 I paid a surgeon to repair the huge gash in my head, the result of a kick, and reduce it by plastic surgery to the one-inch scar it is now.

I estimated that during playing weeks, I paid doctors a minimum of $10 per week to stitch, suture, X-ray and set bones and perform other minor tasks. That came to about $260. Adding them all up, I found I'd laid out $795 while taking in $1,610, for a net gain of $815.

And that net didn't include the gauze, adhesive tape, arnica, Absorbine Jr., rubbing alcohol, iodine, Mercurochrome, Ace bandages, zinc oxide ointment and other such medicine, tinctures and curatives.

Somehow it just didn't seem worth it. And so, at the height of my sterling football career, I hung up my cleated shoes. Right beside my mildewed boxing gloves.

And I decided to concentrate on acting.

Chapter Twelve

I AM well aware that stars like John Barrymore, Edwin Booth, Otis Skinner, Richard Mansfield, Joe Jefferson and John Drew used to look back on their Hamlets, Iagos, Macbeths, Shylocks, Romeos, Caesars, Lears, Othellos and Rip Van Winkles and describe them as their greatest portrayals.

But I look back upon my portrayal of Tom Mix as the finest thing I've ever done.

The only regret I have is that very few people ever got to see it—only my mother, father and brother, my aunts and my uncle, the Jerue family that lived next door, and three or four kids in the neighborhood. Tom Mix, who died in 1940, unfortunately never saw it either, and I don't believe he even knew that I was portraying him.

But I assure you that my representations of Tom Mix were magnificent. In fact, I believe I'm safe in going so far as to say that my performances as Tom Mix were much better than the ones that Tom, himself, gave.

I first began seeing Tom on the silver screen when I was about six years old, and I instantly became devoted to him and his wonderful horse, Tony. Just what fascination he held for me, I cannot tell you. But, brother, was it powerful! I saw every single Tom Mix film at least three times, and I went every Saturday to see the latest episode in whatever serial motion picture he was starring in. I hardly could bear to wait through the week to see whether on the following Saturday he was going to be pushed off the cliff, drilled through the head from behind or actually cut in two, tied as he was to the log moving into the buzz saw.

I saw all the other cowboys, too—William S. Hart, Jack Holt, Hoot Gibson, Milton Sills and William Farnum—but to me they were nothing more than pallid imitators of my hero. I had glossy photographs of him tacked up in my room; I had possibly a hundred facsimile reproductions of his signature; I had dozens of magazine articles about him, complete with fuzzy pictures, and, most precious of all, I had a PERSONALLY SIGNED photo.

The signature read: *For Gordon, with kindest regards, Tom Mix.*

Despite the slight misspelling of my name, that picture was my proudest possession.

Shortly after I first saw Tom Mix (on the screen; I never saw him in person) I badgered my father into buying me a complete cowboy outfit—ten-gallon Stetson (I think mine was only two gallons), chaps, plaid shirt, bandanna, boots and, of course, a Western six-shooter, complete with belt and little leather loops carrying a dozen extra bullets. The bullets were wood, painted silver, and they could be fired from the gun. They traveled about five feet.

I wore that outfit every afternoon when I got home from

school and I didn't even take it off for dinner. I think this was the happiest period of my life.

There was only one flaw. My father wouldn't buy me a horse. So, in the long run, I built my own Tony.

He was only a sawhorse on which my father cut up planks when he was doing carpentry, but oh, what a saw horse he was! I got some old blankets and threw them over his back and with a piece of tarpaulin and some strips of leather, I fashioned a saddle. And I made stirrups out of pieces of rope and some heavy iron rings.

Tony had a fine tail, made out of a scraggly mop that had been thrown away, and he had a marvelous head. This head, incidentally, was a great piece of luck.

It was a papier-mâché model of a wild-eyed, snorting animal that occupied the center of a window display of riding apparel and equipment in Abel's Department Store. The moment I saw it I fell in love with it, and I went inside to ask Mr. Abel if I might have it when he was finished with the display.

He saddened me no end by telling me he was sorry but the horse's head had to be returned to the window dresser—the man who furnished all the effects for the displays. Then, miraculously, one day a week or so after the display had been removed, I was poking around in the junk behind the department store—an industrious boy often could find some mighty valuable things that way—and there on top of a pile of cartons lay the head!

It took me only two seconds flat to grab it and dash home! Then I nailed it to the front end of Tony. It couldn't have looked better. I raced to the blacksmith shop and got an old bit and bridle that the smithy had tossed into a dark corner of the place. I cut a slit in the horse's mouth, slipped the bridle over his head, and I was in business. Just as I was the better Tom Mix, so it was that my Tony was the finer piece of horse-flesh.

I used to ride Tony for hours, sitting there in the backyard, with all the Western plains, the mountains, the mesas and the deep, black forest flying past me with amazing speed. Sometimes Tony and I got into swift, treacherous rivers, but we always managed to get out. Sometimes I killed rustlers with my popgun rifle which was slung in a canvas holster on Tony's right foreleg. And always when our ride was over, I dismounted, gave him a friendly pat on the flank and then bent over and kissed the white star on his forehead.

My Uncle Al, who, as I've said, then was manufacturing portable steel garages, had a small one made for me—about 10 by 6 by 6—and I converted it into Tony's stable. Across the wide front door I painted TOM MIX in letters a foot high, and underneath I painted: Tony's Stable—Keep Out. Nobody was permitted in there unless he was an exceptionally good friend of mine—and, more important, a devout believer in Tom Mix.

This euphoria went on for some time, but it ended in calamity. One afternoon when I got home from school I was appalled to find that some workmen who were building a glass-enclosed porch at the back of our house had taken Tony from his stable and changed him back into a sawhorse. They had removed his head and tail, stripped off his blanket, saddle and stirrups and, when I arrived, they were carelessly cutting into his sides as they sawed some boards.

I ran to my room and cried and cried. Never have I cried so much, before or since. With Tony dead, I put away my cowboy suit and never wore it again. And I gave up my portrayal of Tom Mix.

Overnight, I became Douglas Fairbanks. I'm sure that my impersonation of Mr. Fairbanks never touched that of Tom Mix, but it was a pretty good one all the same.

Swashbuckling and filled with derring-do, I swung by ropes from trees, landing on porch tops, ready and eager to smash a window and leap in and save the beautiful girl from the villain. I leaped from rock to rock, I hurled myself across streams, I even tried to run straight up a wall now and then.

One afternoon, seeking to rescue a young lady who was being tormented and who was shrieking to me from a second-floor window, I took a long ladder, placed it at a precarious angle against the house, and swiftly climbed up it.

As I reached the top and swung at the biggest and most menacing of her captors, the ladder slipped and crashed. I fell into a clump of rosebushes and impaled my lower lip on a stake. I bled for an hour until a doctor came and put three stitches in my lip—and my career as Douglas Fairbanks was over.

It was about then that I decided that impersonations would get me nowhere. Much better to act in plays and create an identity of my own—something that would stand up against such players as Dick Powell, Alan Ladd and Bela Lugosi.

From time to time, I had a role in one of the plays being put on by my class at school, but usually these things were ridiculous little allegories in which the players had to impersonate trees, buttercups, toadstools or maybe a woolly bear or Reynard the Fox. I got absolutely no kick out of portraying a tree, and so I began to write some plays of my own to jazz up the theatrical atmosphere in school and, incidentally, to thus assure myself of a good role.

"If I can't play the lead," I once told my fouth- or fifth-grade teacher, "I won't let you use my play."

I wrote one play called *Couldn't Get Me*, which I have before me now, and I'll tell you a wee bit about it. It featured a Detective Henderson (played by me) who, in trying to catch a criminal, gets a jagged hole torn in his head by a heavy paper weight, gets hit in the face by a rock thrown through a window, gets bludgeoned unconscious in a dark alley, gets tied to a chair and severely beaten by hoods, gets stabbed by a sadistic criminal, kills a crook by fracturing his skull with a chair leg, gets shot in the shoulder, breaks his hand punching another crook, shoots another hood in the leg, and narrowly misses getting killed when the last crook snatches a gun from another policeman, fires wildly, and finally kills himself. All this was circa 1926, about 30 years before James Bond!

I always packed lots of excitement, action and bloodshed into my plays. And the dialogue isn't bad either.

Here are a couple of samples from one of my masterpieces, a two-acter featuring a master safecracker called the Blue Diamond, which was as outrageous a steal from the Jimmy Valentine series as I've ever seen.

In the first scene, a girl reporter walks into the chief inspector's office (guess who played the chief inspector?) and says: "Howdy, boys, how's tricks? I'm the gal from the Selzwick News. Got any news about the Blue Diamond?"

A corporal gives her some notes left by the inspector, but the other detectives who don't like the girl (I'm still not sure just why) sneak out.

"Thanks, big boy," said the girl. "I guess I'll be leavin' pronto. Good-bye, boys." (She turns to see there are no boys left.) "Well, it seems the gentlemen have flew the coop. I better be flewing too. Bye bye, Mr. Corporal."

Then there's the fascinating scene in the home of Mr. Morris who has been robbed of about half a ton of jewelry. A detective sergeant says: "I'd give up my job to know who the Blue Diamond is."

"I'd give anything in the world," says Mr. Morris.

"Well," says the inspector, "you've done just about that. I'll explain." (He pulls his gun and points it at them.) "My dear friends, *I* am the Blue Diamond. Now, last night when you were watching this safe, I put a little powder in your drinks so you would sleep peacefully while I put you in comfortable positions and looted the safe.

"After that, Mr. Morris, your daughter Margaret here"— Margaret smiles warmly at the Blue Diamond—"went out with me and we had a nice little marriage. Now, gentlemen, you will please excuse us as we make a getaway. Sergeant, you know there won't be any need to pursue me as I have well planned

179

our escape. Gentlemen, bid farewell to a PAIR of Blue Diamonds." (He and his new wife go out.) Then this dialogue ensues:

> SERGEANT: Morris, there's no use to follow. He's gone. At last we have discovered the Blue Diamond.
> MORRIS: Yes, but my daughter! We'll search the world for her.
>
> CURTAIN.

I liked the play a great deal, and I particularly enjoyed the inspector's speech in which he explains all, gets the girl and makes his escape. The only flaw in the play, and it was one that really annoyed me, was that both the sergeant and Mr. Morris got to deliver some lines after my thrilling, fact-revealing monologue, thus stealing some of my spotlight. Eugene O'Neill wouldn't have permitted that, nor would have Elmer Rice or Noel Coward. But *The Blue Diamond* was one of my early plays, and my technique was a little ragged here and there.

I didn't, of course, get to write all the plays I appeared in. There were other good dramatists, even then. But there was a marked difference between my performances in plays I'd written, and in those done by somebody else.

That difference was: in my own plays, I knew my lines. In the others, I floundered like mad. I hated the idea of wasting so much time trying to learn words that somebody else had written, and I argued that I could ad-lib to greater advantage. The directors, I'm sorry to say, never agreed with me.

So I resorted to devious methods to satisfy the directors, and still not learn my lines. I did, grudgingly, become acquainted with those that had to be delivered in stage center. But whenever the action took me near the wings, alongside a breakfront or a mantelpiece, or even behind a chair, I typed out my lines and fastened them to the scenery or the furniture. Out of sight of the audience, of course, but in a position where I could read them easily.

Sometimes I delivered an impassioned love speech while bending over an empty chair on which I'd laid my lines. Once in a while when called upon to point an accusing finger at another actor, I managed to do it with my back to him while reading the lines pinned to the curtain. And once, when the script called for me to come to grips with another actor, grasping him by the lapels and shaking him, I, with his reluctant cooperation, pinned my lines to his shirtfront, and never missed a cue.

There were several instances where I came to grief using this method, but the worst occurred when I was appearing as Joseph in a Christmas pageant given in the auditorium of St. Mark's Parish House.

Although we had four weeks of rehearsal, I never got much more than a tentative acquaintance with my lines. And so, on the night the pageant opened, I had the lines pretty well posted all over the stage. Three pages of script were on the floor behind the manger and there was enough light from a baby spot, directed on the manger, to permit me to read fairly clearly, even though I had to lean way over because of my nearsightedness. The director wouldn't permit Joseph to wear glasses.

The pageant went along without incident until we came to the point where I was to kneel by the manger and deliver my lines. It was then I found that somebody had killed the baby spot—the one that shed light on my pages of dialogue.

I absolutely couldn't see a thing. And not one of the lines would come into my head.

Frantically, I whispered to one of the bigger boys in the cast, a fellow who was playing one of the kings, and asked him to sneak offstage and get somebody to turn on the spot. "I can't see my lines," I said, between clenched teeth.

The boy grasped the situation immediately but, instead of going off to find the electrician, he got out a box of matches and struck one for me. It shed enough illumination and I got back on the track again. However, there was a gust of backstage wind, and the straw in the manger instantly caught fire.

The dry straw burned like you wouldn't believe, and within a moment or so both the manger and the Babe were burned to a crisp. The director, stage manager and two or three other adults all ran out on the stage and tried to smother the flames with a blanket. This didn't work and, in the magnificent illumination, I picked up my pages of dialogue and spouted my lines without cessation.

Then some more men ran onto the stage and they dumped buckets of water on the manger. Steam and smoke rose in the air, but I kept right on with my lines. Kept on, that is, until somebody doused me with a bucket of water—and I stalked off the stage, quite grumpily.

Throughout my career, I always had trouble with my hands. I used them too much. There's an expression—"chewing up the scenery"—and some actors do it with facial expressions, others with body movement, and some with wild gyrations of the hands. I'm the dean of the latter school.

When I was only six, I was given a little recitation to deliver in the auditorium in school and, if I say so myself, I did it very well during rehearsals—but with gestures. The teacher in command of my performance instructed me to hold my hands behind my back and keep them there.

On the day of the performance, I mounted the stairs from the audience, went onto the stage and stood in front of the huge, drawn curtain. I then began my piece.

Within a minute or so, everybody in the audience was laughing. And I became disturbed. Because it wasn't a funny piece. In fact, it was a serious thing, about how all patriots are willing to fight and die for their country.

After I finished, took my bow, and walked down off the stage, I was told the reason for the hilarity. Unable to gesture with my hands, I'd placed them behind my back as I'd been told, but the nervous energy still had communicated itself to my fingers.

And, as I recited, I clutched the heavy velour curtain behind me, and, inch by inch, as I stated line after line, I slowly lifted the curtain. They tell me I had it a good two feet off the floor before I finished, and might well have made my exit through the little aperture I'd opened.

There are many stories about actors who use their hands to excess—like the Jewish actor in a Second Avenue theater who couldn't say his lines one night because he'd hurt his wrist—but those of us so afflicted have a terrible time trying to cut down on flailing the air.

I thought I'd had the thing conquered by the time I was appearing on the professional stage with some regularity. But one night in the summer of 1934 I was given a huge shock.

I was playing the older brother, Kenneth Rimplegar, in Gertrude Tonkonogy's Depression comedy *Three-Cornered Moon*, at the Rockridge Theater in Carmel, New York. The part is described thusly: "Kenneth is 25. He has more dignity than any of the other Rimplegars. He is rather heavily built. His speech is affected, his accent being either Harvardian or English, whichever is most unpleasant to you."

Kenneth, you see, is an emotional role. He wants to kill himself when he finds the family has been wiped out in the stock market crash—but I felt on opening night that I'd handled it with finesse and considerable restraint.

Several friends in the audience complimented me on my playing and we all had a nice party after the opening. The next night, however, just before curtain time, Nathaniel Reid, the owner and producer of the theater, came to me in the wings.

"Norton," he said quietly, "will you kindly hold your hands behind you." I blushed a little and said, "Yes, sir, I will."

"I mean right now," said Mr. Reid.

I put my hands behind me, and Mr. Reid, a tall, ascetic gentleman of infinite patience but firm resolve, quickly whipped a stout cord around my wrists and drew it tight. He took a few more turns and knotted it securely.

"Kindly play that way this evening," he said. "It will do you good. Return to me at the final curtain and I'll remove the cord."

That's the way I played Kenneth Rimplegar that night. And I held myself so that I don't think anybody in the audience had any idea that my hands were tied. Never again did I make enormously exaggerated gestures with my hands. *Exaggerated* gestures, yes. But not *enormously* exaggerated.

Quite a few crazy things happened to me at that Rockridge Theater, by the way. It was there, in that same play, *Three-Cornered Moon*, that I got badly caught up with my practice of pinning dialogue here and there on the set.

In two scenes, I had to come onstage and talk on the telephone to my beloved Kitty, a Brooklyn beauty who, according to the authoress, never was deterred by "a decided ampleness" from wearing a tight dress.

Anyway, I had a whole flock of lines such as: "Hello . . . Hi, Kitty, baby. . . . How's my little baby? . . . Oh, sure . . . Well, no not right now . . . Of course I love you, Kitty . . . Do you love me? . . . Yeah, but I don't want you to see him . . . You just hadn't better . . . Of course, I love you . . . Well, maybe tomorrow . . . No, I can't tonight . . . Of course I love you . . . Do you love me? . . ." and so on and so on.

It was a dead phone and, with nobody to cue me, I had a hell of a time trying to remember the sequence. The whole bit was nothing but a bunch of non sequiturs and it meant nothing to me, and so I decided not to waste time learning the lines.

Instead, I typed out the routine on a sheet of paper and tacked it to the side of a bookcase next to the chair on which I sat. Then, since I was wearing glasses, I could read it with ease.

The third or fourth night of the show, however, I bounced onto the stage in answer to the ringing of the phone, picked it up and said "Hello . . ." Then I looked to the bookcase for my next lines. The sheet wasn't there.

Mumbling a bit, I began searching for it on the floor, under the chair, behind the bookcase. I couldn't find it anywhere. And I couldn't just let the whole thing go because some of the words used in the phone conversation are cues to later questions from other actors.

So, while the startled cast waited, I said, ostensibly over the phone, "Excuse me just a minute, will you? I want to look over some stock figures while we talk." I then marched off the stage, went to my dressing room, got my 'sides'—my lines in the play —returned to the stage, opened the book to the telephone conversation and went on as though nothing had happened.

After the curtain, Mr. Reid said to me, "I don't suppose it would do any good to tie your ankles together tomorrow night, but if you haven't learned that phone bit by then, don't show up."

I learned it.

After *Three-Cornered Moon* closed at the Rockridge, I next played the part of Lord Monkhurst, a foppish Britisher, in the English play *Milestones*. This role I did, indeed, play with restraint, and what happened to me wasn't my fault at all. But it really broke up the play.

It happened on an unbelievably stormy night, with much lightning, thunder and the heaviest, steadiest downpour I'd seen in many years. The theater was out in the country, in a converted barn, and, of course, on a night like that, not many people ventured out. There were, I believe, only a dozen people in the audience. There were 16 in the cast.

The rain came down so hard and pounded the roof with such intensity that it often was impossible for the audience to hear what was said onstage. The wind howled and the crackle of lightning and the roar of the thunder sometimes stopped the action for a minute or two.

Lord Monkhurst, described as "a young man-about-town of 22, tall, hollow-chested, careless in his manners, very self-assured and properly bored," doesn't come on until the third act. And when I walked onto the stage, in white tie and tails, I was struck immediately by what was happening overhead.

The ceiling of our set, the drawing room of an English mansion on Kensington Gore in 1860, was made of canvas. Nothing more. Normally, it was stretched taut and looked like plaster. But that night it had bellied down alarmingly, filled with water that had leaked through the roof of the theater.

Several drops were seeping through the canvas—drip, drip,

drip—and they were landing right on the couch where I was scheduled to loll in a moment or so. Nonchalantly, I moved the couch a few feet and then, on cue, lay down upon it. I adjusted my monocle, lit a cigaret in a long holder, and said to Webster, the butler, "Bring me a Benedictine, will you?"

I drank the Benedictine (sugar water!), chatted with the other actors for a couple of minutes as I was supposed to, and then summoned Webster again.

"Another Benedictine," I said.

"To be sure, m'lord," he replied.

And, as he spoke, the load above became too great. The old canvas split and gallons of water and all sorts of junk that had been tossed onto the ceiling—cigaret butts, paper cups, newspapers and old rags—cascaded down upon me. It's possible that there have been more distinguished performances of *Milestones*, but the dozen hardy souls who were the audience that night will tell you there never was a funnier one.

On the whole, the critics were kind to me that summer and few of them mentioned my overacting. In fact, few of them mentioned me at all! There was one gentleman, however, who nearly gave me a heart attack. His name was Ted Martin, and I'll tell you more about him later. It's enough here to say that he was working on a newspaper and had seen me performing two weeks earlier in Stockbridge, Massachusetts.

So, the day after seeing me in *Three-Cornered Moon* at Rockridge, he went to his paper and wrote a critique which was set in type with a headline, and he sent me a proof of it.

The headline was:

MOCKRIDGE AT ROCKRIDGE
WORSE THAN AT STOCKBRIDGE!

And the lead read like this:

Norton Mockridge, who gave the most uninspiring performance of the season two weeks ago at Stockbridge, Mass., has done it again! This actor is capable of the most remarkable flights of mediocrity and he shares them generously with the

186

audience. In fact, at Rockridge, he over-acts even more than he did at Stockbridge, if such a thing is possible.

Shortly after I got this proof in the mail Ted called me, choking with laughter, and said, "Don't worry, Nort. That's not what's going in the paper. I had it set just as a gag. Actually, I enjoyed your performance—almost as much as a visit with my mother-in-law."

But the craziest thing that happened while I was at Rockridge featured a bosomy, beautiful blonde named Helene Fortescue. She was a member of the company and by far the best known and widely publicized.

Not for her acting ability—which had not yet blossomed and which, I understand, still has not—but because of the fact that she was the sister of Thalia Fortescue Massie who, two years before, had been involved in the most shocking incident ever to hit Hawaii.

Thalia, the wife of Navy Lt. Thomas H. Massie, had been brutally attacked by five Hawaiians and subsequently one of the five accused had been killed. Thalia's mother, Mrs. Granville Fortescue, the lieutenant, and two enlisted men were convicted of manslaughter, and the sentences were commuted.

So Helene was big news in the sleepy little town of Carmel and whenever we went anywhere during the day or when we patronized the gin mills after the show, there were plenty of people to gape and gawk at her.

One Friday night late in August, some of us were sitting in front of a blazing fire in the actors' dormitory (it was mighty chilly in that section of the country), when Helene, who was twenty, said casually, "You know, I'm going to marry Johnny tomorrow."

This surprised us because, while we had met Johnny, a young man she saw once in a while, it hadn't seemed that he and Helene were that close. However, we all got into the spirit of it quickly enough and, sipping a bottle of gin that I got from my room, we began to make plans.

"Make it dramatic, Helene," said one of the actresses.

"Yeah, let's think of something that'll make a big splash," said a director.

Within two or three minutes, it was decided that the wedding would be held late the next afternoon on the huge outdoor stage where Mr. and Mrs. Coburn nightly were appearing in *Lysistrata*.

Helene, who later married J. Louis Reynolds, of the Reynolds tobacco family, had a flair for the spectacular. And she spent most of the night making plans.

"I'll call the minister right now," she said, even though it was about 2 A.M., and she put in a call to Frank H. Wells, who lived in Mount Vernon but who was vacationing at Carmel. Next morning, we got hold of a portable organ and an organist, we arranged for champagne, various actors contributed the something old, something new, something borrowed, something blue, and we rigged up a tiny altar on the great stage and decorated the area with evergreens and flowers.

Helene picked six bridesmaids and six ushers (I was one) and, as the brilliant afternoon sun was lowering in the sky, Helene, with tears in her eyes, marched to the little altar and pledged her troth to Johnny. I had a feeling that the minister, Frank Wells, mumbled and stuttered a bit much, and fumbled with the Bible, but I put it down to the fact that some clergymen on vacation drink a little more than usual.

It was a terribly exciting moment, and everybody wept, and Mr. Reid, who gave the bride away, kissed her several times, and then everybody else except poor Johnny got to kiss her, and she tossed her bouquet to one of the actresses—a gal who'd been married five times—and she and Johnny got into his car and roared away.

It was then that the newspaperman in me began to conquer the actor and I went to Mr. Reid. "Sir," I said, "this will make a great story for the New York newspapers. First, it's a romantic thing, what with being married on the outdoor stage and all, and besides Helene is known to every editor because of the Hawaiian thing. Her picture's been in every paper—and the story will be a good thing for Rockridge."

"My boy," said Mr. Reid, turning up one corner of his thin mouth in what was supposed to be a smile of approval, "that's a top-hole idea. Suppose you write the story, and we'll phone it to the newspapers."

I turned out a dandy story, full of hearts and flowers and outdoor stages, and three or four of us took carbons and got on the pipe and read it to *The New York Times*, the *Herald Tribune*, the *Daily News*, the *Mirror* and the three wire services, AP, UP and INS. Within minutes the story was being flashed around the world, and as we had dinner that night it blared at us over the radio.

I felt pleased with myself and I could tell that Mr. Reid was pleased too. He hardly could wait for the next day to read the Sunday papers and see "Rockridge Theater" splashed all over.

That Saturday night was a gala one indeed, and what with the champagne during the afternoon, and the many subsequent gin toasts to the honeymooning couple, spirits were extremely high. In fact one actor, as I remember, was perched in a pine tree singing "I Love You Truly."

And then, as we were finishing the last of the drinks in front of the fire, the door of the dormitory opened and Helene walked in.

Nobody said anything for a moment. We peered into the darkness behind her to see if Johnny was there.

"Hiya, kids," said Helene, sinking to the floor. "God, do I need a drink!"

We gave her a straight gin. "I've left Johnny," she said huskily. Then, as the questions popped, she told how she'd learned certain things about his background that had convinced her their married life would be unhappy, and she went on and on like that, hamming it up, crying and sobbing, and telling everybody how sorry she was that she'd made such a big mistake.

Finally, we all of us were crying in our beer (we'd run out of gin) and then Helene, sensing the proper moment, stood up, swaying in front of the fire, and began to laugh.

"Ha, ha, HAH!" she roared. "I put it over. You all believed it. Some acting, huh? Hell, I'm not married at all. The whole thing was a hoax. Johnny and I didn't even *want* to get married. We just wanted to put on a show."

"But," I asked stunned, "what about the Reverend Mr. Wells?"

"Ha!" said Helene. "He's no reverend. He's just an insurance man that Johnny knows. He's a friendly Elk and he did it just as a gag."

With that she took off up the stairs for bed, laughing all the way.

I was chilled. I thought of the news services, the radio, tomorrow's papers. I raced up the stairs to Helene's room.

"For God's sake," I yelled, "what'm I gonna do now about the newspapers? How can I stop the story?"

Helene calmed down. She paled a bit. "The . . . ah . . . newspapers?" she said.

"Sure," I said. "We've given the story to all the papers, the wire services, the radio. What the hell do we do now?"

"Oh, my gawd," cried Helene. "You shouldn't have done it!"

It was then about 3 A.M., but I dashed to the phone in the office and I began calling the New York papers. All, of course, had been locked up hours ago and were on the streets. Trucks even then were speeding north into Westchester and Putnam counties to bring the happy news to Mr. Reid on the morrow.

I called the radio stations and the wire services and, without exception, the various editors gave me hell. I tried to explain the situation as a madcap thing engineered by Helene, but solemnly believed by all of us. The editors marked it down as a publicity stunt.

And they were profanely bitter about it. I, who had entertained thoughts of some day joining a New York newspaper, kept telling them that the story had been given out by a friend of Helene's named Norman Farnsworth (a name I made up on the spur of the moment) and that nobody at the theater had been guilty of sending in the false information.

I got Helene on the wire to talk to the editors, telling them that it hadn't been a publicity stunt—merely a local gag that got out of hand.

"It was just a joke," said Helene. "Mostly a joke on myself. I told everybody around the theater on Friday that I was going to get married the next day, just as a joke. But I found they were taking me seriously, so I said to myself 'What the hell? Let's do it.' We didn't even have a license, but Johnny got this Mr. Wells to act as the minister and we had a ceremony. I never dreamed anyone would tell the newspapers."

I was practically a nervous wreck by the time we made the last call. My acting career was pretty shaky at best, and now my newspaper career was going out the window.

"Helene," I said, angrily, "I think you've just destroyed me as a newspaperman."

"Oh, well," said Helene, wearily, *"c'est la guerre.* I was only trying to liven things up a little." And she toddled off to bed.

Chapter Thirteen

PRODUCTIONS at the Westchester Playhouse just outside Mount Kisco, then run by Day Tuttle and Richard Skinner, were a lot more professional than the haphazard affairs at Rockridge, where a cow might wander into the theater at any time. But even so, the Playhouse had its moments.

I created one of them one night when, playing a lackey in *The Swan*, which starred Henry Fonda, Geoffrey Kerr, Francesca Bruning and Viola Roache, I somehow misjudged the time. A minute or so before my entrance, I was lolling in my underwear in a dressing room beneath the stage, a cubicle, incidentally, that once had been a horse stall.

"Good God," cried the stage manager, "get dressed! You go on in a minute!" He then relayed word to Myron McCormick and Geoffrey Kerr, who were on stage, that they'd have to ad-lib for a while—vamping till Mockridge was ready.

I flung my clothes on, a pair of silk breeches, boiled shirt with stand-up collar, white waistcoat, tail coat and black bow tie, and rushed to the rear of the stage where I was to make an entrance with Miss Bruning and one or two other actors. As I ran, I combed my unruly, wavy reddish-blond hair (today only a tiny handful of that hair remains, and most of that is in a cigar box) and straightened my clip-on bow tie.

"Do I look all right?" I whispered to Francesca in the dark little space between the rear wall of the theater and the flats which formed the back wall of the set.

"Of course, of course," she hissed, impatiently. "Let's get onto the stage."

And so, we made our stately entrance. Francesca, wearing a tiara, moved with regal bearing to stage right and I, walking stiffly erect, moved to stage left. Suddenly, there were a couple of titters from the audience. Then a loud laugh. Guffaws broke out all over and soon the audience was hysterical with laughter.

Francesca and I exchanged glances. I looked around at the other actors. And then my fellow players began to laugh, too. They all stared at me. Francesca began to choke with laughter. It was one of those moments that all actors fear—and I knew it had come to me.

Even though I didn't want to do it, my head was magnetically tilted forward and I looked down and saw that my fly was open. Wide open!

I blush easily, but that night I set the record. They tell me I was a combination of cerise, vermilion and purple. I fled the stage. I buttoned the breeches and waited till the laughter had died down and then made another entrance. I was still scarlet but the audience, except for a few snickers, let me off the hook. And the play went on.

Francesca kidded me a lot about that incident, as did most of the other players, but two nights later something happened that took the heat off.

As Francesca was making her courtly entrance, her long,

trailing skirt caught on one of the wing bolts that held a steel brace from the flat to the floor, and the skirt, having been fastened only with snappers, instantly was whipped off.

Unable to halt, Francesca walked on stage beautifully dressed from the waist up, but attired only in a short petticoat below. The audience got quite a kick out of that. But it really went into spasms when I disentangled the dress from the bolt, carried it on, held it out to her and said, "Your skirt, madame."

Oh, we had some interesting times at the Playhouse. Like the night that a scenic designer, a very sensitive soul, was insulted by some stagehand. He ran out the stage entrance and threw himself into the grass, in full view of the audience strolling in the courtyard during intermission, and beat his fists into the ground and cried and cried.

And there was the night that I was standing backstage, about to make my entrance, and I was visibly nervous, shaking, even. Some of the other actors badgered me about it, and they continued the kidding at the party after the show. Jane Cowl, who was rehearsing for a subsequent show, was at the party and she heard them and came over and comforted me.

"Young man," she said, "don't let nervousness bother you. I've been in the theater since before you were born, and there's never a night I go on with really dry panties."

There were loads of stars and featured players, such as Ina Claire, Peggy Wood, Tamara, Norma Terris, John Emery and Tom Powers, around the Playhouse all the time. Of course, the atmosphere was charged with temperament, theatrical jealousy and all sorts of other interesting emotions.

One of the most interesting situations occurred when Margaret Sullavan, starring in a show she was taking around the summer theater circuit, came to the Playhouse for a week's performance at the same time that Henry Fonda was rehearsing for the next week's show. Hank and Maggie had been married and divorced, and all of us at the theater expected fireworks. None developed, however, and the ex-partners spent quite a few happy hours on the lawn in the afternoon—playing mumblety-peg.

One afternoon as I was walking across the courtyard to get my car and drive into the village, I saw a wisp of a girl with a thin, peaked face, a large nose and expressive eyes trying to push a small, battered coupe.

"Oh, dear," she said. "I've got to go into Mount Kisco, but my car won't start."

I worked on it a bit, tried to push it and, I think, even kicked it after a while. But it wouldn't start. So, I offered to take the young lady into the village in my car. As we were driving in, I, from my exalted position as a seasoned performer, sized up this plain-looking little girl as one of the kids who'd enrolled at the summer acting school that was run in conjunction with the Playhouse.

"You in the school?" I asked.

"No," said the girl. "I'm an actress. My name is Mildred Natwick."

Another time I was introduced to a striking-looking actress and I caught the name Carlisle. "Ah, yes," I said. "I think I've seen you in pictures."

"No," she sighed. "I've made only one picture and that was a madhouse thing called *A Night at the Opera*, with the Marx Brothers, and I don't think you remember me from that. You're probably thinking of a fat blonde named Mary Carlisle. But you know, I have a feeling you'll be hearing more of me in the future. My name's *Kitty* Carlisle."

And then there was the day when a new batch of eager, young acting students arrived to start courses conducted by Maria Ouspenskaya, the drama coach, and Tamara Daykarhanova, the makeup expert. I looked them over with my professional eye and saw nothing that was going to make sparks in the theater of the future.

But there was one girl who, it seemed to me, didn't even *belong* in the class. She was older than the others, by at least ten years, I figured, and while she had a nice face, she certainly wasn't good-looking, and she had a sort of angular, awkward way of moving and handling herself. And I didn't like her voice much, either.

I got talking to her a few days later, and she told me she'd been a teacher, that she had just married a bank employee named Keith Urmy and that she and her husband had decided to invest a little money in getting her some acting lessons.

"For heaven's sake, why?" I asked.

"Because," she said shyly, "I've always wanted to act. I've acted a little and I always felt that I could be a good actress. I thought I'd like to give it a try before I become too old."

"Well," I said, in a tolerant but worldly-wise way, "I guess it's all right to go ahead and spend a few dollars. Probably won't hurt you. But, my dear, when you don't get anywhere, don't let it break your heart. Too many people have tried the impossible and had it ruin their lives."

"Even so," she said, "I think I'll try."

"Okay," I said, "but don't forget I warned you."

That girl's name was Mildred Dunnock.

But the damnedest thing that I remember in connection with the Westchester Playhouse was something that involved my father and mother.

All through my alleged acting career, I'd lied about my age. In addition to not being a good actor, I had other problems. For one thing, I never was good-looking enough to be a leading man. (Today that ain't no problem—look at guys like Tom Ewell, Jack Palance, Orson Bean, Ernest Borgnine and Cantinflas and Fernandel—but in those days you had to look like Valentino.)

For another thing, I never looked like a juvenile (I had that tired, worried look at eighteen). And for a third thing, I was pretty young to play character roles. You had to be at least forty then to be permitted to play a character role on Broadway. Today, the youngest Lennon sister could get away with it.

So, whenever I applied for a part I added as many years to

my age as I thought necessary. I lied about it so much that many times I wasn't sure exactly what my age was.

Anyway, I was just eighteen years old when I performed along with Fonda, McCormick, Natwick, Dunnock, Bruning, Richard Gaines, Day Tuttle, and Johnny Monks (who later co-authored *Brother Rat*) in *One Sunday Afternoon*.

And on opening night, my mother and father were present in a front row, along with a dozen or so friends for whom they'd given a dinner. It was my debut at the Playhouse and the gentleman who wrote the biographical notes for the program had been especially kind to me. He made mention of some of my past exploits, said I had a promising future in the theater, pointed out that I already was doing newspaper work, and that I'd played football and boxed a bit.

The little bio closed with this paragraph:

> The fact that Norton Mockridge has packed all of this busy career into his few years, is really remarkable. He is to be congratulated—because he's only 21.

This item caused an astonishing stir in the audience, and several of the patrons who knew my parents well became almost apoplectic with laughter. This was because, only two nights before, my mother and father had given a large party, to which possibly one-third of the people in attendance that night had been invited—to celebrate their *20th* wedding anniversary!

It was during my work at the Playhouse, incidentally, that I decided to give up my acting career. There were several reasons. One was that I already had become deeply involved in the newspaper business, and another was that I didn't think I could stand any more cannelloni.

For quite a few years, I, as a young actor, had frequented such New York restaurants as Sardi's and Lucca's, both on West 44th Street and both noted for their distinguished theatrical clientele. They were the "in" places for young, aspiring actors, and we went there as often as possible, hoping to be discovered by producers, directors, and managers.

The proprietors of those meccas, Vincent Sardi and Bartolomeo (Pop) Rissetto, the owner of Lucca's, were happy to have actors dine there, but they were shrewd enough to know that actors very often couldn't afford it. Whenever a performer was working, the two restaurateurs presented him with a check. But when he wasn't working and probably didn't have a dime, the hosts proved what generous, hospitable, and truly magnanimous gentlemen they were.

"Welcome, my boy," Sardi or Pop would say. "Come in. Sit down. And tonight I would like your valued opinion on one of the *spécialités* of the house. No check tonight. I just want your opinion."

And then they would serve us heaping dishes of cannelloni —an Italian concoction of rolls of pasta stuffed with highly seasoned baked minced meat. This was one of their staples, and they were almost always overloaded with it.

After about 15,000 dishes of cannelloni, I began to feel that I really ought to get into some paying profession that would permit me to *buy* what I wanted. However—I guess the main reason that I left the theater was Henry Fonda.

Fonda was ten years older than I and he'd been around a long, long time by my standards. He'd never done anything notable on Broadway (he'd had bits in Leonard Sillman's *New Faces* and a couple of other shows, but no big parts had been offered him) and he'd played stock, road shows and summer theater. He wasn't making enough dough at the Playhouse to keep the wolf from ripping off his pants.

I watched him closely, admiring his acting technique, his easy manner on the stage, and the appeal he had to theatergoers. And I figured that if this guy, who had twenty times as much talent as I, had been able to get not a hell of a lot farther in the theater than I had, despite the fact that he had a ten-year edge on me, where would I be in ten years?

Nowhere, I decided. So I began to make tentative plans to get out of the theater. And my plans became almost concrete overnight as a result of a little foray to the movies made one evening by Messrs. Mockridge and Fonda, and two beautiful actresses named Martha Hodge and Joan Tompkins.

I was much enamored of Miss Hodge, the daughter of the late, great actor, William Hodge. (Later in the season she discarded me and up and married Myron McCormick but I simply put that down as one of those things. Some time after Myron died, Martha married my good friend Cleveland Amory, and, so far as I can see, she's fully recovered from the traumatic effect of the affection I offered her.)

But to get on with the story. The sparkling, red-haired Miss Hodge, the lovely blond Miss Tompkins and the slightly humpbacked, drawling Mr. Fonda and I drove to the Mount Kisco movie theater one free evening, there to take in the delights of a motion picture, the name of which I've long since forgotten.

We arrived at the theater in good shape, but when Henry and I dug into our pockets, we came up with only a few cents. And the girls didn't have anything either. So I had to go to the manager's office and explain that I'd left my thousand-dollar bankroll in the dressing room at the Playhouse and would he please let us in and I'd be back with the money tomorrow.

Fortunately, he let us in and we saw the picture. The next day I borrowed the money and paid back the manager. But that little incident, minor as it was, convinced me that the theater was not for me. Fonda was broke, the girls had nothing, and my only asset was that I could borrow from my father.

So I began casting about for other sources of income. And I really felt sorry for Fonda. "That poor guy," I told Martha, "will die of a broken heart. He's a good actor, but the theater demands more than that. He just hasn't got it. He's washed up!"

Well, just two years later I went to the Mount Kisco movie theater to see a great picture. Before I went in, I stood for a moment on the sidewalk and looked up at the marquee. There, in letters two or three feet high was this:

JANET GAYNOR AND HENRY FONDA
in
THE FARMER TAKES A WIFE.

And there were crowds lined up on the street waiting to get in to see the guy who two years before hadn't had enough dough to buy himself a single seat.

His rise had been electric. During the summer that he and I were at the playhouse, a fine actress, June Walker, who was to star on Broadway that fall in *The Farmer Takes a Wife*, had told the producer, Max Gordon, that Hank would make a good leading man. Gordon hired Hank, and he did make a good leading man.

So good that when Fox decided to make the film version, they looked right over June Walker's head and hired Fonda to play opposite their star, Janet Gaynor. After that, Fonda was on his way, and I'd say that today he can take anybody to the movies any time he wants to.

I was a little staggered by this meteoric success, and every once in a while I sort of kicked myself for having given up the theater. I was doing very well in the newspaper business, making like about $35 a week, but I decided that dabbling in the amateur theater and the semi-pro theater wouldn't hurt me. Just to sort of keep my hand in, as it were.

Snatching what time I could, here and there, I got back into the whirl again. For a summer, I played Rip Van Winkle in a company that toured the amphitheaters and some of the larger barns. This was the show, I hope you'll remember, in which, 14 years before, I had played a child under the monocled eye of Charles Coburn, unable to remember whether I was supposed to say "Fazzer" or "Grandfazzer."

I worked with the Mount Kisco Little Theater for a time,

doing some acting and a little directing. It was with this theater, incidentally, that I did my first—and last—singing on stage. I played a hick doughboy in a wartime musical called *Buddies,* and my big moment came when the sergeant handed me a letter informing me my mother had died. I sat down and read the letter and, as four violins and a harmonica began to play softly behind me, I raised my shaky baritone in a musical tribute to mother—"My Buddy."

I cried all through the song, the violinists sobbed and got their instruments wet, the harmonicat blubbered so much he blew a few clinkers, and the audience—especially when I hit lines like "I long for you all-l-l-l through the day," and ". . . your buddy, mi-i-i-i-sses you"—wept out loud. I felt it was a great moment in the theater, but, for some reason, no producer ever asked me to sing again.

For two seasons I worked with an outstanding company called the Bedford Community Players, directed by a grand old British professional, Rebekah Garden. It was this organization that gave me a chance to perform for the first time as a Negro. I played the part of Florian Slappey in Octavus Roy Cohen's wonderfully funny play, *Come Seven.*

On opening night, I do believe, I made history. I had used the wrong kind of grease paint to blacken my face and, what with the burning spotlights and the heat of a blistering summer night, perspiration cut long, white streaks down my darkened face. I think I was the first, and maybe the last, zebra-striped Negro performer.

I did several Lula Vollmer plays for that company, but the one I remember best is—for a very special reason—*Moonshine and Honeysuckle,* a story about feuding mountaineers that had been broadcast in serial form for three years on radio station WEAF in New York.

My role was that of Tom Bevins, ". . . large and chunky, sandy in coloring, something of a bully . . ." and throughout the play Bevins is trying to shoot and kill his mortal enemy,

Peg-Leg Gaddis. And Gaddis is trying to kill Bevins. Something or somebody always stops them, but whenever they meet they exchange lines like these:

> BEVINS: Hit don't take but one Bevins to kill Peg-Leg Gaddis, and that's me.
> PEG-LEG: Ye bloated-faced catfish, I'll live to spit in yo' grave.
> BEVINS: Ye'll spit from the other world if ye do, ye white-livered weasel.
> PEG-LEG: I 'low to kill ye, ye pop-eyed buzzard a'fore the day fades.
> BEVINS: Ye one-legged sour-faced ape of Satan, ye—take aim.
> PEG-LEG: I'll give ye eternal peace in 'bout one minute more.
> BEVINS: Come on outside, ye hunk of carrion.

I played Tom Bevins quite a few times as we toured that show around and then, one afternoon sometime after our run ended, I got a call from the director of a Peekskill, New York, acting company.

"We're opening *Moonshine and Honeysuckle* tonight," he told me, "but the fellow who plays Peg-Leg Gaddis just has been taken to the hospital. Do you think you could take over the role?"

I didn't really know Gaddis' lines fully, but I'd heard them so often that I thought I could master them in half an hour. So I said yes.

I tried to find some time that afternoon to go over Gaddis' lines, but half a dozen things came up and I never got to look at them. That evening I drove from Mount Kisco to Peekskill and arrived at the theater only a few minutes before curtain time. As I made up for Peg-Leg, I kept glancing at the book.

So it was that when I finally made my entrance as Peg-Leg, I had only the slightest grasp on his lines. And there was no place I could tack them up. This made me nervous of course, and so, instead of roaring the first line that Gaddis throws at Bevins: "Ye low-down scum of a Bevins," I lapsed into the old rut and threw *Bevins'* line at him:

"Hit don't take but one Bevins to kill Peg-Leg Gaddis, and that's me."

This really staggered the poor actor playing Bevins and he looked at me in amazement. He'd never even seen me before —and here I was reading HIS lines. He was so surprised that he didn't know what to do and he mechanically repeated the line:

"Hit don't take but one Bevins to kill Peg-Leg Gaddis, and that's me."

I didn't know what to do either, so I plunged on with Bevins' lines. The dialogue for a full minute went something like this:

ME: Ye'll spit from the other world if ye do, ye white-livered weasel.

OTHER ACTOR: Ye'll spit from the other world if ye do, ye white-livered weasel.

ME: Ye one-legged sour-faced ape of Satan, ye—take aim!

OTHER ACTOR: Ye one-legged sour-faced ape of Satan, ye—take aim!

ME: Come on outside, ye hunk of carrion.

OTHER ACTOR: Come on outside, ye hunk of carrion.

And so it went. The audience was quite confused, but the whole play is pretty confusing, too, so I guess they didn't think it too strange. The actor playing Bevins, however, was damn mad and he demanded that I be fired. But the director, apparently feeling that a Bevins-line-reading Gaddis was better than no Gaddis at all, refused. He begged me, though, to try to study the part and throw in at least a few of Peg-Leg's lines. I did, and the next night's performance was much smoother, but not so interesting.

The wildest night I ever had as an actor came when I was appearing in Emlyn Williams' play, *A Murder Has Been Arranged*. After the show had run some time in Bedford, we took it one Sunday night to Sing Sing prison in Ossining, New York.

It was customary then for theater companies to perform for the prisoners once in a while and when our producer received an invitation from the warden, Lewis E. Lawes, he arranged for us to present the show on Sunday, our free night. Nobody, oddly enough, gave a moment's thought to what effect a play like *A Murder Has Been Arranged* might have on the prisoners —burglars, thieves, rapists, con men and killers.

I played the role of Maurice Mullins, a suave, ingratiating, but thoroughly vicious young criminal who intends to murder one of his relatives in order to inherit £2,000,000. And believe me, those convicts ate up my every word. They loved everything I said.

Unexpected laughs from the cons began coming early in the play, before I made my entrance. The first uproar came when one of the performers said: "Do you think this place is haunted?" and at least five prisoners yelled: "You're damn right. . . . It sure is. . . . Ask the Warden. . . ."

Another laugh came when Sir Jasper, in the play, said: "One morning, ninety-five years ago, an old man was found here— murdered."

Some tough monkey shouted: "Ain't that jest too bad!" and the audience was convulsed. And any reference to police— "Charles, will you or won't you call the police?"—brought howls from the convicts.

But it was my big speech, in which I tell how evil I am, that really panicked them. I'd delivered this monologue many times in a most dramatic fashion, chilling and possibly even frightening my audiences, but that night my listeners lapped it up as the funniest thing they'd ever heard. It went, in part, like this:

> I've studied myself for years . . . here are my conclusions. Some men are born good. (BIG LAUGHTER) They grow up to be saints, or heroes, or preachers, or ideal husbands, as the case may be. Maurice Mullins, however, was born bad. (CHEERS) Very bad, indeed. (BIGGER CHEERS)
>
> I like to be very well dressed. ("Me, too," screamed a con. Much laughter.) I like to buy for every woman I like. ("Oh, oh," cried another, "dat's trouble, brother." More laughter.) I'm an

artist and I do things artistically. Anybody can forge a check, anybody can seduce a defenseless female. (HILARIOUS LAUGHTER)

The little nobodies seduce their women, and marry them because they haven't the courage of their convictions; I give a woman a hell of a good time, and then I cut clean. ("Dat's the way, boy. Kick 'em outta bed." Screams of approval.) I've been fulfilling my destiny ever since I extracted chocolates from slot machines with incredible ingenuity. I've been borrowing money, stealing money and marrying money ever since I can remember. ("You *some* cat, man!" Howls of laughter.) I don't take furtive sniffs at the cup of vice. I drink it to the dregs, with a gesture. I am the Complete Criminal. (ROARS OF APPROVAL. SCREAMS. WHISTLES. AND A STANDING OVATION.)

I, of course, never shall forget that speech. But there were two other things that made that night memorable. One was a statement by Warden Lawes to the entire cast while we were having a little supper before we went into the auditorium to give the play.

"Ladies and gentlemen," said the warden, "in a moment you'll go in there and you'll be seen by fifteen hundred criminals. You'll have stagehands to help you who are crooks and arsonists. You'll have electricians who are safecrackers and a head property man who, despite his mild manners and his soft blue eyes, murdered his wife and tried to kill the two cops who arrested him.

"But please, I beg you, don't look down on these people. Don't condescend. Don't treat them any differently than you would the professional people you meet in the theater every day. Remember this—there is only one difference between you people here and the men in there: *they* got caught!"

The other memorable thing that night was that somebody stole my watch! I took it off in my dressing room because Mullins wasn't the type to wear a wristwatch, and left it lying on the table along with my Kleenex, cold cream, grease paint and other makeup. When I returned after the show was over, I couldn't find the watch.

I raised a bit of hell about it, complaining mainly to the stage manager, a balding, gray-haired man of about sixty who was doing life as a four-time loser because he simply couldn't resist the temptation to show the government that he could make better-looking money.

"Well," he said, "I'm perfectly sure that none of my crew touched your watch. I'd check out your fellow players, however. Actors, you know, are notorious crooks."

The watch, naturally, never was recovered. But there's a funny sequel. Four years later, in my capacity as a newspaper reporter, I returned to Sing Sing one evening to watch the Westchester Playhouse present its production of *Ned McCobb's Daughter.*

I have a clipping of what I wrote the next day, July 10, 1938, and I'll quote just a bit of it:

> Fifteen hundred men, their faces eager with interest, fanned themselves in the sweltering heat last night as they watched a performance of "Ned McCobb's Daughter." You might have taken them for rough and ready soldiers, but they weren't— they were convicts, some of the most dangerous in the state. Killers, blackmailers, hi-jackers, thieves and moral degenerates —and they were having the time of their lives.
>
> At the final curtain, the audience rewarded the players with a thunderous burst of applause: furious handclapping, trampling of feet, hoarse cries of approval and strange sounds of delight from men whose customary expressions are more closely linked with frustration and rebellion.
>
> Even though all of the better lines in the play drew belly laughs, pandemonium broke loose when the star, Van Heflin, playing a tough guy from New York, admitted he had done three years and said: "Yes, but I wasn't in no sissy jail. I was in Atlanta. That's a Federal pen. That's class." Nothing was more enjoyable to the boys in the audience.
>
> Other high spots of the night were Heflin's descriptions of how he planned to hide rum on a farm (during Prohibition days), and of how he intended to fool the police.

"Oh, oh," murmured one colored boy near me, "that's bad. That's BAD!"

Naturally, I got a kick that night seeing Van Heflin, Millie Natwick and the other members of the cast catch those unexpected laughs, just as I had done. But I was really shocked after the final curtain when I went backstage to congratulate the performers, to have one member of the stage crew accuse me of stealing *his* watch!

"You took it, you took it, I know," he screamed. "You was writin' at my desk over there, and that's where it was. You took it!"

A little, scholarly-looking man who was doing life for administering lethal doses of arsenic to his landlady, he kept hopping up and down and yelling for the warden. I had, indeed, made some notes at his cluttered little desk but I hadn't seen his watch.

Protesting that I neither had taken it nor seen it, I went over to the desk and began sorting the mess of papers. There, under one pile of papers, was the watch.

"Look, drizzle-puss," I said, rather angrily, "there's your watch. Now, aren't you sorry?"

"Hell, no, I ain't sorry," he piped. "You just stashed it there. You was gonna pinch it later."

My craziest night as an actor, as I've told you, was in *A Murder Has Been Arranged* at Sing Sing. But the blankest night in my sparkling career came in 1940 at the opening of *The Devil and Daniel Webster* in the huge auditorium of the County Center in White Plains, New York. I played the devil (naturally!) and it turned out to be the last role I ever undertook onstage.

I hadn't done any acting for four years, but Carol Field Derby, my dear friend and one of the finest directors I've ever known, prevailed upon me to play Scratch, the devil, in her Westchester Playmakers Company production of the Stephen Vincent Benet classic, for charity.

207

A show of that kind was a bit out of my line, but I was happy to do anything Carol wanted, and so I agreed to appear wearing a black wig with a widow's peak, dark circles under my eyes, heavy lines from nose to lips denoting extreme cruelty, and an all-black suit, complete with black cape and black gloves. I got scared every time I looked at myself in the mirror.

The role is not a rewarding one. The devil, of course, is terribly villainous and his lines, delivered generally in a scratchy voice, are anything but scintillating. Daniel Webster (who was played by Ernest Hanes) has all the good lines and, after a totally mad courtroom scene, he defeats Scratch's attempt to capture a human soul.

In addition, Scratch has to play discordantly on a violin (I had never had a violin in my hands) and recite dreary things at a wedding, lines such as:

> Young William was a thriving boy.
> (Listen to my doleful tale.)
> Young Mary Clark was all his joy.
> (Listen to my doleful tale.)
> He swore he'd love her all his life.
> She swore she'd be his loving wife.
> But William found a gambler's den
> And drank with livery-stable men.
> He played the cards, he played the dice.
> He would not listen to advice.
> And when in church he tried to pray,
> The DEVIL took the words away.

Well, possibly because I didn't like the role, or possibly because I was working all day and rehearsing all night and thus got overtired, I picked up a bad cold about a week before the opening. And the cold got worse and worse.

On the day we were to open, I had pains in my head and chest, my legs were weak and wobbly, and, worst of all, I had laryngitis. But good! I couldn't speak at all in the morning, and as the afternoon dragged on and I absorbed more and more medicines, I was able only to rasp out a few words at a time.

I told Carol that I was sure I couldn't go on that night and she burst into tears. I had no understudy and nobody could have got up in the role in the few hours remaining.

"You've GOT to do it, Norton," she said, forcefully. "There MUST be a way."

I just sat there, moaning and suffering. "You know," said Carol, "some actors, I've heard, have conquered laryngitis by taking a mixture of hot rum and honey. Why don't you try it?"

Inasmuch as I'd tried at least ten different kinds of medicine, suggested by friends and members of the cast, I mumbled hoarsely that it certainly didn't make any difference whether I tried another nostrum or not. So, I went to Carol's apartment and she cooked up a panful of rum and honey, along with quite a bit of butter.

Much to my surprise, a glass of that mixture did a lot to loosen my voice, and so I had another. Within a short time I was speaking clearly but loudly and, I gather, somewhat irrationally. Carol suggested that it might be a good idea for me to sleep for a couple of hours until performance time, and I went to the Roger Smith Hotel and did just that.

When I was called by room service, however, I couldn't utter a word. Panicky, I went downstairs to the bar and somehow got across to the bartender that I wanted hot rum and honey. He got me some and within a couple of minutes my voice was restored.

"But look," said the bartender, confidentially, "brandy's just as good as hot rum and honey, and a helluva lot easier to take. That rum 'n' honey'll make ya throw up after a while."

So, I bought a bottle of Courvoisier and drove to the County Center. I placed the bottle on my dressing table, and as I made up and got into costume I nipped steadily at the brandy. My voice was fine and I felt like going out there and really showin' 'em!

By the time I made my first entrance, I had consumed about two-thirds of the bottle. And when I made my first exit, I worked it down until only an inch or so remained. That small amount I polished off between the final curtain and the bows to the audience.

When my friends came to my dressing room after the show, they found me standing on a chair, still reciting and scratching on my violin:

> "I summon the jury Mr. Webster demands.
> From churchyard mould and gallows grave,
> Brimstone pit and burning gulf,
> I summon them!
> Dastard, liar, scoundrel, knave,
> I summon them! Appear!
> Twelve great sinners, tried and true,
> For the work they are to do!
> I summon them, I summon them!
> Appear, appear, appear!"

Everybody, including Carol, congratulated me and told me it was the *best* thing I'd ever done. "I've seen you in almost every play, and this was your greatest performance," said one. "You couldn't have been more magnificent, old man," said another.

I was pleased, of course, in a foggy, befuddled way. But do you know, I couldn't remember then, and I can't remember now, one single, solitary detail of that entire performance. I had no recollection of even being on the stage!

I slept very well that night and the next day my voice was better. The honey-and-rum-and-butter-and-brandy apparently had done the trick. But it's a cure I wouldn't recommend to everybody.

Moments of madness like this, however, were not necessarily confined to my stage appearances. I had some pretty trying times both in radio and movie work. I made a number of movie shorts, none of which amounted to anything, but my greatest sorrow came when I was screen tested for film roles that I'd played on the stage.

Although I'd played these parts quite well in stock and on

the road, I never was picked to play one of them in pictures. After one test that produced nothing, I complained to the director, Richard Knight. "Look, Dick," I said, "I think that damn cameraman shot all the footage from the right side. That's my bad side."

"My boy," said Knight, "you have *two* bad sides."

After that I sort of forgot about movies, and concentrated on radio. I worked for a time with the late Bide Dudley, who then was running the Theater Club of the Air on WOR and reviewing Broadway shows at midnight on WOR. It was fun getting guests and performing on the Theater Club, but Bide had no budget and so I received nothing.

I covered the second-best Broadway openings on nights when there were two or more premieres and laboriously wrote scholarly reviews for Bide (who covered the main opening) to read on the air. But generally, after Bide had devoted a good amount of his five minutes to his own review, he didn't have enough time left to read my carefully written review. He usually settled for saying something, hastily, like: "And my colleague had a good time at *Black Panther*. He says it's a nice show." The whole business was very exasperating.

About that time, I decided to become a radio soapbox actor and my French actress friend Babette, who was appearing in several serials, got me an audition with an important producer at NBC. The producer set a date and told me to bring three scripts to read.

I selected these samples carefully from well-known plays and studied and rehearsed them for nearly two weeks. I had them letter perfect and hardly needed to look at the paper I'd typed them on.

Then, the day of the audition, I met Babette at her hotel— she was going with me—and she asked me to let her see the scripts.

"Ooooooooh," she cried. "Zey are much too long. Ze producer weel 'ave a 'eadache. We mus' cut zem a great deal."

Then with a heavy pencil, she sat down at a desk and trimmed all of my beautifully balanced scripts. I'll give you just one example. Script No. 1 was a sort of monologue from Siegfried Geyer and P. G. Wodehouse's *Candle-Light*. Josef, a valet (originally played by Leslie Howard) impersonates his master on the telephone and invites a lady to visit him:

> What a sweet voice you have . . . Me? . . . Oh, *my* voice isn't sweet. No, really . . . My dear lady, you make me blush . . . A tenor? No, I'm not a tenor. I'm a light baritone . . . No, of course I'm not offended. Even tenors are God's creatures, aren't they? Ha, ha . . . What a delightful laugh you have— Do go on. Yes, go on laughing. I could listen to you laughing forever . . . Do you know, I was thinking only this morning that a woman's smile is like a bathtub . . . ah . . . tap . . . What sort of man am I? Well, why don't you come around and see?
>
> Oh, do. Pop into your car and come round . . . Do come and cheer my loneliness . . . What lovely teeth you have . . . Eh? Oh, yes, you can always tell by a woman's voice what sort of teeth she has . . . Please don't ring off. Those whom Central has joined together, let no man put asunder . . . You *will* come? Wonderful! Eleven Ringstrasse . . . apartment number three on the first floor . . . Oh, yes, a very exclusive neighborhood . . . Yes. Goodbye.

Babette scratched furiously. "Ees *so* long," she said. "Ee mus' be made short and 'ow you say? creeesp."

By the time she had finished editing all three scripts, slashing out huge hunks and writing in little bridges in her foreign scrawl, punctuated by a French word here and there when she couldn't think of the English equivalent, it was time to go to the audition.

I tried to read the revisions in the taxi, but I couldn't make out much of her handwriting. I figured I'd have time at the studio, but when we got to NBC, the producer met us in the reception room and said, "Come right into the studio. We're on a tight schedule so I'm glad you were prompt."

Babette gave me her best "See-I-told-you-so look" and the producer stood me in front of a mike and went into the control room. "Please start, Mr. Mockridge," said a voice over the amplifier.

"This is Josef on the telephone, from *Candle-Light*," I said and then I started:

"What a sweet voice you have . . . Me? . . . Oh, *my* voice isn't make me blush . . . A tenor? . . . No, I'm a light offended . . . Even tenors are God's creatures, so do go on laughing . . . I was thinking only this morning that you are like a bathtub . . . So, why don't you come around and see? . . . *Voilà* . . .

"Oh, do. Pop into your car . . . and show me what lovely teeth you have . . . Please don't ring off. . . . Let no man put asunder apartment number three on the floor, very exclusive . . ."

At that moment, the terribly amplified voice from the control room cut in and said, "Thank you, Mr. Mockridge. That will be enough."

"Ahhh . . . er . . . I have two other scripts . . . er . . . don't you want to hear them?" I asked.

"No, thank you, Mr. Mockridge," said the voice authoritatively. "And don't call us. We'll call you."

Chapter Fourteen

As I've indicated, I think, my acting and newspaper careers overlapped here and there and the overlapping was the result of financial necessity. All actors, of course, have "at liberty" periods every year. And I was no exception. The only difference in my case, however, was that some of my at liberty periods ran like from January 1 to December 31. That's why I was open to job offers.

In 1933, during one of my longer at liberty periods, I was

standing outside an ice cream hideaway in Mount Kisco called The Goody Shop. I was eighteen years old and tastefully attired in my rehearsal togs—yellow corduroys, black sweater, maroon ascot and once-white sneakers, the very things that actors like Henry Fonda, Jimmy Stewart and Charles Boyer wore for rehearsal. I was wondering where my next dollar was coming from when I was approached by one of the strangest characters I've ever met—a man who not only was to change my life but to drive it into a channel from which I've never escaped.

This man, whom I shall call Lemuel Snodgrass, was a very unusual man, as you will see. I had never met Mr. Snodgrass, but I knew that he was the editor and publisher of the venerable, considerably decayed Mount Kisco *Recorder*, a weekly newspaper that nobody read.

It had a circulation of about 700, some of it paid, but even most of those who sent Mr. Snodgrass their two dollars for an annual subscription never bothered to unroll the paper when they got it in the mail.

The paper's newsstand circulation can best be described by citing the fact that every Friday, publication day, Mr. Snodgrass would tie a string around 50 copies of the *Recorder*, hoist the bundle to his shoulder and carry it down the street to Carpenter's stationery store, and drop it on the counter.

He then would pick up the 50 copies he'd placed there the previous Friday and carry them back to the plant. He stacked them in his cluttered office, saying, "I'll keep 'em here in case somebody wants some extra copies." Nobody ever did.

I had heard all this from friends, including Walter Huelle, editor of the village's successful weekly paper, the *North Westchester Times*, and so I was quite surprised when Mr. Snodgrass walked directly up to me, hitched up his suspenders, cleared his throat five or six times and said, "Do you want to be a reporter for me?"

I surveyed him coolly, the way I had seen John Drew stare down upon a tradesman who had dared to approach. I asked why he was offering me this great honor. He explained, haltingly, that he'd just lost his only reporter, an octogenarian who had fallen off a curb, but that he'd been planning to get a younger reporter anyway.

As I stood there in front of The Goody Shop with my hands in my empty pockets, knowing full well where my next acting jobs were *not* coming from, I got a giddy sensation that I couldn't analyze. The idea of working as a reporter, a job about which I knew absolutely nothing, was wild. But the idea of working for the *Recorder* was insane! Yet—somehow—the combination appealed to me, and so I said yes.

Mr. Snodgrass grunted and said he'd see me tomorrow morning. Then, as an afterthought, I politely inquired as to how much salary I might expect. Mr. Snodgrass' tanned face paled. He hunched his shoulders, and grunted. His thumbs flicked his suspenders and he shuffled through a nervous little dance. I could see that talk of money was distasteful to him but he made a great effort and blurted out, "Ten dollars a week, and not one penny more."

Ten dollars seemed almost insignificant to me, an actor who had made up to $375 a week—even though I now wasn't getting it—and I asked hopefully about expenses.

"No expenses," he said, with chilling finality.

I felt it would be rude to embarrass him with any further talk about money, so I held out my hand. He took it and the deal was sealed.

Next morning I dressed as carefully as though I were going to be screen tested by MGM. I wore a slightly starched white shirt with French cuffs and my best gold links, a tan, silk gabardine suit, my new camel's hair coat and a practically new brown velour fedora. I got into my secondhand but very spiffy long, yellow Chrysler Imperial, on which I'd paid a down payment and two monthly installments, and drove excitedly to my new place of employment.

I was buoyant with enthusiasm as I stood outside the old

building which housed the paper and inspected what was left
of the faded gold letters on the dirty, gray-black sign:

M UNT KIS O ECORDER, *Est. 1879*
LEMUEL SN DEGRASS, ED. & PROP.

I walked up the steps to the front door, a huge door with
plate glass in the upper half. Both the wood and the glass were
covered with dirt and dust, except around the brass knob and
lock where fumbling hands had manufactured a small oasis of
partial cleanliness.

Dimly visible through the dirty window were three index
cards which, it seemed, had been pasted there some years before. Each was lettered with purple ink. One read: *Gone to
lunch.* The one below it read: *Back in 15 minutes.* And the
third read: *At the post office.*

I opened the door and stepped into a long, dark hallway
barely illuminated by a dust-covered, 25-watt bulb. A mouse or
a small rat, its claws screeching on the bare boards, raced
madly off into the gloom at the far end of the hall. And then,
from out of the darkness at the end, I saw the figure of Mr.
Snodgrass coming toward me.

He was dressed in a frayed woolen, long-sleeved undershirt
unbuttoned to his abdomen, and a pair of loose-fitting, baggy
pants precariously supported by stringy suspenders which were
coated by the grime of inky thumbs. One of the braces was fastened to the pants in front by a large, rusty horse blanket pin.
His dark hair was shot with gray and his unsmiling face, with
bushy eyebrows and turned-down mouth, was forbidding and
streaked with ink and grease.

"C'mon in," he said, jerking a thumb over his shoulder.
"Mind your clothes. We're workingmen here. Everything's
dirty. Can't get janitors anymore. Nobody wants to work."

He led me into the combination composing room and job-
printing room and I stood there appalled. Never had I seen

217

anything so dirty, so cluttered, so disordered. An L-shaped room, about 30 feet at its longest point and 20 feet wide, it contained three relatively open areas around the two inky, grease-covered, dusty job presses which were used to print tickets, handbills, letterheads and such; around the four stones, or tables, on which the type for the newspaper was assembled; and around the single, dust-covered Linotype machine.

The rest of the room was stacked from the floor almost to the cobwebby ceiling with boxes, crates, barrels, tables, chairs, reams of paper and cardboard, bundles of old newspapers and magazines, books, fonts of type, and hundreds of items of assorted junk.

There were several windows but because they hadn't been washed in many years, only the faintest suggestion of light penetrated from the outside world. The room was black and gloomy, except for the dim circles of amber from dust- and rust-encrusted, green-shaded lamps that hung over the stones and the job presses, and a little light that flickered on and off over the keyboard of the Linotype. Cockroaches more than an inch long clattered over the type that lay in forms.

Instinctively, I held my expensive camel's hair coat close to my legs, and I looked nervously to see whether the sleeves were touching anything. Mr. Snodgrass noticed this, grunted a couple of times and said, "Black clothes are best in here. Don't show the dirt and the ink."

He then led the way to the Linotype and grunted again. A white-haired, bespectacled man wearing a heavily ink-stained printer's apron emerged from behind it. This was Mr. Snodgrass' only employee—Mr. Ted Martin of Brewster, New York, who operated the Linotype and the job presses, and who later was to write some articles and drama criticism about me, including that dandy headline about Mockridge, Rockridge and Stockbridge.

"This is Ted Martin," said Mr. Snodgrass.

Mr. Martin looked at me in what I took to be a surly manner and said, "Whatever in the hell do you want to work *here* for?"

"Well . . ." I said.

"Christ, kid, get out of here while you can," said Mr. Martin, and he returned to his machine.

"Never mind him," said Mr. Snodgrass, with a couple of grunts. "He's hung over."

He then stalked off, nimbly pursuing a labyrinthine path through the jumble, and I followed as best I could. Presently we came to a cubicle at the front of the building in which there was a dust-covered, splintered wooden desk, an ancient L. C. Smith typewriter, a sagging swivel chair and a rickety table laden with hundreds of rolls of blueprints, catalogs, builders' magazines and boxes of yellowed envelopes and writing paper.

The large plate-glass window, overlooking the street, was so dirty I couldn't even see through it, but I was able to make out, in reverse, the words *General Contractor*, lettered in a half circle.

"Used to rent this room to a builder," said Mr. Snodgrass. "But he went broke. Been dead thirty years. Can't rent it to anybody else. You can use it to write in—if you want."

I was numb. I just stood there looking at the thousands of dead flies on the large windowsill, the cobwebs, the stubs of scores of long-forgotten cigarets and cigars, the quarter-inch layer of dust on virtually everything in the room.

"Here's some scratch paper," said Mr. Snodgrass, and he reached for a pile of yellow copy paper that had turned brown around the edges. As he picked up a few sheets, they crumpled, flaked away and fluttered to the floor.

"Dried out in the sun," he said, wiping his hands on his pants. "Well, some of us gotta work around here. Copy deadline's Wednesday afternoon." And he turned and went back to the composing room. The place was chillingly quiet except for the buzzing of big black flies against the window and the clump of Mr. Snodgrass' feet as he vanished into the black depths in back.

And then, in a mournful, hollow, reverberating tone, I heard Mr. Martin yelling, "Lem, that kid must be nuts! You oughta get him outa here."

I looked around the room again. This was *my* office. This was to be the nerve center of the newspaper. This was, in effect, the city room, the editorial office, the communications center, the link between the publisher and all those readers in the great big wonderful world outside that dirty window! I thought I'd throw up.

I wanted to sit down, my legs were that weak, but there wasn't anything clean enough to sit on. I was perspiring, and I took my hat off and found to my horror that it not only had collected a huge, dusty cobweb as I'd come through the door, but that the big greenish spider whose home I had ruined was now trying to burrow under the feathered band.

I threw the spider to the floor and stepped on it, cleaned my hat with my handkerchief and then, gathering my clothes about me like a woman Turkish-toweling her way out of a shower, I picked my way back through the composing room. "You must be crazy to wanta work here!" cried Mr. Martin. I went down the long hall. "You quittin' already?" cried Mr. Snodgrass. I went out through the front door and into the clean air and stood for a moment, breathing deeply.

I got into my beautiful yellow car and caught a glimpse of myself in the mirror. I had dark smudges all over the right side of my face and dirt streaks on the right shoulder of my coat. There were tears in my eyes and to this day I don't know whether they were from rage or just plain self-sympathy.

I drove home, hung up my fine clothes and used some cleaning fluid on the coat. I put on old slacks, an old football sweatshirt, worn tennis shoes and a battered old hat. I went to the cellar and got a bucket, mop, broom, dustpan, soap and a lot of old rags. Then I drove back to the M unt Kis o ecorder, Est. 1879, and spent the entire day cleaning up my office—my new home.

When I finished, the place looked quite presentable and I felt a little pride in my desk, my chair and my typewriter and table. But I found that with the window clean, the setting sun poured through with a glare that made the room seem as though it were on fire.

I stood on the desk and reached way up toward the ceiling for the huge, 8-foot shade, tightly rolled up over the top of the big window. I wiped the dust off it and saw it was white, but when I began to pull it down I discovered that the sun had bleached the outer roll of it and the shade was really green.

As I got off the desk, pulling the shade down, the brittle, bleached fabric fell apart, the stick came off in my hand, and the shade shot up with a clatter, leaped from its moorings and came crashing down on my toe. I yelled in agony and Mr. Snodgrass rushed in.

"You've ruined my shade," he shouted. Then he looked around the office and his eyes bugged out. "Good God!" he cried. "What happened here?"

I explained that I'd cleaned up a bit and I apologized for the shade. But, I said, I'd cut it off evenly, tack it back over the stick and it'd be as good as new.

"Well," he said, "that shade's been there for more'n twenty-five years and nobody *ever* fooled with it." He surveyed the office with distaste. I had pushed the desk and chair near the window, and I'd placed the table at right angles to the desk.

"Everything's moved around!" he said. "What was the matter the way it was? Everything's changed. Everything's different. I don't like changes. I don't like any kind of change at all."

He gave the room one more withering glance and turned and stalked out. I sat down in my creaky chair which tilted and nearly threw me over backwards. I put my feet on the desk, pulled my hat down over my eyes the way I'd seen Lee Tracy do in a newspaper movie, and grinned. "Mr. Snodgrass, maybe you don't like change," I said to myself, "but, boy, oh, boy, Mr. Snodgrass, I think you're gonna get it."

The following morning I presented myself to Mr. Snodgrass and asked for instructions. I had no idea of what he wanted me to get to put into the paper and no idea, either, of how to get it.

"Well," he said, "get the news from the police station and from the village clerk, and then there's a village board meeting tonight, and tomorrow night the board of education meets."

I got in my car—incidentally, I now was dressed in an old dark suit, a black English raglan coat with slash pockets that I'd inherited from a mystery show role in a stock company, and a fairly weather-beaten brown hat with a broad brim that I turned down all the way around—I must have looked like a cross between Sherlock Homes and Mike Hammer—and I drove to police headquarters.

There was an old fat, white-haired sergeant sitting at the desk when I entered and I walked up smartly and said, "I've come for the news." Without looking up, he said, "Kid, ya kin buy it at any newspaper store. Now scram."

I was, to say the least, quite hurt. Carefully, I explained to him that I was the new reporter from the Mount Kisco *Recorder* and that I had been authorized by my employer to get all the news that the police had, good, bad or indifferent.

The sergeant stared at me in amazement. Then he yelled, "Hey, Chief. C'mere. I want ya to see something."

In a moment, Police Chief Ed McCall walked in from his office and he too stared at me. "What do you want?" he asked.

"I'm a reporter . . ." I started.

Both the sergeant and the chief laughed and winked at each other.

". . . from the Mount Kisco *Recorder*," I finished.

At this, both men howled. They laughed and they roared and the chief clapped the sergeant on the back, and the sergeant put his head on his desk and laughed some more.

Eventually, however, Ed McCall (who later became one of my best friends) opened the record book and pointed out some of the hen scratching the policemen had put in it. I made notes, even though I understood little of what I was doing.

"Take what you want," said the chief, "but for the life of me, I don't know what you're gonna do with it. Lem Snodgrass

222

hasn't printed any news for years. Or if he has, I haven't seen it."

"And neither has anybody else," said the sergeant. And both men started laughing again. They were howling like mad and clutching each other as I got into my car and drove away.

Each morning for a week I went to the police station and copied everything I found in the book—arrests for drunkenness, auto accidents, fires, lost dogs, noise complaints and one assault and battery—and I wrote these things for the paper in just about the same language I found in the book.

Since most of the nine cops on the force hadn't got beyond the sixth grade, hardly anything I put in the paper was intelligible to my friends—all of whom began to read the paper out of curiosity, and strictly for laughs. It wasn't until my third or fourth week in the business that I finally began to "interpret" the police reports.

Meanwhile, I covered village board meetings, the board of education meeting, an American Legion meeting and an outdoor rally called to stamp out ragweed. And I wrote what I thought had gone on, although some of the speakers later told me I was wrong. I attended sessions of the PTA, Free Library, town board, Mount Kisco Garden Club and so on.

Dutifully, I wrote stories about everything I observed—stories of bewildering length—and Mr. Martin set them in type on the Linotype machine. Mr. Snodgrass put the type in the forms, and the stories came out and, all in all, I felt I was moving ahead.

There was only one thing that troubled me a good bit. That was money. At the end of my first week, Mr. Snodgrass said nothing about my $10 salary, and I was too polite to bring it up. Then another week slid by—lots more reporting, lots more writing—but again he said nothing about money.

By the end of the third week I was still unpaid and I was beginning to have doubts about the whole thing. Mr. Snodgrass went on bustling about the place each day, putting type in the forms, locking them up, doing a bit of job printing and such, but he never mentioned money. I consoled myself with the thought that maybe he paid only once a month.

I was getting so financially pinched that I couldn't buy gas for my car which consumed about a gallon every ten miles. I borrowed from friends, charged where I could, and bravely carried on. At the end of the fourth week, Mr. Snodgrass still failed to mention money and I got desperate. I went to Mr. Martin, who had turned out to be a lot more friendly than he was on that first day, even though he was convinced that I was crazy, and asked whether Mr. Snodgrass was in the habit of paying every two months, or every three months, or something like that.

"Hell, no," said Mr. Martin. "He won't pay at all, if he can get away with it. I *make* him pay me every week. Every Friday I tell him I won't be in Monday unless I get my money, and somehow he scrapes it up. Hasn't he paid you?"

I explained the situation and Mr. Martin got taken with a laughing fit. When he calmed down, he wiped his steel-rimmed eyeglasses and said, "Kid, the only thing for you to do is get tough with him. Go to him and demand your money. Get tough. Make him scared of you."

Thus advised and armed, I went down into the cellar where Mr. Snodgrass was tinkering with the unbelievably old, decrepit and cantankerous four-page, flatbed press. "Mr. Snodgrass," I said, my voice unaccountably rising to a high pitch, "I've worked for you for four weeks now, and you owe me forty dollars, and I need it very much, and may I have it now?"

He looked at me as though stricken. He dropped the hammer and the pliers with which he'd been attacking the press and the clatter rang through the stone-walled cellar like steel doors being clanged in a prison. Mr. Snodgrass gurgled and choked, and I could see he clearly felt I had gone mad.

"Money!" he roared. "You talk about *money? You*—just started in the business!"

I was a little frightened, particularly when he leaned over

and picked up the hammer, but I felt I hadn't made my situation clear. I explained that I didn't have enough money to buy gas for my car, that I had no money for food, that I couldn't afford to clean my clothes that had been all but ruined by contact with the greasy machines, the grubby makeup tables and the dirt-covered type fonts.

Mr. Snodgrass shook his head and sighed. He put down the hammer and reached out an ink-stained hand and took me by the arm. "There goes another jacket," I said to myself.

"Come with me," he said, grunting and snorting, and he led the way up the narrow, cobwebby, littered staircase, illuminated by a single 15-watt bulb. (Mr. Snodgrass always contended, irritably, that the staircase needed no light bulb, but that the fire department, wastefully, made him keep one there anyway.)

We went through the composing room, down the long front hall and into Mr. Snodgrass' private office. It was the first time I'd been invited in, and the décor all but overwhelmed me. I must have stood there in a state of shock for a full minute. The office, a room about 15 feet square, was crammed to the ceiling with stacks of ancient newspapers, magazines, boxes, cartons, bundles of old rags and old clothes, and hundreds of empty cigar boxes which he obviously had been saving for many years. Everything slept solidly under a thick blanket of dirt, dust and cobwebs.

I hadn't yet heard of the recluse, pack-rat Collyer brothers, but I can tell you that this was an office of which they would have been very proud indeed.

The wall to the right had a sort of opening in the stacks of junk, and in this little eddy stood Mr. Snodgrass' desk and chair. The chair was a thing of beauty, a swivel that once had been handsomely upholstered in leather. Now the leather, long since shredded like dried cod, hung in jagged strips. The seat had broken through and clumps of it were clinging to the screwlike post that held the upper portion of the chair to the legs at a jaunty 15-degree angle. Mr. Snodgrass had neatly filled the hole in the decayed seat with an assortment of dirty pillows, blankets, newspapers and bits of cardboard.

His roll-top desk was a W. C. Fields creation, almost invisible under the tremendous piles of papers, books, boxes and other odds and ends. It was obvious from the layers of dust that hardly anything on the desk had been touched for a decade or more, although some of the things on top, near the ceiling, had a little less dust, indicating they had been placed there more recently.

Mr. Snodgrass fished somewhere deep in the interior of the lower portion of this dust-adorned mountain. He stirred up a cloud which made both of us cough, and extracted a thin cigar box.

He opened it and, like a jack-in-the-box, up popped a great batch of dunning letters, please remits and FINAL notices. He lifted them out and placed them on the desk's only clear space, and there, on the bottom of the box, I saw some $1 bills. Mr. Snodgrass picked them up and began counting them out in two piles on the desk.

"One for you, one for me . . ." he said, laying down the bills. "Two for you, two for me . . ."

I watched him in disbelief, but he never looked at me. He went on counting: "Three for you, three for me. . . . Four for you, four for me. . . ." Then he stopped because he had counted out all eight bills. He picked up one pile of four bills, folded them and jammed them in his pants pocket. He handed me the other four dollars.

"There you are," he said. "Four for you, four for me. An even split. That's all I've got."

I really don't remember what I said and did. I was too numb for sensations to register. My first month in the newspaper business had netted me just $4. I took the money, and I think I mumbled my thanks, and I went out of the building and walked to my car. I wanted to get away, anywhere at all—but just get away. I got into the car, stepped on the starter and it whined and whined, but the motor didn't start. In a moment or so, I realized I was out of gas.

Still quite numb, I walked about a mile to the nearest garage and as I walked I debated what to do. My first inclination was to quit. But then I thought of how hard I'd worked that month, learning the newspaper business and getting to know which end was up. I'd begun to make contact with interesting people in all fields, and I enjoyed writing about them. In short, I already had printer's ink inside me, as well as on my clothes, and I was hooked.

I walked into the garage, intending to buy a can of gas, but instead I found myself saying to the proprietor, "How would you like to buy a nice, yellow Chrysler Imperial?"

Then I remembered that I really didn't own it, but after a bit of discussion, the garageman agreed to take over the rest of my obligation on the car, swap me a serviceable little fourth-hand Plymouth, and let me have what he called "forty dollars in walkin'-around money." Since I had only the four dollars and needed both walkin'-around money and *drivin'*-around money, I accepted.

I drove away in a daze, but I'd learned one of the cardinal rules that all newspapermen have to learn sooner or later—the rule of economy. I knew I'd have to cut down on all expenses. I estimated that I could support the Plymouth, but not the Chrysler of course, on whatever I might make from Mr. Snodgrass, but I also realized that something had to be done to get me more money than four dollars a month.

It was then that I decided to sell advertising. This seemed like a great idea at the moment, but when I sat down and tried to make a list of merchants to approach, I got the chills. I was well aware that not too many merchants thought much of the Mount Kisco *Recorder*.

However, I remembered my old friend Phillip Sussman, owner of the Mount Kisco movie theater—the man who had let me cuff my way in with Fonda and the young actresses—and so I went to him. I presented my proposition quite clearly, I thought, but I got a strange reaction.

Mr. Sussman sat down in his office chair and laughed and laughed. He mopped away the tears with a large handkerchief, and laughed and stamped his feet on the floor and slapped his thighs.

"Take an ad in the *Recorder!*" he cried, and he howled some more. "And I suppose you'd even have the nerve to ask money for it!"

I carefully explained to Mr. Sussman that the *Recorder* was about to be reborn, that I personally was going to put lots of news in it every week. I said that I would write his ad for him and see that it was set without more than three or four typographical errors, and that I was going to launch a circulation campaign so *some* people, at least, would read the ad.

"My boy," said Mr. Sussman, "why should I pay for an ad in the paper? Nobody else pays for any of the ads."

This staggered me. The paper carried quite a few ads, eight or nine of them on page one, and I had supposed they were paid for. "Nah," said Mr. Sussman. "I don't think anybody pays. Snodgrass carries those ads on an exchange basis. Like he's got the drugstore in there every week so he can get a soda at the counter each day—for free. And so on."

"Well," I said, evenly, "all that is over now. But you've got to help me. Will you be the first to take an ad—and pay for it?"

Mr. Sussman started to shake his head, but then he squinted at me and he began to laugh again. "Y'know," he said, "you might just do it! God, what an idea! Okay, I'll give you one ad a week. Make it just one column, about eight inches, and I want my complete week's billing in there. How much?"

Without batting an eye—or even knowing what advertising was worth—I said, "One dollar an inch. Total, eight dollars."

"Okay," said Mr. Sussman, and he gave me the eight dollars and a program from which to prepare the copy.

I was overjoyed and I couldn't wait to get to the office. I

found Mr. Snodgrass, splattered with ink, running the large job press. I yelled at him over the clatter and he stopped the press.

"Will you please come into my office?" I asked.

He looked surprised, but he followed me. I sat down in my chair, took out the eight dollar bills and counted them out in two piles on my desk. "One for you, one for me . . ." I said. "Two for you, two for me . . ."

Mr. Snodgrass' face was blank. "What's that for?" he said, picking up his four dollars.

"I sold an ad to the movie house," I said. "Eight bucks a week. Four for you, four for me."

"Now wait a minute," said Mr. Snodgrass, reddening. "It's all right if you want to sell an ad, but I give only ten percent commission."

"*Fifty* percent," I said. "An even split—like my salary."

"Twenty percent," said Mr. Snodgrass grimly.

"*Fifty* percent!" I said. "Take it or leave it."

Mr. Snodgrass debated for a long, long time, standing there, saying nothing. Then he looked at the four dollar bills and nodded his head.

"Now, Lem," I said, smiling pleasantly, "there's something else I want to tell you. Please sit down." (By then I had added a kitchen chair to the furnishings for the comfort of an occasional visitor.) Deliberately, I outlined my plan to Mr. Snodgrass—the tossing out of every ad that didn't pay!

He was, to put it mildly, thunderstruck. "I can't do that," he said. "Some of those ads have been in there for years. My father put some of those ads in there."

I picked up a copy of the paper and pointed to a large two-column ad on page one, extolling the virtues of the Mount Kisco Mattress Co. "Is this a paying ad?" I asked. "I never heard of that company."

Mr. Snodgrass squirmed a bit. "Well, no," he said. "The factory burned down about fifteen years ago."

"Then there is *no* Mount Kisco Mattress Company?" I cried.

"Nope," said Mr. Snodgrass, "but I keep their ad in 'cause I've got nothin' else to fill the space."

I nearly choked on that, and even Mr. Snodgrass could see that his reasoning had been something less than top-hole. He shrugged his shoulders.

I pointed to more ads—a company that advertised evergreen trees, and Mr. Snodgrass explained he was running the ad because six years before the company had given him some trees— A shoe store, and Mr. Snodgrass said that was where he got his shoes, and so on and on.

There were five or six stores that actually paid for their ads, but they paid so little that the sum was more of a contribution than a payment.

"Well, Lem," I said, "starting next week, we take out all the nonpaying ads, and gradually we'll replace them with the ads I sell. And we'll raise the rate for those stores that are now paying."

"They'll quit advertising entirely!" moaned Mr. Snodgrass.

"No, they won't," I said. "Not when they see how we're going to dress up the front page."

There was genuine alarm in Mr. Snodgrass' eyes. "Dress up the front page? What do you mean?"

I picked up the copy of the paper again and we both looked at it. There across the top of the paper was its title, MOUNT KISCO RECORDER, in great black capitals of about 120-point type. Then, under that, the paper's seven columns were filled with church notes, social notes, legal announcements, public notices, a column of ads down the left-hand side, and a batch of ads across the bottom.

There wasn't a single news story on page one (what stories we had were on inside pages) and there wasn't even one headline. The nearest things to headlines were one-liners, set in 10-point (the largest type on the Linotype) which read: PUBLIC NOTICES, CHURCH NOTES and SOCIAL NOTES. That was page one!

"From now on," I said, "we're going to have news stories on page one, and we'll push the churches and socials and like that, inside. And we're going to have big headlines on page one."

"We'll *never* have headlines on page one," cried Mr. Snodgrass. "My father never had 'em and his father never had 'em."

"We're going to have headlines," I said, quietly.

"That would mean tearing up the whole page and shifting things around," wailed Mr. Snodgrass. "And we'd have to set the headlines by hand. Haven't got any big type on the machine. That would be a hell of a lot of work!"

"Yes," I said.

Mr. Snodgrass jutted his jaw and glared at me. He looked pretty fierce and I thought he was going to punch me. I braced myself, but he just stood there. "NO headlines!" he yelled.

"All right," I said, "I quit! Give me back the four dollars and I'll give the eight back to Mr. Sussman. That's the end. I quit."

I got up and pulled my four dollars out of my pocket.

"Now, wait a minute," said Mr. Snodgrass, nervously hitching up his pants. "There's no need to quit."

His tongue flicked quickly over his lower lip and he grunted a couple of times. "We maybe . . ." he said, slowly, "we maybe could have . . . well . . . a couple of headlines a week. Probably wouldn't hurt *too* much."

"No, Lem," I said, with a smile, "we're going to have headlines on *every* story *every* week—from now on."

Mr. Snodgrass glared at me malevolently.

"All right, all right!" he shouted. "But *you'll* have to set 'em. You won't get any help from me!"

And he turned and stalked out of the office.

Chapter Fifteen

FOR quite a few minutes after Mr. Snodgrass left my office I just sat there grinning and basking in the warmth of victory. I felt absolutely certain that I'd be able to completely rebuild the *Recorder,* change its whole mode of existence and brighten it to the point where it would compete with all other papers.

I saw myself throwing away the old title at the top of page one: MOUNT KISCO RECORDER, which was too large and too black and etched with scraggly white lines where scratches in the type made it impssible for the ink to smoothly cover the whole letter. I wanted to replace it with a specially drawn title which would look something like the title of *The New York Times.*

And I envisioned a sparkling page one, filled with one-, two- and three-column headlines, a seven-column streamer headline over all, and two, three or four pictures, preferably of pretty girls. I planned headlines for the inside pages, too, lots of pictures and live, well-designed advertisements. Little did I know what a task I was undertaking. It would have been easier to have cut a tunnel through the Rock of Gibraltar with a dentist's drill.

But I wasted no more time in launching my program. I got out a piece of paper and drew up a dummy—or layout—for the following week's front page. It was the worst layout ever prepared for any newspaper anywhere, but it had ten headlines and I was very proud of it.

In the next seven or eight weeks, we threw out all the junk ads and replaced them with dozens of ads that I sold in what I laughingly called my "spare time," time that I found between covering police, fire, village affairs, politics, school boards, weddings, parties, plays and a thousand other things.

It was a seven-days-a-week operation, 10 to 15 hours a day. And Mr. Snodgrass fought me seven days a week, 10 to 15 hours a day. I thought he was going to have a heart attack when I took the first dead ad and broke it up, putting the type back into the fonts.

"That ad's been in the paper for at least fifteen years," he said angrily. "And what's the good in taking it out now?"

"I want to replace it with a live ad," I said. "A paying ad."

"Well, put the live ad on top of the other one," yelled Mr. Snodgrass. "No need to break up an ad that's already set."

"Can't do that, Lem," I said. "That would cut down on the space available for news."

"Well, then, don't put the news in," said Mr. Snodgrass.

In time, however, after all the junk ads had been eliminated, he seemed quite satisfied and he never mentioned the subject again. He did, however, continue the war along other lines—almost every line I took.

"I'll NEVER permit a picture on page one," he told me the week that I ran a picture on page one.

"I'll NEVER permit a seven-column streamer on page one," he told me the week I ran a seven-column streamer on page one.

"I'll NEVER permit a story about a divorce on page one," he told me the week I ran a story about a divorce on page one.

And so it went. He fought me when I raised my salary to $25. He fought bitterly when I stopped mailing the paper to people who hadn't paid. And he fought me powerfully and successfully when I tried to buy a less-scarred title for the top of page one.

"That's been there as long as I can remember," he roared, "and it's gonna stay there." And stay there it did till the paper's death during World War II.

Mr. Snodgrass was one of the most eccentric men I've ever met but, truth to tell, I became very fond of him. I began to like his eccentricities and the little games he played to try to trick me into giving up a project. And I even enjoyed it when he blew up a storm over one of my changes or ideas, raged and ranted around the shop, and then calmed down and said something like, "Well, all right. Have it your way. I'll not interfere. But do it yourself. You'll get no help from me."

Then, trickily, he'd try to circumvent me. A good example of how he operated came when he fought my plan to stop mailing the paper to the non-pays. He argued for two or three weeks, then gave in. I suspected something, of course, and one night about midnight I returned to the office after covering a show and, instead of going to my own desk, I went down into the basement.

There, in the light of a single dim bulb, stood Mr. Snodgrass, running papers for the unpaid people through a stamping device which contained galleys of their names and addresses. I said nothing, but the next day when he was out I threw away all the type containing the names and addresses.

Mr. Snodgrass was violently angry when he discovered this, and he tried another tack. Unbeknownst to me, he'd sit in his living room late at night (he had an apartment on the second floor of the building) and address the papers by hand. He wrapped the papers in newsprint and then scratched the names and addresses on the wrappers in the purple ink that he used for all correspondence.

I found out about this, however, when I went to the post office one day and the postmaster invited me into his office. He pointed to a pile of about 500 *Recorders*, all scribbled with purple ink, and said, "You can't send stuff like that through the mail. The handwriting is so terrible we can't make out the names or the addresses."

I took the papers back to the *Recorder* and, while Mr. Snodgrass was in the composing room, I piled them neatly on his desk, his chair and in the little open area around the chair, and I placed a note on top of the pile:

> Lem, these papers were returned by the post office because the addresses are undecipherable. If the subscriptions are paid, let's run them through the addressing machine.
>
> NORTON

I never heard another word about it, and from then on, people who didn't pay didn't get the paper. Meanwhile, I had a score of boys out selling and delivering the paper—they got prizes and a percentage of their sales (Mr. Snodgrass fought me on this, too!) —and the circulation rose to 1,700—all paid.

In time, Mr. Snodgrass came to tolerate nearly everything I wanted to do. One of the few things, however, that I simply couldn't get him to agree to was either to modernize or replace the unbelievably decrepit flatbed press. This monstrous thing, of uncertain vintage, clanked and crashed and shook and groaned until I was certain it would fall into a thousand pieces. But Mr. Snodgrass, a good mechanic, somehow kept it running.

It was driven by, of all things, a gasoline-powered motor. I doubt that, then or now, any publisher in the country operated on a flatbed newspaper press driven by a *gasoline* motor.

There were no advantages to using a gasoline motor, and at least twenty disadvantages. The worst was that it gave off smoke and fumes so dense that we coughed and choked and cried a lot. And I was afraid we'd both die of carbon monoxide poisoning. Even on the coldest day in winter, I had to insist that we keep all doors and windows open. And we worked in the basement wearing overcoats, mufflers, wool stocking caps, galoshes and gloves.

The other really big disadvantage was that the motor, unlike an electrical unit, often would sputter, die down and then roar back into action with a tremendous jerk. This put a severe strain on the 10-inch-wide, old leather belts that ran up from the machine, across the ceiling and down onto the big wheel that drove the press.

When these belts suffered so sudden a strain, the rivets that Mr. Snodgrass had painstakingly installed to hold them together often gave way or ripped through the decaying leather. Then 30 to 40 feet of heavy leather belting would whiplash through the air, flapping and flailing and damn near decapitating anybody who happened to be in the way.

After the first crack on the head that I suffered, I always took up my station on the opposite side of the press, where I could rescue the papers from the creaky old, canvas-tape paper-folding machine (another monstrosity if ever I saw one) in comparative safety.

But Mr. Snodgrass, whose duty it was to feed the sheets of newsprint onto the barrel-like cylinder which rolled down and pressed the paper against the pages of type, had to stand on a platform high up on the flatbed, directly under the leather straps. Whenever one snapped, it was almost certain to get him.

Time and again he got whapped on the head and shoulders, and once, just as I happened to glance up at him, I saw a belt writhe through the air, wrap around him cobralike, lift him from his perch and toss him headfirst to the floor. He landed in a pile of mailbags and was relatively unhurt. I suggested that thereafter he lash himself to the press so he wouldn't be hurled through the air. "Yeah, and get my head cut off!" he growled, looking at me as though I were trying to do away with him.

And in those very early days there was one other great disadvantage in using a gasoline motor. That was that its tank had to be filled with gasoline. Gas cost 17 cents a gallon at that time, and there were Fridays when neither of us had 17 cents.

Upon occasions like that, I'd be put in the embarrassing position of having to go out on the street and search for a friend who would lend me the cash. This annoyed the hell out of me because I felt it damaged my image both as a distinguished journalist and a suave advertising salesman.

On those days I was especially bitter toward Mr. Snodgrass, and I kept snarling, "Buy an electric motor on the installment plan, buy an electric motor on the installment plan . . ." I'd keep it up until he'd stalk out of the basement in search of some peace and quiet. But he never bought a new motor.

He won other little wars too, but the biggest one—the one in which he outsmarted me—had to do with my income. Just four months after I started selling advertising, Mr. Snodgrass talked me out of keeping 50 percent of everything I took in.

In one of his more impassioned and eloquent speeches, he pointed out that, even though my sales were pulling him out of the hole, putting some money in his pocket and permitting him to start dining out with a girl he'd been courting for some thirty-five years, it was he, and he alone, who had to pay the expenses of maintaining the plant. He had to pay Mr. Martin and buy paper, ink and other supplies. Therefore, he argued, wouldn't I reconsider our arrangement and give him a little more money?

I solved this, neatly, I thought, by saying that thereafter we'd

237

deduct all business expenses first, and then split 50-50. And we did this for months, but I still have the feeling that there was an inequitable element.

My income dropped sharply, of course, but I was quite surprised some weeks when it got down to only $10 or $15 over my basic weekly salary of $25. I asked Mr. Snodgrass about this and he said that business expenses had been unusually heavy. And he quickly brought out the books he kept in which to record all purchases and payments.

Proudly, he turned over the pages of the ledgers, showing me hundreds of items all written in purple ink, detailing, he said, just what everything cost and to whom it had been paid. I studied those books, and studied them and restudied them, but for the life of me I couldn't make out more than two or three words he'd written. And when I asked him what the other words were, he puzzled over them too and mumbled that the damn ink had smudged so much that he couldn't really tell me.

Finally, I found I was wasting far too much time on the accounting and I just gave it up. Mr. Snodgrass had won again.

While Mr. Snodgrass and I incessantly argued about everything in connection with the *Recorder*, from headlines to pictures to expenses and even to who got the passes to the movies, he never once during all the time I was on the paper said anything, pro or con, about my writing.

In all the books and magazine articles I'd read, and in the plays and films I'd seen, editors always were editing, rewriting or killing reporters' stories. Mr. Snodgrass, however, never edited, rewrote or killed anything of mine. In fact, I'm not sure he even *read* anything I wrote.

I'm the first to admit that many of the stories I turned out in those days were pretty dreadful things indeed. In the first months on the *Recorder* I had no idea how to put together a news story and I frequently wrote everything chronologically, which gave the reader scores of paragraphs to plow through before he came upon the big fight at the village board meeting, or the homicide on Maple Avenue.

But the cruelest blow came the day I asked Mr. Snodgrass about something to do with a local story and he gave me information which I recognized immediately to be wrong. And this error had been made in the rival weekly newspaper's account! It was then I realized that Mr. Snodgrass not only didn't read my stories, but depended for his knowledge on the opposition!

In time, largely due to the kindness and guidance of an experienced reporter on that opposition paper, Mr. Alvin Mills, I got a grip on news reporting technique and things became a bit more intelligible.

In addition to reporting, selling advertising and fighting with Mr. Snodgrass, I set all the headlines by hand and put them in the forms, stacked the type from the Linotype machine beneath it in the proper places, locked up the forms, carried them to the dumbwaiter and lowered them to the basement, where Mr. Snodgrass put them on the press.

I learned to run the Linotype machine—albeit slowly—and time and again when Mr. Martin was otherwise occupied or recovering from what he described as "weekend madness," I set many of my own stories on the Lino. I also learned to make up the job presses and run them so I could help out when we were printing tickets, programs, contracts or letterheads. But running a job press is the most boring thing in the world, and I avoided it whenever I could.

Another important part of my job was the handling of the items sent in by anywhere from 10 to 15 special correspondents in surrounding villages. These reporters, mostly elderly ladies who knew everybody in their towns, provided us with what Mr. Snodgrass called "personal intelligence." And that's how their columns were headed—until I came along.

Not one of these ladies knew how to write, professionally that is, but they were getting 10 cents an inch for this "personal intelligence" and they were remarkably adept at padding their paragraphs.

For instance, if the lady who handled the social items from Bedford Village wanted to tell the world that Mr. and Mrs.

Jack Smith entertained Mr. and Mrs. William Wilson on Saturday night, she usually wrote:

> Mr. and Mrs. Jack Smith, of Craven Avenue, who only six months ago returned from a delightful trip to Miami, Florida, where they and Mr. and Mrs. Charles Johnson, who used to live eight miles north of here, went to visit a lot of friends in that southern city, including Mrs. William Wentworth, the widow of the Mr. Wentworth who owned the Central Produce store in Bedford Hills until he died, entertained at a party in their spacious home on Saturday night. Their guests were Mr. and Mrs. William Wilson of Mount Kisco, who last year toured through Europe with their four children, Mary Jane, Sue Ellen, Jonathan and Charles, and visited many countries including England, Ireland, Scotland, France and Germany, and who are planning another trip next year, probably to Canada or maybe to Mexico. Delicious food was delightfully served.

These items, and there were hundreds of them, took a little editing, as you can see. This I did, most laboriously. Mr. Snodgrass never objected to my shortening and tightening these items because it was saving him quite a bit of money. But the *ladies* objected. They howled at me over the phone and once in a while one of them would come in and upbraid me. One lady of about seventy-five rapped sharply on my desk with the handle of her umbrella and informed me that if I touched her copy again, she'd rap sharply on my head.

But the dean of our staff of "personal intelligence" columnists was a tiny, bent, henna-haired lady whom I shall call Mrs. Henry J. Dempster. She was the Mount Kisco "personal intelligence" columnist and her efforts put all the other correspondents to shame.

Mrs. Dempster could write longer than anybody. She could get more names into a story—one of her ploys was to mention all the relatives of the person she was writing about, and then mention all the relatives of the relatives!—and she could get more stories into her column concerning what was really a single story than anybody else.

Her column might include something like this (after editing, that is) : "Mr. and Mrs. John Golden entertained Mr. and Mrs. Howard Sampson at dinner Tuesday night."

"Mr. and Mrs. Howard Sampson visited Mr. and Mrs. John Golden for dinner on Tuesday night."

And each week (once again highly edited down), she'd have these items about herself:

"Mrs. Henry J. Dempster of Kisco Avenue entertained Mr. and Mrs. Marvin Smith of Kisco Avenue at dinner on Wednesday night."

"Mr. and Mrs. Marvin Smith of Kisco Avenue entertained Mrs. Henry J. Dempster of Kisco Avenue at dinner on Thursday night."

They lived right across the street from each other, and saw each other every day.

Mrs. Dempster had several other strings to her bow, as she would have said. She was, primarily, a classicist. Nobody who appeared in her items, and there were many, ever served refreshments or cookies or punch. Her items always concluded with: "Delicious comestibles were delightfully served."

And Mrs. Dempster was an amateur theatrical director. She staged plays like *Up in Mabel's Room* at the American Legion Hall, church pageants, patriotic extravaganzas and passable renditions of *Getting Gertie's Garter*.

She reviewed these shows herself: Every one was a smash hit. Never before had there been anything like it in Mount Kisco, or anywhere for that matter. And never had any direction been more superb. A typical review, written by Mrs. Henry J. Dempster, under the byline of Mrs. Henry J. Dempster, started like this:

Mrs. Henry J. Dempster directed a magnificent production of "Up in Mabel's Room" last Saturday night at the Legion Hall. Folks said it was the finest directed show they ever saw and they paid high compliments to Mrs. Dempster who has a long string of successful shows to her credit. This remarkable woman will be doing a lot of shows in the near future, so watch this paper for announcements about Mrs. Dempster.

Mrs. Dempster had been an actress and, when opportunity offered, she was willing to leap into one of her own superbly directed shows. And once, writing about the fact that she'd played one of the characters, she said: "Mrs. Dempster not only directed the show with better-than-Broadway skill, but also took a roll [*sic*] for herself in the third act."

Mrs. Dempster and I had many a heart-to-heart, but nothing that I said—or that she readily agreed to—changed her copy one bit. It just went on and on until this spirited lady, who was in her eighties, died of old age. And then we found that she'd written her own obit. I don't have to tell you how it started!

Somewhere along the line during the two years and six months that I spent at the Mount Kisco *Recorder*, I began to yearn for better things. And so, one night after attending a local Boosters' Club dinner, a village board meeting, an Italian block party on South Moger Avenue, and a dance at the Masonic Hall, I returned to my office, typed out my stories and then wrote a long, fervent and enormously detailed letter to B. O. McAnney, the city editor of the New York *World-Telegram*.

I told Mr. McAnney quite fully what I had achieved in Mount Kisco, what I had failed to achieve because of lack of cooperation from the publisher, and I outlined copiously what I believed I could do for the *World-Telegram* if Mr. McAnney would give me a job.

I think I also threw in a menacing line to the effect that if the Scripps-Howard *World-Telegram* wouldn't or couldn't take me right away, I probably would have to join the Hearst organization in New York, but I pointed out that, at that moment anyway, I preferred Scripps-Howard.

The letter I received from Mr. McAnney was, I thought, a gem of brevity. It read:

DEAR MR. MOCKRIDGE,

This is to thank you for your letter of application for employment here, and to tell you that at the moment there are no vacancies on the staff.

However, even if there were, I feel that your lack of experience would not warrant giving you a tryout. Why not get in touch with me again in about five years?

Sincerely,

B. O. McANNEY, City Editor.

PS—Acheivement is better spelled achievement.

This was quite a blow! (I didn't know then, of course, that Burnett Olcott McAnney, city editor and later managing editor of the *World-Telegram,* eventually would engage me and groom me for the city editorship of the *World-Telegram* which was given to me by the executive editor, Lee B. Wood, on February 22, 1956.) I didn't like that Mr. McAnney at all, and I decided to present my great talent to someone else.

Sort of jolted by the New York reaction to my readiness to conquer, I brought my sights a little lower. I looked south of Mount Kisco, about 16 miles, to the city of White Plains, county seat of Westchester. And there was the *Daily Reporter,* a fine, prospering newspaper of about 10,000 circulation. And it was a *daily!*

So I wrote to the city editor, Milton Harker, and told him that I had spurned innumerable offers from New York and that I'd like to be a member of his staff. Mr. Harker's reply was about as brief as Mr. McAnney's but infinitely more pleasing.

"Dear Mr. Mockridge," it read. "We have no openings on the staff at the moment. However, if you are interested in helping to cover northern Westchester for us on an assignment or stringer basis—we pay 10 cents an inch for whatever is published—please give me a ring."

I gave Mr. Harker a ring and within a day or so I was the northern Westchester correspondent, or stringer, for the White Plains *Daily Reporter.* I couldn't have been more excited.

Mr. Snodgrass didn't like this at all. "Here I am, paying you for working for me, and then you're going to give all the news to that daily paper down there," he said. "They'll run me out of business!"

I explained that first of all, I'd give only a relatively few stories a week to the *Reporter*; secondly, that if *I* didn't cover the stories the *Reporter* wanted, they'd send a reporter up to our area or get another stringer; and thirdly, the *Reporter* circulated only a few copies in northern Westchester and not at all in Mount Kisco and so how could they run the *Recorder* out of business?

"Nevertheless," said Mr. Snodgrass grimly, "they'll do it."

Within a few days, I fell into the pattern that most stringers adopt. Whenever I came across a story that I thought might interest Mr. Harker and the other editors of the *Reporter*, I telephoned them (collect) and outlined it.

If they wanted it, they took what facts I had and/or authorized me to go out and get additional facts. In addition, whenever anything was taking place in the northern part of the county that they were interested in, they'd call me and direct me to get the story. And they paid me for what appeared in the *Reporter*, plus expenses. This was a nice arrangement inasmuch as I was covering 90 percent of the stories for the *Recorder* anyway, and so made quite a lot more money merely by making phone calls.

I got to know most of the reporters and rewrite men on the *Reporter* telephonically, although I never had seen anybody but Mr. Harker, and I had my favorites. Some of the men—one in particular, Denslow Dade, who later went with the New York *Herald Tribune*—were wonderful to talk to. There was only one man with whom I had any trouble. His name was William L. J. O'Donovan and this is what happened.

Mr. O'Donovan had taken my calls occasionally, and he'd been a bit more acid than the others. I, I have no doubt, had returned the acid a little. And so, one day when I was phoning in some hastily gathered details about a big fire, Mr. O'Donovan turned on the pressure.

"Is that all you've got about a big fire like this?" he yelled over the phone. "Why, the lousiest cub would have found out more than this before he called in!"

I tried to explain that I'd just been informed of the fire, had had only a quick look at it, and had raced to a phone because

I knew the *Reporter* was just about to get out its second and last edition and I wanted the paper to have whatever I had at the moment. "I'll go back and get more if you want," I said.

"The hell with that," roared Mr. O'Donovan. "If you haven't got it now, it'll be too late. We lock up in six minutes."

I then told Mr. O'Donovan what I thought of his criticism, he told me what he thought of my reporting, I told him where I thought he should go, and he told me what he thought of my ancestors.

All in all, it was quite unpleasant. And the following day, I phoned Mr. Harker, told him what had transpired, and said that in the future I'd appreciate it if, when delivering a story by phone, I'd be connected with anybody but Mr. O'Donovan. In fact, I said, rather deliberately, I would have to refuse to deal with Mr. O'Donovan in any way in the future.

"I'll tell him," said Mr. Harker, "and hereafter you'll get Dade or one of the other men."

Mr. Harker did tell Mr. O'Donovan, as I learned from some of the other reporters, and, apparently, there was a rather acrimonious exchange.

Anyway, a few weeks later Mr. Harker called me and asked whether I'd be interested in giving up the correspondent's job and taking a regular job as a staff reporter. He said he would pay me $35 a week to start, which was anywhere from $10 to $30 less than I was making as a combined *Recorder* reporter and *Reporter* correspondent, but I decided to accept.

I had spent the two years and six months with Mr. Snodgrass, and, as I think back on it, they perhaps were the most exciting years of my life, but I felt I wasn't getting anywhere. Many big city newspapermen I know keep telling me that they long for the day when they can retire from big-city tension and operate "a li'l ole country weekly somewhere out in the hills." But as far as I am concerned, they can have it. It's not for me.

Speaking as a newspaperman who started at the top as the editor of a weekly (I was the only steady editorial employee, so I called myself editor), and who worked himself down to a columnist, I can tell you that a seven-day-a-week, 15-hour-a-day routine ain't nothing to comfort you in your old age.

In fact, it didn't even comfort me in my *young* age. So, at the advanced maturity of twenty-one, I said yes to Mr. Harker and then went and told Mr. Snodgrass that I was leaving in two weeks.

"Where ya goin'?" he demanded.

"I'm going to be a reporter for the White Plains *Daily Reporter*," I said.

"I told you no good would come of you stringin' for that paper," he exploded. "They're tryin' to run me out of business. What the hell do you want to work for them for?"

"Well," I said, "I want to work for a daily, and then, in time, I want to go with a big New York City paper, probably the *World-Telegram*."

"I never heard anything so damn foolish in all my life!" he spluttered. "Fleshpots! That's what those papers are! Fleshpots!"

He got up from his chair and shook his finger at me.

"Let me tell you something," he shouted, "if you go with those papers, you'll never amount to a goddam thing."

And that—I think—was Mr. Snodgrass' way of saying, "Goodbye and good luck."

Well, the next two weeks were sort of difficult, with Mr. Snodgrass refusing to speak to me or even acknowledge that I was in the plant, and Mr. Martin getting a little loaded every afternoon "just by way of celebration—thank God somebody's got enough sense to get out of here!" and people dropping in to say good-bye, and everybody bringing something to drink, and the type getting all mixed up and some of the stories getting lost, and I'd say it wasn't a period in which I did my best work.

However, on my last Friday night some of my friends gave a series of little parties for me. Mayor Harry P. Blackeby presented me with a gold key to the village of Mount Kisco (I think it was the key to somebody's barn that he'd had gilded);

Virgil Banks, the superintendent of highways, gave me a typed sheet of paper that entitled me to "a free ride on any village sanitation or dump truck upon any occasion"; and Rockwell Matthews, the village clerk, gave me a certificate that said if ever I owned any property in Mount Kisco, I could have one day's grace in paying the taxes.

My buddy, David Niss, gave a party for me in the Royal Restaurant, where everybody ate huge mounds of French fried potatoes drowned in catsup and, because Prohibition was ended, consumed quite a lot of spirits. Several other friends had impromptu gatherings in their houses, at which more booze was served, and here and there a lot of pals got to weeping about my departure and some of them sobbed openly on my shoulder.

"Good luck in the big city," they said. "We always knew you'd go to the big city sooner or later. You'll be a big success. Nothing between you and New York now, except White Plains. You'll go on to Washington, maybe to London, to Paris, to Rome. Maybe you'll be President some day."

Well, it was all pretty heady, and I was happy. Ted Martin wrapped his arms around me and said, "Kid, from the day I met you, I knew you wouldn't last here. You ain't got the guts. So go off to the big city and ruin your life. What the hell do you care about your friends here, friends who've sweated for you, died for you, friends who . . ."

And then he sat down and cried.

It was quite a send-off, and after I'd rested under ice packs all weekend, I got into my car on Monday morning and drove to White Plains. I entered the Daily Reporter Building, walked through the downstairs business office, mounted the stairs to the second floor, walked over to Mr. Harker's desk, smiled at him and said, "Good morning, sir. I am here."

"So I see," said Mr. Harker wryly. I think he wanted to add: "I just hope we'll measure up."

He took me aside then, and explained that he was firing a man whom we'll call Tommy Denson for a series of incidents involving some pretty heavy drinking. "However," he said, "this Denson is a hell of a nice guy and he's volunteered to take you out on his beat and show you around. He's a little drunk, but I'm sure he can show you the ropes."

He introduced me to Denson, a good-looking, balding chap about ten years older than I, who was, indeed, pretty well tanked. He sat there at his typewriter, hat on the back of his head, lids lowering over his bloodshot eyes and said, "What you wanna work here for, I'll never know. But what the hell, it's your own funeral."

He wasn't being nasty. He merely was stating a fact from his point of view. He got up, pulled down his sweater and put on his coat. It was then he noticed that he was wearing two ties. The ends of both, a blue and a brown, were peeping out beneath the sweater.

Tommy tugged at the blue one. It didn't respond. He then tugged at the brown one and, inch by inch, he pulled it out.

"Put this one on this morning," he said, slurring his words. "Must've forgot I had the other one on."

"I gather you didn't undress last night," I said.

"Haven't undressed for a week," he said. "A week, at leas'." He leaned forward, smiled at me, winked and added, "Been on a little bender. Thas why I got fired."

Tommy and I went downstairs and he told me that he'd show me the beat—the villages and towns of Scarsdale, Elmsford, Greenburgh and Tarrytown.

"You got a car?" he asked. I said yes. "Well, then drive me, and we'll pick up mine," he said.

He directed me to a nice residential area on the outskirts of town and when we came to a graveled driveway which had a small metal sign reading JUDGE GOLDSTEIN, he said, "Go in there. Lef' my car here las' night. Or, anyway, I think it was las' night."

Tommy was right. He had, indeed, left his car there. I was staggered when I saw it. The front end of it was on the gravel courtyard in the rear of the house, the middle of it rested on a stone retaining wall, and the rear wheels were hanging over a formal garden ten feet below.

"Nearly went over the wall," said Tommy, laughing and rubbing his hands together. "Backin' around, and didn't see the wall. Nearly went over. Les' see if we can pull her off."

I got a chain from the trunk of my car, fastened it to the front end of Tommy's car and, gunning the engine, tried to drag the Chevrolet coupe off the wall. It never moved. I gunned the engine again—and stripped my clutch! So, we had to call for a wrecker which lifted the Chevvy off the wall and towed my car to a garage for the installation of a new clutch.

The rest of the day was a nightmare. We drove around in Tommy's car, stopping successively at the Scarsdale police station, a bar, the Scarsdale village hall, a bar, the Elmsford police station, two bars, Elmsford village clerk's office, a bar, Greenburgh police station, a bar, Tarrytown police station, two bars, various offices of various officials, various bars, and, here and there, the homes of friends of Tommy's who, hospitably, fed us booze.

By the time we got back to the office that night—actually, I got back in Tommy's car; he'd gone to the Court Bar and Grill and fallen asleep on a banquette—Mr. Harker looked at me most suspiciously. I'm sure he didn't know whether he'd hired an improvement or not.

Anyway, he took me to an inner office where we could talk without being heard and said, "As I told you, I fired Denson and hired you. But the editor of this paper, Walter V. Hogan, is vacationing in Florida and I did it without consulting him. So this morning I sent him a wire which read, 'Fired Denson. Hired Mockridge. All is well.' Just a couple of hours ago, I got this telegram from Hogan."

He handed me the yellow piece of paper and I read:

DO NOT FIRE DENSON. DO NOT HIRE MOCKRIDGE. ALL IS NOT WELL.

I was chilled, and if I'd had a slight alcoholic edge when I entered the office a few minutes ago, I didn't have it anymore.

"What . . . what . . . does this mean?" I quavered.

"It means a showdown," said Mr. Harker. "When Hogan went south he told me I was running this shop. And now that I do something, he tells me I'm not. Well, I'm not gonna work for a guy like that. Here's what I wired back."

He handed me the carbon of another telegram. It read:

DENSON STAYS FIRED. MOCKRIDGE STAYS HIRED. OR I QUIT.

I never had felt so terrible in my life. Here I was causing all this trouble for a man I admired so much, a man who was opening for me the gateway to the great life. And who was going to suffer for having done it.

"What . . . what do you think Mr. Hogan will say?" I asked.

"Damned if I know," said Mr. Harker. "But I mean what I say. Either my decisions stand, or I go."

"Well, what . . . what . . . should I do?" I asked.

"Nothing, right now," he said. "Go on home and get a good night's sleep. You look as if you need it. And come in tomorrow morning at eight."

Numbly, I said good night, and I left the building, got into Tommy's car and drove to the garage that was repairing my Plymouth. They lent me another car to drive home in.

All the way home I suffered as I'd never suffered before. Suppose I was fired? What would my friends say? Here they'd given me all those wonderful parties, said so many kind things, expressed so many big hopes. And now, after only one day in the big city, I was fired. A failure. A has-been before I'd even started.

I'd like to be able to claim that I didn't sleep that night, but the truth is, I slept solidly. So solidly that I didn't hear my alarm clock, and my mother had to come to my room to wake me up.

I told her nothing of the mess I was in and, after a good breakfast, I got into my borrowed car and tooled off for White Plains.

My heart was pounding as I went into the building and up

the stairs. As I approached the door to the city room, every instinct told me that calamity waited inside. I pushed open the door and walked in.

Some changes had been made.

Mr. Harker was nowhere to be seen.

Sitting at the desk to which I had been assigned the day before was Tommy Denson. He was typing furiously. His hat was on the back of his head, he was wearing only one tie, and he was sober!

My eyes then lifted and swung to the left. There at the desk at which Mr. Harker habitually sat—the city editor's desk—was my nemesis—William L. J. O'Donovan!

I froze on the threshold. I wanted to turn and run. I wanted to yell. I wanted to do something—but I didn't know what to do.

In a moment or so, I found myself walking slowly over to Mr. O'Donovan.

"Good morning," I said. "Mr. Harker told me to report at eight."

"Mr. Harker," said Mr. O'Donovan, "is no longer here. *I* am the city editor now."

Chapter Sixteen

THE stillness in the city room of the *Daily Reporter* was so oppressive that I hardly dared breathe. I was afraid it would make a shattering sound. Everybody had stopped work. Everybody was staring at O'Donovan and me—George Cummins, the assistant city editor; Courtney B. Mabee, the sports editor; Denslow Dade, Tommy Denson, Theresa Flintoft, the society editor, and her assistant, Libby Craig, white-haired old Ella Housefield Lowe and perhaps ten other staffers I didn't even know.

Mr. O'Donovan, red-faced and prematurely gray, stared at me over the tops of his rimless glasses, and his clear blue eyes were cold, cold, cold.

"Well," I said, in a shaky voice that seemed to reverberate through the room, "my congratulations to you. Ah . . . well, I'll be going now."

I turned to say good-bye to Denson and take my leave when Mr. O'Donovan spluttered a bit and said, "Where are you going?"

"Home, I guess," I said. "Mr. Harker showed me the telegram from Mr. Hogan. He doesn't want me hired."

"Hmmmm," said Mr. O'Donovan. "But since Milt Harker's gone and I've moved up, that leaves a vacancy on the staff. So I'd like to have you stay—if you want to."

He grinned in a boyish way and all the antagonism I'd ever felt for him melted instantly. I liked him enormously and I knew we'd grow to be the best of friends—which we did, and are to this day.

"Oh, thank you, sir," I said. "Thank you so much. I want to stay more than anything in the world. I love this paper, and I love everybody here and I . . . well . . . I just want to be one of you."

Applause broke out all over the room and I turned and smiled at all the reporters. Old Ella Housefield Lowe, practically blind and bent way over, really unable to work anymore, got up from her chair and came over to me. She took my hand and said, "Goldie, that was a fine speech. One of the finest I ever heard. We're glad to have you with us."

(I didn't know it then, but I discovered in a day or so that she had decided to call me "Goldie" because when she'd first seen me I was sitting in sunlight streaming through the window and, to her dim eyes, the sun transformed my reddish-blond hair into a crown of gold. "Goldie," she used to say, "I like it when you're sitting there in the window with the sun on your hair." Then she'd muss my hair and go back to her desk. What she'd say today if she could see the sunlight on my bare scalp, I cannot imagine.)

There was some more applause after Miss Lowe's little speech and Mr. O'Donovan, clearing his throat several times, said, "All right, all right, we've got a paper to get out today. So let's try to do a little work."

He then asked me if I knew Tommy's beat well enough to go

it alone and when I said I thought so, he sent me off. It was one of the proudest moments of my life. I was working for a DAILY and I was on my own!

I had expected that I'd meet lots of fascinating characters as I made my daily rounds, and I surely did. There was an aging police chief who was drunk all day and who once lost his service revolver; there was a big, fat, jolly surrogate who always was the life of the party, but who got his affairs so mixed up that one night he walked off the top of Kensico Dam, on the dry side, and crashed to his death on the plaza far below.

And there was the town supervisor who hardly ever attended meetings of the Board of Supervisors but who got reelected time and again merely because he always gave the biggest and best clambakes and cocktail parties; there was an assistant district attorney who got and held his job because he was a fine tennis player and was willing to give lessons to his chief; there was a judge who was so blotto most of the time that his law clerk made the decisions and wrote all of the judge's opinions; there was a socially elect, middle-aged ladies' club president who, whenever the moon was full, loved to take off all her clothes and dance on the lawn; and there was a town cop known as "Wild Bill" who got his kicks by going into bars and lunch wagons late at night and shooting the clocks, bottles and glassware with his .38.

There were many, many more, and I enjoyed them all, but much to my surprise I found that my newspaper associates were infinitely more entertaining.

Tommy Denson, of course, was always good for a laugh. He had his spells of sobriety when, unfortunately, he was rather dull, but when he was a bit tanked, he was one of the most amusing and engaging fellows alive.

One night, for instance, I parked my brand-new Studebaker behind his car in the driveway of a friend's house and went in to the party. Seeing the condition Tommy was in, I warned him several times that I'd parked in back of him and urged him to go forward when he left and drive out the other end of the driveway.

Fifteen minutes later there was a terrible crash outside. Tommy had backed right into my front fenders and headlights. Yessir, a laugh every minute!

One night at a party Bill O'Donovan gave at his farm some 20 miles north of White Plains, Tommy decided to go for a swim in the pond. He stripped to his undershorts, went out into the dark, climbed a tree, crawled out on a branch that projected over the pond, and dived in.

There was only one thing wrong about this. The pond had been drained and Tommy went headfirst into three or four feet of mud. Fortunately, somebody saw him dive and gave the alarm. It took four men to pull him out.

Another night when he, his wife-to-be, and Carol Derby and I were attending a black tie dance at the Orienta Beach Club on Long Island Sound, Tommy said something about it being too hot inside, so we all strolled onto the long pier which reached well out into the water.

Before I even realized what was happening, Tommy tossed off his dinner jacket, boiled shirt, pants, shoes and socks and dived into the salt water. The splash attracted attention, of course, and within a couple of minutes nearly 300 people were out on the pier. By then Tommy had lost his shorts and was afraid to come out of the water.

Finally, a couple of men hauled him into a rowboat, wrapped him in a blanket and took him to a bathhouse where I handed him his clothes. As I was leaving the bathhouse, the club manager rushed up to me and gave me hell for letting my friend swim naked.

Tommy, incidentally, was known to just about everybody in the county and was loved by all. People liked him so much they sought him out to give him stories. And Tommy dutifully would pull out a batch of folded scrap paper that he always carried in his back pocket and make notes.

Sometimes these notes got transformed into stories when Tommy got to the office, but many times Tommy would have a few snorts after making the notes and forget that he'd ever written them. Then, two or three weeks later when another

paper would come up with a big headline such as METROPOLI-
TAN LIFE TO BUILD $10,000,000 OFFICE IN WHITE PLAINS,
Tommy would stare at it and say, "Hell, there's nothing new
about that." He'd pull out his notes, open them up, point to
some scratching and declare, "Why, I got that story three weeks
ago!"

There were a couple other newsmen around in those days
who drank as much or more than Tommy. One was a fellow
named Harry who worked as Westchester representative for the
New York *Daily Mirror.*

When I met him he shared an apartment with three other
bachelors, O'Donovan, John Stevens of the Standard News
Association, and Archie Miller of the New York *Tribune.* One
night the four gentlemen tossed a swinging party in their dig-
gings and the applejack flowed like right out of a spigot.

The party broke up about 4 A.M. and the bachelors retired
for a fast bit of sleep before reporting to their offices at 8. But
when O'Donovan, Stevens and Miller awakened and took turns
in the cold shower, they became aware that Harry wasn't
around.

Thinking that he might have risen earlier and gone to the
office (although they realized that was a pretty slim possibility),
they forgot about him and went to work. About noon, however,
O'Donovan began to get worried. Nobody had seen or heard
from Harry.

We began phoning the various police stations and hospitals,
and checked out all the bars and grills. We cautiously called a
friend of Harry's at the *Mirror* office in New York and asked
him to quietly check around and see whether Harry might be
in a nearby pub. Meanwhile, we covered his beat for him and
phoned stories in to his city desk, saying that Harry had given
us the notes and now was off on another story.

Well, he never turned up all day, and that night when Stevens, Miller and O'Donovan returned to their apartment and
mixed some martinis, they began to try to think of what else
they could do. Wearily, Miller dropped onto the sofa and in-

stantly there was a loud but muffled, "Aaaaaaaaaaaggggggg-hhhhhh!"

Miller shot out of the sofa and O'Donovan and Stevens lifted up the huge cushion. There, snug as a bug where he'd somehow crawled the night before, lay Harry!

Harry was a born loser. Almost every time we reporters tried to cover for him at his office, he'd do something to louse it up. Once he sat fairly stoned in a chair in the county courthouse and listened to a reporter phone a divorce action to his desk, explaining that Harry was working on another story.

After the reporter finished, Harry staggered to his feet, solemnly dialed his office, got the city desk and said, "Thash a lotta crap. Tha' dizzy bashtard's drunk. Lemme give ya the whole shtraight shtory. . . ."

And then there was the time I phoned his city editor with a story and explained that Harry was over at the county jail interviewing a prisoner.

"That's funny," said the city editor, "then it must be Harry's twin brother who came in to cash an expense voucher about ten minutes ago!"

The other very heavy drinker at that time was a fellow named Mike, who was a fine newspaperman, a top-notch copy editor and a man with a great sense of humor. But when he got loaded he'd slither to the floor, yell out that he was having a heart attack and beg us to rush him to the hospital.

I used to go to his house each morning about 7:30 and drive him to work in my car. The ritual was to stop first in front of the old Carpenter House and wait while Mike went around to the back door—the front door didn't open till 8 A.M.—and downed a couple of shots. He also filled a pint flask which he carried in his hip pocket.

Then we'd drive the rest of the way to the office. Mike, who knew every cop in the city, would wait till we came to an intersection where a cop was directing traffic and he'd yell at him, something like, "Hello, you lousy son of a bitch!"

Then he'd duck down in the car so he couldn't be seen and the cop would whirl and glare at me!

Mike's habit of ducking, incidentally, once brought me one of the most powerful punches on the jaw I ever got. Mike and I were standing at the bar in the Carpenter House one lunch hour. I was having a beer and Mike was working on the day's second pint of bourbon, when suddenly Mike got into an argument with a huge construction worker standing on the other side of him.

I was chatting with the man to my left and wasn't paying any attention. Mike, who was Irish and intensely proud of it, could become extremely belligerent when crossed and then he wanted to indulge in fisticuffs. Unfortunately, however, he was tall but very thin and he had the muscles of a paper dolly.

Whatever the man said to Mike that provoked him, I never did learn, but I heard Mike yell, "Harrrrrr! Ye'll niver survive that insult to ould Ireland . . ." And he pulled back his right arm and punched the man with all the power of an aging flea.

I turned to see what was going on just as the man countered with a mighty right overhand. Mike ducked under it and it caught me right on the tip of the chin. I found myself on the floor about five feet away and, not realizing the man hadn't meant to punch me, I bounced up and lashed him with a couple of uppercuts. He fell backwards. He grabbed a bar stool, but I grabbed it too. It came apart in our hands and I was just a little quicker. I cracked one of the heavy legs over his head and the fight was finished.

"Harrrrrr!" shouted Mike. "I told him he'd niver survive that insult to Ireland. Let's have a drink."

Mike was lots of fun in the office, too. Once when I was writing a story about a burglary ring in the town of Bedford that had been broken up by police, I told Mike the main facts so he could write an eight-column headline for page one.

"This ring," I said, "consisted of six brothers, all of whom live in Bedford."

"How did the cops catch 'em?" asked Mike.

"One of the brothers was caught in something else and he ratted on the rest," I said.

"Harrrrr!" said Mike.

I finished writing the story and then picked up the headline Mike had written to go with it. It read:

BASTARD BEDFORD BROTHER
BETRAYS BURGLAR BRETHREN

He turned out another masterpiece when Manuel Luis Quezon, then president of the Philippines, visited the United States in, I think, 1937. I must explain, by the way, that although Quezon is pronounced kay-son, many people in those days believed it was pronounced *kee*-son.

Anyhow, on this particular day we were within ten minutes or so of locking up the final edition of the *Daily Reporter* when a stringer from northern Westchester phoned excitedly that Quezon, who had been visiting the governor in Albany, had stopped in the little village of Armonk on his return trip.

"He's here right now," the reporter told me over the phone. "Oh, this is a great honor for Armonk."

I told Mike to hold me space on page one for about four paragraphs and to write a 9-head—which was a one-line, two-column headline.

"What's he stopping in Armonk for?" asked Mike.

I asked the reporter. "Well," said the reporter, "it's a long drive down from Albany, and I think he's gone into the drugstore just to use the men's room."

I told this to Mike, who snorted and laughed. I took the story from the reporter, including the facts that Quezon had emerged from the drugstore, reentered his limousine and driven off toward New York.

Hastily, I typed my story and took the headline from Mike. It read:

QUEZON
PEES ON,
GOES ON.

Oh, there were many other fascinating things that Mike did —like hiding his empty pint bottles every day on top of a huge wooden cabinet and then feigning complete astonishment one day when the cabinet was moved and nearly 500 bottles crashed to the floor—but I think I'll conclude the saga of this wild Irishman with just one other anecdote.

Throughout the time I knew him, Mike, in addition to drinking, had one thing that he mightily wanted to do. And that was to go to New York on St. Patrick's Day and march in the great Fifth Avenue parade.

Each year, several weeks before March 17, Mike would make arrangements with the editor, Walter Hogan, to be off that day. He'd work nights or Sundays afternoons or something, but it was well understood that on March 17 there'd be no Mike in the office. He'd be in New York, smartly attired, flamboyant in his green suit with shamrock, green shirt, green tie and green derby, helping to lead the parade!

Unfortunately, however, he never made it. Each St. Patrick's Day he made the same mistake. He went to the Carpenter House first.

I was there one St. Patrick's Day morning and, they tell me, it was relatively representative of all the other St. Patrick's Days. Mike apparently had arrived at the Carpenter House on the stroke of eight and had had his first two slugs.

Then, as was his custom, he had had his pint filled and he'd placed it carefully in his hip pocket. After that he had had four or five more slugs.

When I reached the Carpenter House about 10 A.M.—I was working an early shift and that was my lunch hour—I was surprised to find Mike still there. He was exuberant and in marvelous spirits, but I wondered why he hadn't taken off for New York and the parade.

"Ahhhh, me bye," he said (the more he drank, the thicker the brogue), " 'tis the God's truth, I'm waitin' for me delegation to forrrrm."

He explained that he'd cajoled one of the regular patrons of the bar into driving him to New York and that he'd invited six or seven other loyal sons to join him on the trip and take part in the parade. They even then were laying in a supply at the bar, making ready for the long journey.

In time, Mike marshaled his little group, lined them up for inspection, stalked back and forth in front of the thin, wavering line and finally pronounced them fit.

"Ahhhh," he cried to the bartender, "it's a grrrrreat day for the Irish. We're off for the big city. We're off to New Yorrrrk. We'll be marchin' in the grrrrreat parade."

With that, Mike turned sharply on his left heel, high-stepped five or six feet to the swinging doors and struck one of them with his hand. Even then he might have made it, but as the door swung out, Mike halted a moment, turned back to the bartender, waved one last farewell and cried out, "Long live the Irish!"

At that moment, the heavy swinging door came back, and as Mike turned toward it once more it caught him right on the nose and forehead. It opened a three-inch gash in his head and pitched him to the floor at the feet of his troops. He landed on his pint and within a few seconds, claret was mingling with bourbon.

Well, we loaded Mike into a car and took him to St. Agnes Hospital where they did some stitching, top and bottom, and then we took him home. All the time he railed at us, screaming that he wanted to go march in the parade, and telling us what he would do to us when he got his strrrrenth back. And when we got him to the house, Mike's wife gave me a tongue-lashing for "encouraging" him to drink so much! It was a memorable St. Patrick's Day.

We were quite a group at the old *Daily Reporter*, with talent, drive and energy all sort of mixed up with eccentricities, some of which were more or less controlled, some of which were not. Dear old Ella Housefield Lowe was one of the most fascinating. She'd hobble around the city room and every once in a while she'd sit down at her desk and place a stack of yellow copy paper in front of her.

Then, bent over so that her nose almost touched the paper—

she really couldn't see across her desk—she'd take a stub of soft pencil and start to write a review of a musicale she'd heard. Sometimes it was a musicale of the night before; sometimes it was one she'd heard 40 years before.

She wrote in a shaky handwriting with letters fully three inches tall and it was impossible for her to get more than a few words on each sheet. When she was finished, she'd give the stack of papers, which by then had got out of sequence, to one of the deskmen and they'd thank her and then later they'd give the papers what we called "the deep six"—filing them in the wastebasket.

This in no way harmed Ella because she never bothered to find out whether her reviews got into the paper, and she couldn't have read them if they had. She just wanted to write them; she was still on the staff, she was paid every week, and that made her happy.

She really didn't even want the money. She had enough. I found this out one humid, summer day when she came over to me, placed a hand on my shoulder and said, "Goldie, will you please come over and open my right-hand top drawer. It's stuck and I've got my pencils in there."

I went to her desk and pulled at the drawer. It was, indeed, stuck. I tugged at it three or four times but it didn't budge.

"Oh, don't bother," said Ella. "It's too hot."

I didn't listen. I'd got mad at that drawer and I was determined to open it. Hooking the fingers of both hands under the handle, I placed one foot against the desk, leaned back and gave a mighty yank.

The drawer suddenly came free. Still holding the handle, I fell on the floor and the drawer, shooting out of the desk, flipped right up in the air and dumped its contents all over me.

And the contents were 5-, 10- and 20-dollar bills!

Money showered down on me as I lay there on the floor, intermingled with about two dozen pencil stubs and some paper clips. Hundreds of dollars, possibly thousands.

"Oh, dearie me, Goldie, did you get hurt?" cried Ella, kneeling down beside me and pressing her face against mine so she could see. "I told you not to bother."

Well, I got up and with the help of other people in the office I put the money back in the drawer and shoved it back into the desk. I then lectured Ella on leaving that much money in a desk drawer, stuck or not. Somebody might steal it, I said.

"Oh, my goodness," said Ella, "it doesn't matter. I don't need it. I have lots more than I want."

She explained that she would cash her pay check each week —"For a long time I didn't even bother to cash the checks," she said, "but Mr. Keefe [the business manager] got upset about that"—and then put a few dollars in her purse and dump the rest into the drawer.

"Once in a while," she said, "the drawer gets full, so I take a purseful home to my apartment and put it in the laundry hamper."

I asked her why she didn't deposit it in the bank and she laughed and slapped her leg and said, "Oh, no, no, I won't do that. If I put the money in the bank, then they'll give me a deposit book and that's just another thing to read. I don't see as good as I used to, and I don't want to be troubled by another book to read."

A couple of years later, when she became fatally ill and we took her to the hospital, several of us went to her apartment. And she hadn't been fibbing. Over the years she'd taken thousands of dollars in cash to the apartment and, as she'd said, a lot of it was in a hamper. But there were hundreds of other bills lying around in clumps, just where she'd dropped them when she came in.

My good friend George Trow, who then was a reporter on our staff, was, I think, the first one in Ella's apartment. And when he came back to the office he still was a bit bug-eyed.

"Norton," he said, "I don't believe I've ever seen so much money in my life. And it's all out in sight, just lying around the apartment."

George, incidentally, was the man who succeeded me as northern Westchester correspondent. He had a job on a Pleasant-ville weekly called the *Townsman*, which was owned by John McAllister, now a senior editor of *Newsweek*, and he strung for us just as I had done in Mount Kisco.

He did such a good job of it that one day Editor Hogan said to Bill O'Donovan and me, "That kid's good. Why don't we put him on the staff?"

So, George was offered a job on the *Reporter* and he quickly accepted. His starting salary was only $17.50 a week, but, he reasoned, he'd made the leap to a daily and so it was worth it. In a few weeks, however, he had second thoughts and he told me that not only had he lost his *Townsman* salary, which was about $20, but he'd also lost the $30 to $40 a week he had made stringing for us.

"Never mind," I consoled him. "You're on your way to fame and fortune." (And for once, I was right. Today George Trow is night managing editor of the New York *Post*.)

A couple other gentlemen of note worked at the *Reporter* in those days for only $17.50 a week. They were Roger Williams Straus Jr., now head of the publishing house of Farrar, Straus & Giroux, and Mel Heimer, the author and nationally syndicated Broadway columnist.

The $17.50 that Straus got wasn't enough to buy gas for a week for his Chrysler Imperial, and Heimer, who had the ex-citing job of taking box scores for baseball and basketball games over the phone from high school kids, said that his $17.50 didn't really cover his lunches.

Money, as I've perhaps indicated, was a bit tight on the *Re-porter*, even though it was a most profitable paper. I think that the editor, Walter Hogan, was basically a fairly liberal man—he supported one brother who always was losing jobs, and he supported another brother who, so far as I could see, never took any jobs—but the publisher, W. Lee Tuller, was a man who broke out in a rash when he saw the checks being handed out on payday. He nearly dropped dead one afternoon when I put in an expense voucher asking reimbursement of $2.85 for drinks I'd bought two lawyers in getting the biggest scoop of the year.

Tuller was at his best when, as, and if, any member of the staff got up enough courage to go to him and ask for a raise.

"A what?" he'd cried. "What did you say? You want *what?* You want a *raise?*" His face would flush and he'd stagger around a bit—he had a slight limp anyway, and you always felt as though you'd done something to make his infirmity worse— and then, finally, he'd let his shoulders drop, and he'd hang his head, and say, with a deep sigh, "Welllll, come on in the office and we'll talk about it. A raise, you said, huh? A RAISE?"

Once in his nicely furnished office on the first floor of the Reporter Building, Tuller would settle you in a chair in front of his desk and he'd hobble painfully around to his swivel chair, drop in it as though shot and begin to mop his head with a cotton handkerchief he kept in his desk. There was a silk one in his breast pocket, but he never used it.

I shall not forget the one time I asked Lee Tuller for a raise! He went through the preliminary moves and then, after we'd sunk into our chairs, he squinted at me across the desk.

"Didn't Mrs. Tuller and I have you out to the house for dinner one night last month?" he asked.

"Yes, sir," I said. "Yes, you did. And it was very nice. You invited me, as I remember it, so I could take your niece to the theater afterward." He didn't say so, but he gave me the impression that he had a low opinion of anybody who would take a free dinner and then ask for a raise.

I explained that I was only asking for a $5 raise, that I felt that I merited it since I'd been doing very good work and had never had a raise, and that I was very sorry that I was causing him such anguish.

"Well," he said, his face suddenly creasing in a smile, "I'm glad that you're so understanding. You know, Norton, I like you very much, and I've been watching your work. You're coming along, and one of these days. . . . well, I think you've got a future with this paper. . . . One of these days you might even. . . ."

He let his voice trail off and I never did get to hear what I "might even" but I tingled with the anticipation of it. Tuller clasped his hands in front of him on the desk, leaned over, smiled at me and said, "Why don't we have a drink on that?"

I modestly lowered my eyes but said, "I think that would be nice, sir," and when I looked up, Tuller was opening the liquor cabinet that stood beside his desk. He took out a bottle of 100-proof Mt. Vernon straight rye—the kind you can't hardly never get today—and set it reverently on his desk.

"This is the greatest, my boy," he said, licking his lower lip. "Only thing I ever drink. The finest, the greatest and the most expensive."

He pushed a crystal glass in front of me and splashed in some whiskey.

"Two fingers enough?" he asked. And then, before I could answer, he added at least another finger. That was quite a bit of booze, the glass being as large as it was, and I thought to myself, Good Lord, I've never seen this man so generous. But I pushed the thought out of my mind because I felt guilty about having it.

"Cheers," said Tuller, lifting his glass.

"Ah . . . er . . . ah, I'm sorry to . . . ah . . . but could I have a little water in this?" I asked.

"Water!" cried Tuller, his hand shaking and sloshing the liquor about a bit. "Water in this! You want to kill it? Good Lord, boy, this is the drink of the gods! And you want to ruin it with water?"

Well, I assured him that I certainly didn't want to ruin it, but that I'd been accustomed to mixing water with liquor, although I'd be very happy to try it this way, and I really was very sorry about having asked for water, and I certainly was sure that I certainly would enjoy it without water. I certainly would.

I lifted the glass, smiled at Tuller and tossed it down.

Nothing happened for a second or two. Then, suddenly, I felt as though a piece of dry ice had been jammed into my throat. And then, in the next moment, I was sure it wasn't dry ice—it was molten lava.

The burning sensation was so acute that it spread through my neck to my ears. I knew they were smoking. It shot upward into the front of my head and the roots of my hair were burning. My eyes puffed up and tears poured down my cheeks and I began to cough, and I coughed and coughed and choked and sneezed, and my teeth hurt. And then there was something burning so deep and down and far inside of me that I knew I was going to die.

"Well, my boy," I could hear Tuller saying, off in the distance somewhere, under a blanket, "it's been nice to have had this drink with you. And you know, maybe you're right. Maybe you *do* need a bit of water with it. Never touch water myself, but maybe it would be good for you. Here, come on—I'll take you out to the fountain."

Tuller took my arm, escorted me from his office and led me to the drinking water. I think he depressed the button himself. I don't know. I only know that a stream of water came up and hit me in the face, and splashed into my mouth, and soothed my tongue, and dribbled down my tortured throat and, I guess, partly put out the fire below. It was the most welcome relief I'd ever had and I stood there with my face in the stream of water, crying all over again.

"Well, my boy," I heard Tuller say. "I've got an appointment so I'll leave you. You probably have a lot of work to do. Nice to have had a drink with you. And do drop in again."

He walked away, and I staggered upstairs to the men's room.

It was two days before I remembered that what I'd gone to see Tuller for was a raise.

At first I laughed at myself, telling myself what an idiot I'd been. But then as the days went by, I began to get angry, and when I get angry, I can get quite angry. My first instinct was to walk into Tuller's office and punch him on the nose. Then I thought that it might be better to get him locked in his office, put him on the floor with my foot on his head, open his mouth with a crowbar and pour about 10 gallons of Mt. Vernon down throat.

Then I decided that the latter punishment might, indeed, be

something he'd like, and I didn't want to take that chance. On the other hand, I got to thinking, maybe I'd misjudged him. Maybe he *had* only wanted me to have a drink, and hadn't realized what that straight stuff would do to an inexperienced drinker.

So, being straightforward and honest like the Rover Boys and Dink Stover at Yale, I went to him one afternoon and said, "Mr. Tuller, you remember I came in to see you the other afternoon to ask about a raise . . ."

I stopped for a moment while he blanched and gripped his bad leg as though a terrible pain had surged through it.

"And," I continued, "I choked on that nice drink you so kindly gave me and so I never did get to asking you for the five-dollar raise that I think I'm entitled to."

Tuller's face contracted and his lips thinned.

"Look, Mockridge," he said, "you're the first one I've worked that on who ever came back. Didn't you catch on? Whenever anybody comes in here and asks for a raise, I slug 'em with the Mt. Vernon. It always works."

He turned and pointed out the window to the new LaSalle that stood at the curb.

"You see that car?" he asked. "I *bought* that car with raises that I didn't have to give in the last few years. And I didn't have to give 'em because of my little friend here." And he lovingly tapped the bottle of Mt. Vernon. He leaned forward and leered: "Would you like another drink?"

I looked at him for 10 or 15 seconds and he stared right back at me. Then I turned and walked out. I went upstairs to my desk, put paper in my machine and started to write a story for the next day's edition.

I didn't know what to think. I knew only one thing—I no longer wanted to work for Tuller.

As I wrote the story, I began to think of ways I'd notify Mr. Lee W. Tuller that I no longer was going to be his slave. I thought of all sorts of interesting things—like standing on his neck, like taking him up to the roof and holding him over the edge, upside down, by his ankles, and so on.

But then I said to myself, "Whoa, boy. No need to cut your own throat. Much easier to get a job when you've got a job. Let's just take our time."

And I did. I began, however, to write letters of application for various jobs. I wrote to Mr. McAnney at the *World-Telegram* and told him that I thought his publication had been falling off quite a bit lately and that here, sitting lonely and underpaid in White Plains, was the very person who could spark it up.

Mr. McAnney politely replied that he felt the paper could survive another year or so without me, but that he'd give the matter some thought and maybe somewhere in the future I'd hear from him.

Then something happened that reinforced my decision to leave the *Reporter*. I was sitting in the office one Saturday about 11 A.M. when I got a call from Tuller, who was at home.

"Norton," he said, "Mrs. Tuller and I want to take some friends to the Federal Theater Circus this afternoon. Will you leave eight passes for us at the box office?"

I was amazed beyond belief. I was well aware that Tuller was a first-class Freebie who always wanted passes to theatricals, movies and band concerts, but I'd never once considered that he and his wife wanted to see the Federal Theater Circus.

First, the one that was in White Plains wasn't a very good circus, and second, the matinee would be loaded with kids, screaming, yelling and running all over the place. I couldn't imagine the Tullers wanting to go—and besides, I'd given the 50 passes I'd had to the printers, the pressmen, some of the junior reporters, the restaurant man next door and the delivery truck drivers.

I didn't have a single pass left and, it being Saturday morning, I didn't have any idea how to get any more. I told this to Tuller.

"Well," he said, evenly, "the performance doesn't start until two-thirty. You have until then to leave eight passes at the door for us and our friends."

I hung up and did the only thing I could do. I started to hunt for the show's press agent, Paul Lutz. I phoned the box office but nobody answered. Probably nobody had shown up yet. I phoned Lutz's roominghouse. No answer there, either.

I recalled then that Lutz usually spent Friday nights playing poker with some of the circus people and that he probably hadn't got to bed until dawn. So, I decided to go to his room and wake him up. My car, however, was in the garage having the brakes relined, so I phoned for a taxi and took off.

Lutz wasn't in his room and his bed hadn't been slept in. A man sitting on the porch told me he thought he'd seen Lutz going into a bar called Johnny's about 8 A.M. So I dashed there. Yup, Paul had been there, but he'd gone. Probably to Sammy's.

We drove there. Lutz had left an hour before. And he hadn't said where he was going. "But it'll be another bar," said the owner. "I cut him off here."

Well, there were maybe 50 bars in and around White Plains in those days and so the taxi driver and I began to cruise around to all of them. Finally, a little after 1 P.M., we stopped at a dingy dive on the road from White Plains to Elmsford, and there, seated at the bar drinking boilermakers, was a beautifully loaded Lutz.

He recognized me, however, greeted me effusively, insisted that I join him in a boilermaker and said that he and the bartender were going to sing a song for me—"Flat Foot Floogie."

Somehow I got through to Lutz that I needed eight passes for the circus. This jolted him almost sober. "You're crazy," he said. "Who the hell wants to see that circus?" When I told him, he nearly fell off the stool.

He kept shaking his head. He ordered another boilermaker and insisted I have one too. "Well," he said, "I ain't got any passes with me. We'll have to go to the office." I said that would be fine, I had a taxi waiting.

Lutz peered out the window. "You got a taxi out there with a driver?" he mumbled. "Well, that's a hell of a howdy do. That man's too good to drink with old Paul Lutz, eh. Well, you just get him in here so we can have a friendly old drink, or I won't go get the passes."

There was nothing to do but get the driver in. He refused to drink boilermakers, however, and insisted that he drank nothing but beer. Lutz was insulted and he said that if that was the case then he wouldn't ride with that lousy driver.

In time I got his mind off the insult by buying him another boilermaker and joining him in two choruses of "Flat Foot Floogie—with the floy floy." Singing lustily, we left the gin mill, got into the cab and drove to the circus's office.

There was nobody in it, all the personnel having gone to the school in which the circus was being staged. And the door was locked. I chased all through the building but couldn't find the janitor. Somebody told me they thought he'd gone to a bar and grill down the street for some lunch.

I left Lutz and the driver in the cab and ran down the street. I prayed that Lutz wouldn't notice I'd gone into a bar. The janitor was there, deep in conversation with a pretty waitress, and he was in no mood to go back and unlock the door for me. But he relented when I gave him $2 to pay for his lunch and drinks.

Lutz got the passes and scratched his name on eight of them. It was 2:15, and it was a good 10-minute ride to the school. I could visualize Tuller and his wife and their six friends all standing at the box office, barred from the circus—no passes available. And I didn't like the picture.

We got there in time, however, and left the passes. We were driving away from the school just as the Tullers arrived in two cars. I had planned to go directly back to the office but the sight of the party gliding past me in a LaSalle and a Cadillac to go to a Federal Theater circus on eight passes—when admission to the circus was only 15 cents per person—did something to my equilibrium.

"To the Court Bar and Grill, James," I cried to the driver. "The drinks are on me."

Late that evening, I sat at my desk in the office, drinking my fourth container of black coffee and holding my aching head with one hand.

With the other I jotted my day's expenses on a piece of paper:

Taxi fare—3½ hours—$14.00	
Driver's tip	— 2.00
Drinks for Lutz	
and driver	— 9.75
Tip to janitor	— 2.00
	$27.75

This, incidentally, didn't include my own tab at the Court Grill—$6—but I was appalled. I'd spent $27.75 to save my employer $1.20!

I also felt quite sure that Tuller would explode when he saw my expense voucher, and I decided to take the first job offer that came along.

Oddly enough, there was a phone call for me on Monday morning from Mr. McAnney. He said he still didn't have any opening on his staff, but he said that a very good friend of his, Earl Newsom, owner of a fine public relations firm at 597 Madison Avenue in New York, was looking for a writer and that he, Mr. McAnney, had recommended me.

I got away from the *Reporter* early that afternoon, drove to New York, was interviewed by Mr. Newsom—and I took the job. It paid $50, $5 a week more than I was making.

The next day I told Mr. Hogan I was leaving, and he said he was genuinely sorry to see me go and that if ever I wanted to come back, he'd be glad to have me. Then I told Mr. Tuller I was departing.

There were two remarkable things about the little chat we had that day in his office.

One—he never even mentioned the huge expense slip I'd put in.

Two—when he asked me why I was leaving and I said that it was because I hadn't received the $5 raise I'd asked for, he replied, "Good Lord! You're leaving just for that? Why, I had no idea you wanted a five-dollar raise. You should have come to me. I'd have given it to you right away!"

Chapter Seventeen

THE very first minute of the very first day that I went to work for Earl Newsom, I knew I wouldn't like it.

For one thing, the office was entirely carpeted. I'd never worked in an office with carpeting and it seemed strange and unnatural to me.

For another thing, the typewriters were noiseless. I'd never even seen a noiseless typewriter let alone operated one and these machines were cold, friendless, uncommunicative things. Newspapermen generally develop a kind of relationship with their noisy, clattering typewriters to the extent that they feel the machine is talking back to them and giving them inspiration —much the way a dialogue develops more inspiration than a monologue. I know I feel that way and I hated those noiseless, hostile machines the moment I touched one.

Then too, I instantly felt a funny kind of sensation in my

stomach when I realized that from now on I wouldn't be reporting news but trying to sell products. I'd never sold anything except newspaper advertising (and I didn't even like doing that) and now I was going to push products that I really didn't care about.

The Newsom office at that time had, so far as I know, only four major accounts—glass, wool, tea and wallpaper. It handled these on the industry level in an attempt to promote greater use of all four.

We didn't, thank heaven, have to promote any brands—just the product itself. That made the job much easier. It was possible, for instance, to get a beautiful, busty girl, dress her in a tight wool sweater, get her to hold a glass filled with tea and photograph her in front of some wallpaper and thus hit all four products at once.

Then all you had to do was to get the editor of some paper or magazine to publish the damn thing. Most of the people in our shop did this with ease, but it somehow or other was very difficult for me to go, hat in hand and, in essence, beg an editor to do something. A public relations friend of mine years later said that he constantly hated the business because, he said, "You're always on your knees," and that's about the way I felt.

Anyhow, during the next six months I pushed glass, wool, tea and wallpaper like mad. We invented a rum and tea drink, called it the "Skiball," and spent a lot of time in the Stork, El Morocco and other posh joints trying to popularize it.

We invented a thing we called the tea caddy—a little cart that featured pots of bubbling, boiling water, tea bags, lemon, sugar, cream and so on—and induced department stores to have a pretty gal push it around in the various women's departments every afternoon for the benefit of the customers.

We had the serving girl wearing a wool sweater, there were glasses on the cart for the tea, and one side of the cart was tastefully decorated with red-rose-imprinted wallpaper. Oh, we were the tricky ones, we were!

I did loads of other things along that line, making movies to teach grocers the best ways of selling more tea; writing funny little things about glass, wool, etc., etc., for radio commentators to use on the air; writing funny little things about glass, wool, etc., for columnists to use in their columns; writing long stories about glass, wool, etc., etc., for publication in trade papers; writing speeches for our clients' executives and making sure that they mentioned glass, wool, etc., etc.

And I loathed the whole business.

I shrank from going to work in the morning and I couldn't wait for quitting time to arrive. And oh yes, there was another thing I detested. And that was tea.

I'd always liked tea before I joined the Newsom company—especially iced tea—but at Newsom's it practically was forced down your throat. The secretaries went around serving tea in the office every day, at least twice a day. There always were bubbling, boiling pots of water here and there in the office and if you didn't make yourself a cup or two, in addition to those that were served you in your own private office, you felt like a cheater. And if you had a cup of COFFEE with your dinner, you felt as though you'd committed treason.

In time, I got so sick of tea that I can stand neither sight nor smell of it even today. I have nothing against glass or against wool, especially when it's properly filled out, but I really don't like wallpaper. I saw so much of it that the sight of a nice plain, painted wall is as soothing to my eyes as a balmy tropical paradise.

Some of my feeling must have got through to Mr. Newsom because one day he called me into his office, peered at me through his glasses—he was the first man I ever saw who wore harlequin frames—and said, "Norton, you're no longer writing as well as you did when you first came here. What's wrong?"

I told him frankly that while I liked him immensely—in my estimation he was then and is today one of the finest public relations counsels in the country—and while I liked everybody I worked with, I just didn't like the work.

This surprised him not at all, and wisely and kindly, he suggested that I return to the business I loved—newspapers. He told me to take my time in looking for a job and not to quit until I found one I wanted.

"We shall miss you," he said, "but I think it would be a shame for you to stay in this business. Not so much because you don't like it—I think you might adjust to it in time—but because I believe it would be depriving the newspaper business of a fine and dedicated writer. Norton, I think one day you will be tops in your field."

It was the nicest thing anybody had ever said to me, and I almost wanted to weep. In fact, I think I probably would have but at that moment Mr. Newsom's secretary shattered my sentimentality by walking in with a tray and saying, "Here we are, Norton. Here's your tea."

Urrrrgh!

That night I did what now seems to me like a funny thing, but which then seemed quite natural and the only thing to do.

I drove to White Plains, went back to the Daily Reporter Building, walked into Editor Hogan's office and said, "I don't like it at Newsom's and I'd like to get my old job back."

Mr. Hogan was mildly surprised but he put down his pencil, leaned back in his chair and said, "All right. When can you start?"

I told him I thought I had to give Newsom's two weeks' notice and then I added, "Oh, yes. Just one other thing. I really can't come back unless I get a five-dollar raise."

Mr. Hogan looked at me owlishly and said, "Well, I guess you'll have to ask Tuller about that. He handles the budget, you know."

"I don't think there'll be any trouble there," I said. "On the day I left here Mr. Tuller told me that had I asked him for a five-dollar raise he would have given it to me."

"Ho, ho, ho!" roared Mr. Hogan, almost choking with laughter. "Couldn't keep his mouth shut, eh? Well, he'll be sorry he ever talked to you. Ho, ho, ho! I can't wait to tell him!"

Well, tell him he did, and Tuller had to admit he'd com-

276

mitted himself and so with one of the most grudgingly given $5 raises in the world, I went back to work for the *Reporter*. I couldn't have been happier.

The next couple of years were, up until the two or three months before the end, filled with fun, excitement and accomplishment. I wrote a series on the slums in White Plains—it started off: "White Plains is the city of beautiful homes. But have you ever seen her slums?"—that won prizes and helped clean up the worst areas.

We ran contests and gave prizes to people who beautified their homes. We sponsored little theater drama festivals and gave statuettes to the best directors and actors. We operated The Daily Reporter Summer Camp Fund and raised thousands of dollars to send needy kids to the country. We developed extravaganzas like our annual *Night of Stars*, staged in the White Plains High School football stadium and featuring dozens of big-name entertainers from New York, for the benefit of the camp fund.

We had art and literary contests for kids in school and gave substantial prizes (most of which were contributed by local merchants; not by the paper!). We helped organize the White Plains Civic and Business Federation, a sort of chamber of commerce which still operates today.

And we either founded or helped scores of other organizations such as garden clubs, women's clubs, art clubs, music clubs, jazz and classical orchestras, little theaters, baseball and other athletic groups, golf tournaments, horse shows and I don't know what all else. Even a Wednesday evening poetry group.

I worked anywhere from 60 to 80 hours a week, six days a week, and sometimes six and a half—all without overtime. And I was, under the guidance of Bill O'Donovan, a lot of things, including assistant city editor, picture editor, drama editor, amusements columnist, rewrite man, reporter, special editions editor (we used to get out 96-page special supplements on grocery stores, electrical appliance outlets, cars, real estate and so on), editor in charge of correspondents and sort of head of the Friday Night Press Club, a loosely knit organization that gathered in the Roger Smith Hotel every Friday about midnight when we'd completed our work for Saturday's first edition and were in the mood to unwind a bit.

Unwind we did—O'Donovan, George Trow, Eddie Tompkins, Jack Page, Marjorie Welch (the school page editor), Terry Flintoft, Libby Craig and others—as fine a set of drinking newspapermen and women as you'll ever find.

We always wrapped up each evening in the cocktail lounge (or sometimes in the men's room when other patrons of the lounge complained) singing the most beautiful rendition of "Somewherrrrrre, over the rainbow, blooooo birds fly." It was truly beautiful and a lump comes into my throat even today when I think of it.

Lots of fascinating things happened in those years and I never had a dull moment. One Saturday morning in 1940, for instance, I was sitting at my typewriter when one of our advertising men, a fellow named Jerry, came to me in a state of agitation.

He told me his sorry tale. The night before, having a few with some of the boys, he'd been talked into betting on the Kentucky Derby, which was being run that afternoon.

"Isn't that terrible?" he asked.

I said I didn't see why it was so terrible.

"Well," he said, "I bet twenty dollars [which was nearly half his salary] and I bet it on a pig named Gallahadion. This Gallahadion is ninety to one in the morning line, and he's up against the great Bimelich and Bimelich will run right over him. Oh, if my wife ever finds out! What am I gonna do?"

Jerry went on to explain that the $20 loss would mean that he and his wife would subsist on sardines for the coming week, that there were three little mouths that would be denied milk, and that he'd get behind in his rent.

He ended his recitation with: "And so I thought that maybe you'd like to take the bet off my hands."

I was shocked. He'd just told me that Gallahadion didn't

have a chance, and now he wanted me to take the $20 bet! However, I could see that he was desperate. Money didn't mean as much to me then as it does now, and so I said, "Well, I can't go for the full twenty. But I'll take half of it."

Jerry almost fell to his knees. He clutched my hand and thanked me over and over. When I gave him a $10 bill he kissed me on the top of my head.

"Thank you, thank you, thank you," he cried. "I'll never forget you for this." And he went home a relatively happy man.

Well, I forgot all about the thing and, working that afternoon, I didn't even turn on the radio to listen to the Derby. But about 6 P.M., as I was riding home in my car, I switched on the radio and heard the announcer say: "In one of the most startling upsets in the history of racing, Gallahadion, a horse that wasn't rated as having even an outside chance, today won the Kentucky Derby."

I was elated, of course, and began to figure out how much I'd made. Although the track price for winning was $35 for one, the bookies—and Jerry had placed his bet with a bookie—never paid more than 30 to 1. However, I was happy to know I'd picked up $300.

And I was happy for Jerry, too. I looked forward to seeing him on Monday morning to congratulate him and, of course, get my winnings.

But at 9:30 on Monday morning when Jerry reported for work, he stomped up the stairs to the city room, marched over to my desk, flung a bundle of bills on my desk and said, "Of all the goddam things that ever happened to me—I pick the biggest winner of all time and *you* take half of it away from me! I think that's a goddam shame and as far as I'm concerned, the hell with you!"

He turned, stamped out of the place, and didn't speak to me for weeks.

While I'm on the subject of betting, I think I'd better tell you about another chilly Saturday I experienced. I was alone in the office, writing a delicate little story about a praying man-tis, I think, when an expensively but sharply dressed man walked in.

He wore a tightly tailored black cashmere coat, a black velour hat, and a white silk scarf about his throat. I recognized him immediately as the king of the Westchester County bookmaking and policy rackets, and frankly, I was scared. I glanced out the window and there in the street was this huge black Cadillac. Two men, both in black, stood outside it, looking up at me.

"Hullo, kid," said the king, in his Italian accent. "I come to put in a social item, ya know?" Then he laughed as though this were the funniest thing ever said.

I explained that I was not the society editor but that I would be glad to take the item. Then he lowered his voice and asked me if we were alone. I shuddered a bit and said yes we were.

"I'm Gene Cabrizzi," he said (and I'm not using his real name because he's still around!) "I thought you and me could talk a little business. I got my eye on you for some time." He smiled and let this sink in.

I was shaking inside—Cabrizzi had had his eye on *me* for some time!—but I controlled myself and said I was flattered, even honored.

Without being invited, Cabrizzi sank into the chair beside my beaten old wooden desk and told me he was gonna level wid me. And he did. In less than two minutes, he made this proposition:

Each day about 5:30 P.M., one of his boys would drop in to see me, ostensibly to deliver pictures and items for the paper. In the envelope, however, would be tally sheets for the day, lists of bets, policy numbers, checks and cash.

"There'll maybe be as much as ten Gs in cash," said Cabrizzi, "but I know I could trust you." And his laugh reminded me of an electric saw cutting into steel.

All I had to do, he said, was to take this envelope to the Roger Smith Hotel where Cabrizzi had noticed that I repaired each day at sundown for cocktails and/or dinner, and there I was to deliver it to a certain man I'd meet in the men's room. For this I was to be paid $125 a week which, as Cabrizzi noted, was "big dough compared wid the fifty bucks peanuts you gettin' every week."

"There ain't gonna be no risk involved to you," Cabrizzi said, "because every cop in town knows you and they all know you're above the board, and they wouldn't think nothin'. And besides, I got every cop tooken care of."

I asked him why, if he had every cop tooken care of, he needed me. His answer was a classic.

"Well," he said, "I got every police department in dis county in my pocket. But, kid, it's like a game, see? A guy might be layin' down for ya, but he don't like nobody to know he's layin' down. If he's takin', he don't like his nose rubbed in it. So, if I got the right word, he don't like it should be obvious."

Cabrizzi admitted that sooner or later every cop would know I was his runner, but, he insisted, the general public wouldn't know, wouldn't even dream of it, and therefore "there couldn't be no stink, and nobody's nose would get rubbed in."

Well—I sat there for a minute, not knowing what to say. I was overwhelmed by the enormity of the whole thing, the brazenness of Cabrizzi, the certainty with which he made his proposition, and with his contempt for the police.

And I don't mind admitting that I thought for a moment about the $125 which, my buzzing brain told me, was indeed big dough for those days and almost *three* times what I was making. And all for only five minutes' work per day.

Cabrizzi was looking at me coolly, a sneering smile on his face. He had taken out his wallet and was flipping it open, no doubt to lay out the first $125.

I like to think that I surveyed him with all the dignity my twenty-two years could muster, but I don't really know what I looked like. I do know, however, that when I spoke, my voice seemed to be coming from someone else.

"I'm sorry, but I don't think I could do this," I said. "No matter what you say, sooner or later some cop would arrest me

—I don't think you have them *all* in your pocket—and in addition, I would get involved in gangland affairs, or my sudden riches would cause talk, and I certainly would lose my self-respect. And besides—it isn't honest!"

Cabrizzi sat there for a full minute, staring at me with little darts of hatred shooting from his black eyes. Finally, he snorted and lifted himself from his chair. He stood over me and flicked his suede gloves.

"Kid," he said, "I think you some kinda jerk." Then he turned and walked out.

I sat there for a long time. At first I felt quite cold, but then as I thought back over the conversation, I began to perspire. Nobody, I thought to myself, ever has told Cabrizzi just what he could do with his "job" offer and I began to feel that sooner or later I'd have to pay the price.

But nothing, of course, ever happened to me. I saw Cabrizzi many times after that and sometimes he ignored me and sometimes he said "Hullo." Once he put out his hand, took mine and said, "You ain't changed ya mind none?" I said, "No," and he shrugged and left me.

Actually, I suppose, it really made little difference to Cabrizzi whether I took his "job" or not. There must have been dozens of others almost ravenous for the assignment. And in the next months I often wondered whether I'd been a fool to turn him down. There were weeks when finances were tough and the $125 would have been unbelievably welcome. It was my first, and last, tussle with whether one is morally justified to do what bootleggers and bookies do—break the law to provide people with what they want and with what they're going to get whether there's a law or not.

It was a hard decision to make, especially because I'd seen the hypocrisy of public officials sworn to enforce the gambling laws. Back in 1934, when I still was on the Mount Kisco *Recorder*, I recalled, Thomas F. Reynolds, then sheriff of Westchester County, had announced a gigantic drive to rid the county of bookies. And he had warned the heads of every police department to clean up their cities and towns or be ousted.

Well, there was a good bit of scurrying around, and here and there a bookie was arrested. The sheriff proclaimed that the heat was on, and that nobody could place a bet.

Frankly, the drive *did* make it more difficult to place a bet—you had to go around to the back of the candy store rather than just walking in the front. This lasted nearly two weeks. After that, you could use the front door again.

Then, a couple of years later after I'd joined the *Daily Reporter*, Reynold's successor, Sheriff George A. Casey, held a press conference that I attended and he proudly announced that he had just stamped out gambling in Westchester and that every bookie had been run out of the county.

On my way back to the office to write this momentous story, I stopped in at the Carpenter House for a beer and watched five men placing bets with bookies on tracks all over the country.

During this period, with gambling stamped out, a tobacco store on Martine Avenue underwent extensive alterations. Prior to the elimination of gambling, the store had consisted of a tiny front room which contained a glass counter and a few dust-covered boxes of cigars and packages of cigarettes, and a large back room which contained phones, wooden counters and chairs, cash drawers, tally sheets, scratch sheets, pads, pencils and—lots of money.

Shortly after Sheriff Casey made his pronouncement, business in the back room picked up so much that the operators enlarged the back room right up to the show windows in front. They eliminated the cigar counter entirely and placed large cardboard displays advertising cigarettes in the windows as a screen.

Thereafter, when you walked in the front door, presto, you were in the horse room and, on any given day, you had the honor of rubbing elbows with detectives and patrolmen in uniform.

As I say, I, as a young reporter, was a little confused by this. Especially after I was offered that princely job in the syndicate.

But I became even more confused later when, during the terms of Gov. Herbert H. Lehman, I went to upstate Saratoga to attend the August horse races.

Betting at the track, of course, was legal, but I found any number of gambling casinos running wide open in the big hotels. All the games in them were against the law, but early every morning when the casinos closed, who was it who drove the operators to the banks so they could deposit their winnings? Saratoga policemen, that's who.

I didn't ask any questions about this because, in those days, it was well understood that the Democratic party leaned a little toward poetic license on the part of bookies, but I was enormously surprised to see what happened—or rather, what didn't happen—some years later when Thomas E. Dewey, the racket-busting New York district attorney and the implacable foe of all lawbreakers, became governor of New York.

I returned to Saratoga in August for the races and, making the rounds of the hotels at night, I found the same gambling going on. Maybe even more. I was so surprised that I asked some of the policemen about it.

"How can Dewey permit this?" I asked.

"Oh, Dewey doesn't know about it," said one of the cops with a big wink. "You see, every August he takes his vacation and visits his mother in Michigan."

I talked to lots of cops after that about the difficulties and dangers of protecting bookies and, strangely, many of them were willing to chat about it. They seemed to have little reticence. A lot of them told me it wasn't no picnic, 'cause there was lots of dangers involved, and sometimes a guy could get hoit.

But in all the years I've watched cops mother-henning bookies, I've seen only two of them get even slightly hurt. One, a fellow in Yonkers, was a plainclothesman who got a little too greedy and held out on his captain.

The captain, to teach him a lesson, had him picked up by another cop and when the story came out in the newspapers, it was revealed that the plainclothesman had been netting about $150 a week above his salary.

When he went home that night, he was met at the door by a raging wife. She clipped him over the ear with a heavy poker and screamed, "You bum! You told me you were getting only fifty dollars a week!"

About a year later, a Mt. Vernon cop was badly beaten in a fight with a bookie who got away. We reporters heard about it and went to interview this champion of law and order. But we were met by a lieutenant who took us down the street to a gin mill and invited the proprietor to provide drinks for all of us—for free.

"Lissen," said the lieutenant, "we don't want nothin' written about Joe gettin' beat up."

"Why not?" we asked. "Isn't he a hero? Didn't he fight a bookie?"

"Yeah," said the lieutenant, ordering another free round, "but this was a bookie from New York. He was musclin' in on our territory."

And so it was that I sometimes wondered whether I'd given Gene Cabrizzi the right answer. However, there's no sense debating it now. All I know is that if I'd stayed in White Plains and worked for Cabrizzi—even assuming that I'd never been raised over my $125, which I'm sure I would have—I'd have made to date on that little sideline: $189,500. And tax free, too!

Another interesting character I met in those years in White Plains was Thomas Franklyn Manville Jr., the eccentric and wildy amorous marrying millionaire. Shortly after I got to White Plains, I heard from other reporters that it was great sport on a dull Saturday night to drive to Manville's luxurious, 28-room baronial mansion, called Bon Repos and located between New Rochelle and Mamaroneck, to see what was going on.

"Sometimes," a Westchester county reporter for the New York *Daily News* told me, "we get there before the cops and firemen. You get to see a lot more that way." He explained then that it was practically traditional for cops and firemen, and often for a couple of ambulances, to make at least one trek to Manville's heavily guarded, fenced-in estate every weekend.

The police were summoned to throw out secretaries, ex-wives and sometimes current wives who had incurred Tommy's displeasure; the firemen were needed to put down small conflagrations that broke out with consistent regularity; and the ambulances were for carting off the wounded.

I was so naïve at the time that I ascribed much of this recital to the reporter's inventiveness. But one night, a Thursday, I think, the city desk of the *World-Telegram* (for which I was the Westchester representative) called me and asked me to check a report that Manville was having trouble with his then current wife. Manville had been married only a few times and was a rank amateur in the art of matrimony, and no one then dreamed that he would attain the professional status of about a dozen wives which he holds at this writing.

Anyway, I telephoned him at Bon Repos, which Manville often translated as "Never a Dull Moment," and asked him whether he had plans to shed his wife.

I apologized for interrupting him in the middle of a party, which I could hear in the background, but Tommy was the soul of geniality. He also sounded a wee bit astonished.

"Why, my dear fellow," he said. "I cannot imagine where you heard so sorry a report. My wife and I are as much in love as ever, happy as two little birds in a nest. And, if you don't believe me, come on over and have a drink with us."

Well, I didn't believe him. So I drove to the beautifully land-scaped, five-acre, waterfront estate. I stopped at the gate, presented my credentials to the guard, looked nervously at the three snarling dogs, and then proceeded up the gravel driveway and parked in front of the sprawling house. It was shortly after 9 P.M. Lights blazed in many of the upstairs windows, but the ground floor was dark.

I rang the ornate bell, but there was no answer. I rang again and again. Still no response. So, I tried the front door and it swung open.

I walked in and stood there, uncertainly, in the dark. Suddenly, lights went on all around the big foyer and Manville, his prematurely white hair all tousled and his face smeared with lipstick (which at first I took for blood), came lurching toward me. He was wearing a blue and gold brocade dressing gown which hung open and revealed he had nothing else on except a pair of jockey shorts and slippers. He carried a highball in one hand.

"Welcome," he shouted, lifting high the glass. "Who the hell are you?"

I reminded him of our phone conversation and told him that he had asked me over. He squinted at me suspiciously, but then he laughed a series of short little laughs.

"My wife and I are the happies' people in the worl'," he said, slurring his words and sloshing the drink over both himself and the floor. He blew a kiss in the general direction of the second floor and said, "C'mon, I'll show you."

I followed him across the rich Oriental rug, glancing at the tapestries and oils on the walls, and we went upstairs, turning into a long hall. There on the floor lay a good-looking, red-haired woman. Nude.

"She's drunk," said Manville. "T'hell with her."

He stepped over her body with exaggerated carefulness, and I followed suit. The woman never moved. Manville opened a door and we went into a bedroom, blazing with light, that seemed about 40 feet long and about 20 feet wide. Reclining in a gold, richly upholstered chaise longue in the center of the room was a pretty blonde in her early twenties. She was fully dressed and was smoking and sipping a glass of champagne.

Nearby another girl, also in her twenties, her blond hair in a wild state of disarray, paced nervously back and forth. She was attired in nothing but pajama tops and she was crying. Mascara and lipstick were streaked all over her face.

At the far end of the room was a majestic bed with what seemed like a red damask canopy, and reclining on the bed, propped up by silken pillows, was a woman a little older than the others. She wore a negligee, amply open.

287

Manville waved vaguely in the direction of the girl on the chaise and mumbled, "Thass my sec'tary." The girl smiled sweetly and took another drink of champagne. Manville turned to Miss Pajama Tops and said, "Thass my sec'tary." She brushed her hair back, looked at him for a moment and began to wail hysterically. She flung herself on the floor.

Tommy then advanced unsteadily to the bed, smiled and winked at the woman and said coyly, "And how is my li'l pet?" he leaned over, trying to plant a kiss on her bosom.

The woman kicked at him and screamed.

"Get away from me, you dirty, lecherous old bum," she yelled. "Get out of here! And get those *bags* out of here!"

Manville staggered back and she snatched a highball glass from the night table and hurled it at him. It shattered against the wall. Manville looked as though he might strike the woman but she leaped from the bed and flung herself at him. He pushed her away and she slithered to the floor, scratching at his legs and trying to bite him.

It seemed to me that this was as good a time as any to make a dignified exit. And so, with a polite nod to the woman on the chaise, and a smile for Miss Pajama Tops, who now was jumping up and down with excitement and laughing madly, I hurried out into the hall. I stumbled over the nude redhead and bumped my head against the wall, but I found the stairs and got out of there.

I learned later that the Mamaroneck police went to Bon Repos three times that night—twice on complaints of neighbors who said they heard shots, and once after a hysterical woman screamed into the phone that she was being strangled.

About a year later, I met Manville in the lounge at the Copacabana and we had a couple of drinks together. I gently reminded him of my visit, recounted some of the things that had impressed themselves rather vividly on my memory, and asked him how it had all come out. He told me quite frankly he didn't remember that I'd come to see him and he swore he couldn't recall much about that night, although he did remember that "the damn cops were there a number of times."

He shook his head sadly and offered a word of advice: "Stay the hell away from women. They just get you into trouble."

He went on to explain that he had always tried to act the gentleman, that even after a wife divorced him and, in his own words, had taken him for everything she could get, he still maintained friendly relations with her. He said he often invited his ex-wives to visit with him and with whatever wife happened to be current.

"They're all very nice to each other at first," he told me, "but after they get drinking, the bitch in them comes out and they start ripping each other up the back. Now, that's a hell of a way to act. And in addition, I've never had a wife who didn't scream bloody murder just because I keep my secretaries in the house."

Manville, heir to a huge asbestos fortune and one of the country's largest individual holders of American Telephone & Telegraph stock, said that he got a lot of mail, mostly from people asking for handouts or financial backing of one kind or other, and that he needed at least three secretaries. He admitted that he seldom could keep them long—"Fights are always breaking out and they tear each others' hair and they get sore at me and I have to fire them. I'm sort of like a finishing school. I've had more secretaries than General Motors and, believe me, I get more action out of them."

Next to a spurned wife, there's nothing so fearsome as a fired secretary, according to Manville. Many times he's had to call police for protection when a fired secretary refused to be fired. And once Tommy's friend Max Baer, former heavyweight champion, heard that Manville had barricaded himself in a room while several violent blondes scratched and clawed on the door. Max phoned Manville and offered to go to Bon Repos and protect him from "blonde-annoyance."

"Ah, no" said Tommy, gently. "It's not necessary. Blondes do not annoy me. They surround me, they hang on my arms, they wear my orchids and they clutter my guest rooms—but, positively, they do not annoy me."

I asked Manville that night in the Copa why he felt it necessary to marry the women who attracted him and he seemed genuinely shocked at my question.

"My God," he said, "it's the only honorable thing to do. It's one thing to go to bed with a broad and then forget it. But if you love a girl, hell, you gotta marry her."

I didn't see Manville much after that meeting at the Copa— I was in the *Reporter* office more than I was out, and reporters covered his many exploits and phoned in the facts—but one day in, I think 1939, I met him on the street as I came out of the Court Grill after lunch.

He'd been in the courthouse trying to straighten out some tangled marital mess, and he was in a rage.

"You got any keys with you?" he demanded. "Christ, what a day this has been! I got trouble in court, I got a stiff neck. I'm hung over worse than usual. I got trouble at the house. And now, goddammit, I can't get into my car."

I had a bunch of keys in my pocket, for my car, my desk, my locker, my Roger Smith Hotel room and so on, and we walked over to Manville's gleaming Mercedes which was parked at the curb. The doors were all locked.

"Can't find the goddam key," he said. "Can't find any of my keys. Can't get into this goddam thing."

We tried all my keys. Two or three of them slipped into the lock but none did the trick.

Manville was wild. He pounded his fists on the roof of the car. He punched the windows. He kicked the front door, making several long scratches.

"Goddam car," he screamed. "Never was any good. Been nothin' but trouble since I got it. Sometimes the windows won't open. Sometimes they won't close. Now I can't even get into it."

"There's no sense getting mad," I said. "The best thing to do is call a locksmith."

"I *am* mad, goddammit," he cried. "And I don't want any locksmith. I just want to get rid of this goddam car."

He swung around and faced me, and he seemed to be entirely serious.

"Look," he said, "you gimme a buck and the car is yours. I'll sell it to you. Just take it away. I'm sick of the goddam thing."

I thought he was off his rocker and I told him so. But he took out his wallet and began to fish for the registration.

"Look," he said, "I got the registration right here and all I gotta do is fill it out on the back, and you gimme the buck and the car is yours. I'm sick to death of the goddam thing."

I looked at the Mercedes. It was practically new, a shimmering thing of beauty, worth, I supposed, nearly $10,000.

"Tommy," I said, "don't be silly. I *can't* buy your car for just a dollar. Even if you sold it to me today, you'd regret it tomorrow. Now calm down and go inside and call a locksmith. You'll probably never have any more trouble with it."

"Yes, I will. Yes, I will. Yes, I *will!*" he screamed. "This damn thing never has been anything but trouble. I wanna get rid of it."

However, he calmed down in time, went into the grill, had a couple of drinks, phoned a locksmith, had a couple more drinks and, eventually, got into the car, which had been opened by the locksmith, and drove away.

I thought no more of it until two days later. Then, coming out of the courthouse, I met a reporter from, I think, the Yonkers *Herald-Statesman*.

"Hi," he said, with a huge smile. "C'mon over here. I want you to see my new car. It's a Mercedes. I got it from Tommy Manville yesterday. He couldn't get the windows closed and he got sore at it. You'll never believe it, but he sold it to me for a buck."

Chapter Eighteen

AS I told you earlier, there were quite a few people on the *Daily Reporter* in my era who went on to the bigger and better—Roger Straus, George Trow, Mel Heimer, Bill O'Donovan who became a vice-president of the Celanese Corp. of America, Milt Harker who was named chief of the West Coast bureau of International News Service, and Eddie Tompkins who, strangely enough, became sheriff of Dayton, Ohio!

But one of the most interesting staffers was a little guy named

Willie Turnesa. Willie, who's only a few inches over five feet, stood, however, mighty tall in the golfing world. He was the youngest of the seven famous golfing Turnesa brothers. All of Willie's brothers were professional golfers; only he stayed amateur.

But he was (and still is) a magnificent player. He was the New York State amateur champion when he came to us, and he was destined to go on to win the United States amateur championship twice, once in 1938 and again in 1948.

I was playing quite a bit of golf at that time—I've always had a fierce love for going out on the fairway and smacking a ball into the woods—and when I heard that Willie was joining our editorial staff I was ecstatic. I planned to play with him, study his style, catch on to his tricks, get him to give me a few pointers—and within a month or so I was sure I'd be breaking par just as Willie often did.

He had come to the *Reporter* because he needed a job (you don't make any money out of amateur golf no matter how many tournaments you win) and he believed he wanted to become a journalist. He had a fairly good command of the written word and he felt that he'd improve a great deal if he worked for a paper and wrote every day.

It was—oh, joy!—one of my daily tasks to take Willie in hand a bit, show him the ropes and give him advice on writing. And, in return for this, I made it quite clear that I expected him to go to the golf course with me every afternoon that we could slip away and play at least a few holes. Saturdays and Sundays, of course, Willie was playing with the big boys and I wouldn't have dreamed of trying to intrude.

But Monday through Friday—he was my pigeon! And what a price he paid! He played beautifully on the Gedney Farms Country Club and Westchester Hills courses, shooting par, or close to it, almost all the time, and I played right along with him, bogeying most holes, three- and four-putting here and there, losing balls in the woods and the ponds, driving out of bounds, digging divots like a berserk steam shovel and entrenching myself in sand traps.

He made suggestions from time, to time, he demonstrated grips and swings and stances, he held my left arm straight, he held my head down, he even made me get a set of slightly longer clubs. But, I'm sorry to say, it didn't do much good. I still shot in the 80s, the 90s and sometimes the 100s. The best thing I can say about my game is that, bad as it was, it luckily didn't hurt Willie's game very much.

Well, after he'd been reporting and writing for us about six months, Willie came to me one day in the office and said, "Frankly, Norton, how am I doing? Do you think I'll ever be a good reporter, a good writer? I'd like to know now because I don't want to waste my time if you don't think I'll make it."

I thought back over all of the stories that Willie had covered and over painful attempts to put them into proper form for the paper and I decided to level with him.

"Willie," I said, "to be perfectly blunt, I think you'd do better to stick to golf and give up the newspaper business."

I went on and gave him the reasons why I felt that way. Willie took it like the fine sportsman he is. Then he told me he'd sort of felt that way himself and that he thought it would be best for him to quit at the end of the week and go into some other field of business. We shook hands and then, as he was getting up to leave my desk, he grinned and said, "May I offer *you* a bit of advice?"

I nodded and Willie said, "Stick to the newspaper business and give up golf."

Well, of course, I didn't take his advice. I continued to play and I gradually got worse and worse. Today if I break a hundred I'm lucky, but truthfully I really don't care whether I win or lose the game. Oh, I'd rather win, to be sure, but I don't mind much if I lose. I get such a kick out of playing the game that the bad shots don't bother me too much. I just like to remember the good ones—and that's what takes me back to the course.

Golf, as you probably know, can put a frightening strain on a man who's likely to lose his temper. It not only separates the men from the boys, but husbands from wives, lovers from sweethearts and businessmen from long-trusted lawyers, accountants and doctors.

I had a most vivid experience along this line one afternoon when Clark Batchelder, one of my oldest and dearest friends, was playing golf with me at a course in Lake Mahopac in upper Westchester County. It was a glorious sunny afternoon and I was shooting much better than usual. In fact, I hardly ever did anything wrong.

But poor Batch was hacking his way around. Batch, short, yet powerfully built, weighing about 200 pounds, had been an outstanding football star—probably would have been All-American had he remained in college—and he was twice the athlete I was. He could play any game and play it exceedingly well, but golf was one sport that eluded him.

He shot a lot better than many golfers, of course, but that wasn't satisfactory to Batch. Whenever he hit a gorgeous 260-yard drive and then took a 5-iron and put the ball in a brook, he'd sit down and bang his head with his fist.

Well, that afternoon I was shooting close to par and Batch's score was soaring. Just about everything went wrong and he was getting madder and madder. I made the mistake of suggesting that he keep his head down and he snarled at me. I told him that he was too fast on the backswing and he told me to mind my own damn business.

This I did, from then on. In fact, I didn't even speak to him. But finally Batch got into so much trouble on one hole that I thought I was going to burst if I didn't laugh. The terrible climax came when Batch, lying five on a par four hole, took a wedge and really slashed at the ball. He swung so hard that his right shoulder must have lowered three inches and the wedge dug a trench right under the ball. Grass, dirt and pebbles flew through the air. The ball did nothing but drop into the hole.

I couldn't help it. I laughed.

Batch swung around and punched me right in the solar plexus. It pushed me back about two feet and my breath was gone. He hit me four or five more times, mostly in the midsection. It was some time before I realized what was happening and began to fight back. Then, much to the surprise of our caddies and of a dozen or so other golfers who stopped and stared, we punched each other back and forth across the fairway.

When we both were arm weary, Batch grabbed his clubs, paid his caddy, stalked off the course, got into his Packard and drove home to White Plains, leaving me stranded at the club with no car.

He called that night to apologize. It had taken him about eight hours to cool off. Since then, we've played many games, but I never, never laugh. Hell, I hardly even breathe.

And I always take my own car to the course!

Speaking of cars, it was about that time in my blooming career that I bought a nice new, shiny black Studebaker from my friends and former schoolmates, George and Willie Martabano, who had the Mount Kisco agency. They'd demonstrated with this car and they gave it to me for four or five hundred less than its list price but I well recall that I treated that car with a tenderness that indicated I'd paid many thousands.

It used to distress me to take it to fires, explosions or other disasters because I was afraid that firemen would pump chemicals on it, or back into it, or damage it in other ways. I often left the car half a mile from the scene and then ran the rest of the way.

One day about an hour before deadline, O'Donovan sent me to a farmhouse north of White Plains where some maniac had shotgunned to death a woman and her two daughters. I sped to the place and, seeing a lot of cars and trucks parked close to the farmhouse, I decided to avoid the possibility that some cop in a hurry would sideswipe me as he rushed off on another assignment. So, I parked my beautiful black Studebaker under an apple tree in a pasture beside the driveway leading to the house.

There was a bull grazing in the field, but he was anchored by a heavy link chain to a huge iron spike driven into the ground. He certainly was no menace because he was 50 yards away. Anyhow, I left the car there and went into the farmhouse to get the story.

When I came out, 15 minutes later, and ran over to my car I found to my acute horror that the bull had pulled up the stake, had wandered over to inspect my car and had amused himself by looking at his reflection in the front fenders and the grille. In some manner he had got his chain wrapped twice around the bumper. He now stood, pawing the ground, secured to the bumper, his massive head only inches from the grille.

I was petrified. Any moment, I told myself, that bull will take a step forward and his horns and skull will crush my grille and maybe the fenders, too. I could see two or three hundred dollars' worth of damage hanging on that one step.

I also could see that I might never be able to phone my story to the office in time. The cops wouldn't let me use the single phone in the farmhouse, and the nearest house, which might or might not have a phone, was about three miles away. I thought about running, but the four-minute mile hadn't been invented then, and, even if it had been, I was loath to leave my car to the tender mercy of the bull.

So, I got into the driver's seat and, praying that it wouldn't make enough noise to frighten the bull, I started the engine. The bull raised his head a little and the front end of the car rose with it. He glared at me, but he didn't do anything. Then, hoping that maybe if I backed up, the chain would unwind and free both me and the bull, I shoved the car in reverse, let out the clutch and started to move. The bull came right with me.

He came right with me for a few feet, that is. Then he jammed his hoofs into the earth, and both of us stopped.

I put on the brakes and got out to look. The chain now resembled the Gordian Knot. I didn't like the situation, and the bull didn't either. Setting his feet, he began to try to back up.

The car didn't budge and the bull got angry and stamped his hind feet.

I decided to try diplomacy. I walked up to the bull, which by then had grown half as high as the Empire State Building, and patted him on the shoulder.

"Nice bull," I said. "Nice bull. You're a fine fella. You're a good old boy."

The bull's right eye turned and glared at me like a 1000-candlepower searchlight. He snorted and the wind nearly swept me off my feet.

I'd always been told that you mustn't let an animal know you're afraid of him. But I'd never been told *how* to keep from letting him know you're afraid of him. However, I decided to brazen it out.

"Look," I said, "you've gotta lean forward and loosen that chain. Then I can take it off and you'll be free. Okay?"

I put my hand on the bull's head and pressed down. Instantly, his head shot upward, the chain tightened and the car raised a good 18 inches into the air.

"Nice bull," I said. "Nice bull." And I patted his flank. He let down the car.

With the minutes oozing away, the deadline looming, and the danger to my car increasing, I got a little desperate. Suddenly, without even knowing what I was doing, I ducked under the bull's throat and began to try to slip the chain off the end of the bumper. The bull didn't like me under there and he kept trying to back up. This only tightened the chain.

In time, however, by talking to him—"Okay, nice bull. Take it easy, old man. Move in a little closer, nice fella" and stuff like that—I got the bull to relax a bit. Whenever he did, I shifted the chain an inch or so closer to the end of the bumper. Every time I touched it, I was afraid he'd rear and catch my fingers between the chain and the bumper.

Fortunately, he never did. After a while, I got one turn of the chain off the bumper. The bull then had an extra eight inches of leeway and he began to enjoy it, moving forward against my back and then rearing and jerking the car into the air. Twice I was hit by my own bumper.

But when he got whiplashed forward, pulled by the chain and the weight of the car, I'd take advantage of the slack and move it toward the bumper's end. At long last, I gave a strong push and the chain came free.

I quickly got out from between the bull and the car, expecting him to charge me, or wheel and stomp over me and rush away. He did neither. He just stood there and looked at me. And you know, there seemed to be a friendly, grateful look on his face. Possibly, he felt as the lion did when the thorn was removed, and I had the feeling that he wanted to lick my face.

However, I apologized to him and explained about the deadline, and I leaped into the car, slammed the door and backed like crazy into the driveway. I sped down that dusty road at 80 miles per hour, screamed onto the highway and raced to the nearest house. I phoned in my story of the triple murder and, when I finished, I said to the rewrite man, "That's all on *that* story. But I picked up another one. And I'll give it to you some other time. It's about a lotta bull."

The rewrite man thought I'd gone mad.

When I turned, I found the farmer and his wife looking at me with wide, wide eyes. I glanced into a mirror and got quite a shock myself. I was beet-red, drenched with perspiration, my hair was standing almost straight up, there was dirt from the pasture all over my face, my hands and my suit, and from the right side of my forehead, tracking down across my face, over my collar and onto my light tan suit, were caked rivulets of blood. How I got the gash in my forehead I do not remember.

"I . . . ah . . . I had a bull fastened to my car . . ." I began. But from the looks on their faces, I knew they didn't believe me. I tried to convince them, but they weren't buying one word. And, after a moment or so, I got the distinct impression that these two simple people believed one of two things: either that I was totally crazy, or that I had murdered three people in the farmhouse up the road and had just delivered my confession to the authorities over the phone.

They were glad to see me go, and as I drove away I looked back and saw the farmer hurry to the phone. No doubt to call the police.

One of the most frightening times I ever had with the police, by the way, occurred on a hot summer night when, having nothing particular to do after finishing work at the office at 10 and not wishing to go to bed, I drifted into police headquarters to see what was going on.

I often did this and once in a while the detectives, if they were going out on something, would take me along in the car. This particular night two detectives—let's call them Jack and Charlie—were setting out to find some guy who had knifed two people in a gin mill in one of the slum areas. They told me to hop in.

We went to the joint, found out who the man was and where he lived. In a couple of minutes we were in front of the four-story tenement, a dirty, dark, decrepit old building that should have been pulled down years before. It housed about 20 families, with an average of eight in a family to each three- or four-room apartment.

The stench in the building was terrible, and as we went up slowly from the first to the second floor, from the second to the third floor, it got worse. And it got hotter. Small children raced through the halls and up and down the stairs and, even though the detectives were in plain clothes, the word spread like mad that the fuzz had come.

Doors on each floor opened suddenly, stayed open a second or so while the occupants peered out, and then they slammed shut and you could hear the bolts clicking into place. When we got to the third floor, we walked along the hallway, checking the faded numbers on the door. Then we found our door— No. 3A.

Jack knocked on the door. There was no answer. He knocked

again, really pounding his fist. Then Charlie hammered on the door and yelled out, "Open up. It's the police."

"He's in there," said Charlie, knowing that the suspect always holed up at home after a fight. "Let's bust the door."

The two officers, both heavy men, stood side by side. They took a couple of steps backwards and then smashed their bodies against the ramshackle door. It gave instantly, falling into the apartment. And the two detectives fell right with it.

The knifer stood there, waiting. I could see him outlined against a window. And he had a gun in his hand. Flame came from the gun. Twice. Then I heard the noise of the shots. The bullets zipped past me down the long hall and I heard them crash through the wooden door at the end.

I flattened myself against the wall. The man leaped over the fallen detectives and raced down the hall to the stairs. Both detectives opened fire, lying on the floor, but it was too late. He flung himself down the stairwell and was gone.

Jack and Charlie got up and dusted themselves. Charlie turned to me and said, "A helluva lot of help you were. Why didn't you grab him when he came out? We set him for ya, and you blew it!"

Chapter Nineteen

WELL—that wasn't the only big chance I "blew."

Let me tell you about a most fantastic thing that happened when the *Daily Reporter*, Bill O'Donovan and I tried to strike a mighty blow for liberty and the eradication of tyranny and oppression!

It all began one cold day in January of 1938. That was the year when the New York State Motor Vehicle Bureau issued license plates to all motorists bearing the customary letters and numbers, but also the legend: NEW YORK WORLD'S FAIR 1939.

This made quite a lot of people unhappy. They contended they didn't see why they should be compelled to carry advertising on license plates that they'd paid for, and secondly, some of them thought that if, indeed, they did have to carry the advertising, they should be paid for it.

A number of these "don't-tread-on-me" complaints came into our office and one day Bill O'Donovan and I kicked it around a bit and decided to do something to test the constitutionality of the whole thing. We wanted to find out whether the State Legislature, which had authorized the placing of the legend on the plates, had the right to make citizens advertise something they didn't want to advertise.

We weren't against the World's Fair, of course, but he and I, frustrated lawyers both, thought that this was a matter that ultimately should be taken to the U. S. Supreme Court for a final decision. If the state were permitted this year to advertise the Fair, what would prevent it next year from advertising bagels or hot dogs, all without paying the motorist for the privilege?

At first we thought that we'd take the plates to our own cars and scratch out the legend, or at least paint it out with black paint, so we could be arrested and set the case in motion through the courts. Then we decided that defacing the plate might well be a heinous offense that would land us behind bars, and so we hit upon the idea of merely obliterating the legend with black friction tape that wouldn't hurt or deface the plate at all.

Secondly, we concluded that it would be wrong for a newspaperman to pull the stunt because everybody would say that it had been done merely to gain publicity for the newspaper. So, we did what any good, red-blooded American newspaperman with a flair for public relations would have done. We got a beautiful blonde to take over the assignment.

The lady we selected was a lovely, voluptuous, photogenic society matron by the name of Dorothy Quisenberry, and she, willing to fight shoulder to shoulder with us to prevent tyranny, agreed that she would tape out the legend on her husband, Jack's, car and drive around until she got arrested.

With everything set, Bill and I made one mistake. We told our editor, Walter Hogan, what we were going to do. Hogan listened impassively and then said, "Well, I think your idea is all right, but I don't go for having the dame do it. I think we should use somebody we've got control over. Who knows what the hell this dame might do when the big publicity avalanche starts? When her picture gets in the papers and magazines, on the newsreels, when she's interviewed on radio? We need somebody we can control."

Bill and I fought for the principle of having a beautiful blonde battling for our rights, crying to the world that nobody has to be a mobile sandwich man if he doesn't want to. We argued that she'd get her pretty picture in *all* the papers, *all* the magazines, *all* the newsreels, and that a great surge of public opinion would well up throughout the country, all over the world. The *Daily Reporter* would be hailed in every corner of the globe as the finest champion of human rights since the committee that organized the Boston Tea Party.

"No," said Hogan. "I don't want any dame involved. Let's use Martin McBohin."

Bill and I looked at each other. Martin McBohin was an unemployed squat little guy who hung around the office a lot, who chased out to get coffee and sandwiches and run errands and such, and who, we suspected, was more or less living on what Walter Hogan paid him for these petty jobs. He certainly had no other visible income. And, so far as Bill and I could see, he had no sex appeal. In fact, no appeal at all.

But there was no use fighting Hogan's order, so Bill and I called McBohin into the little office I had at one end of the city room and looked him over. What we saw was most discouraging. Prepossessing, he was not. He was forty-two and looked older, he had a thin, pinched face and shifty, or at least nervous, eyes, and he butchered the King's English quite handily.

We learned that he was a boiler mechanic but that since very few people needed boilers repaired just then, he was unemployed. And had been unemployed off and on for several years. He had a little pad in an apartment house at 1 Battle Avenue, White Plains. There was, so far as Bill and I could determine, only one thing in his favor: he told us he'd been a U.S. Marine sergeant for 15 years and that he'd fought at the battle of Belleau Wood during World War I.

Marines everywhere, we reasoned, would be on his side, and he'd get support from the American Legion, Veterans of Foreign Wars and other service organizations. Mentally, I already was booking him as the main speaker at Legion conventions, Fourth of July ceremonies and such.

We told McBohin what we wanted him to do and he began to squirm. "Jesus," he said. "I could get arrested."

He seemed even more unsettled when we told him that that was just what we wanted. He would be arrested, fined by a local judge, and released while we took the case through the higher courts all the way to the U.S. Supreme Court for a ruling on the constitutionality of the state legislation.

"Well," he said reluctantly, "just so long's I don't hafta go to jail."

Inasmuch as he didn't seem to have the proper spirit, Bill and I gave him a fight talk—here was his chance to do something for his country, he would become the hero of Americans everywhere, he might even go down in history along with Patrick Henry.

"Who's that?" he asked.

Fortunately, McBohin had a jalopy of sorts, but being virtually without funds, he'd left the car more or less abandoned in a lot back of his apartment house for the last four months.

"It ain't got no battery," said McBohin, "and I think the tires is flat. And I ain't got no license plates."

Well, we got a new battery, got the tires repaired and paid a mechanic to get the thing running, which was no small job that cold January, and then we gave our hero $12.50 and he went to the Motor Vehicle Bureau branch in White Plains and bought a set of plates—1V 22 97.

He also bought a roll of black friction tape and then, after he got back to the office, he knelt in the street in front of his car, wound the tape several times over the New York World's Fair legend and fastened the plates to his car. Our one and only photographer, Herman Kartluke, stood shivering in the icy winter air recording the whole thing on his Speed-Graphic.

With the tape in place, obliterating the hated advertising, McBohin was ready to start driving around the city, waiting for a policeman to arrest him. We told him to get going.

"Gotta have some money for gas," he said. We gave him a few dollars.

"And for oil," he said, reaching for more. "She burns a lotta oil."

Well, she burned a great deal of gas and oil that day as McBohin drove slowly all over White Plains—but he never got arrested! He wasn't even noticed by police. Or if any one of them did spot the taped plate, he simply didn't give a damn.

To eliminate the possibility that McBohin might spend the next year or so driving around and not getting arrested, I phoned my good friend, Sergeant John Hergenhan of the North Castle police, a few miles north of White Plains.

"Johnny," I said, "there's some kind of nut driving around the city with the World's Fair inscription on his license plates all taped over. But the city cops aren't arresting him."

"Well," said Johnny, "that's a violation of the law and if he comes up here, I'll see that he gets arrested!"

"He'll be in Armonk tomorrow afternoon at 2:30 P.M.," I said, "and if you happen to be standing in front of the police station at that time, he might just park right there."

"I'll be there," said the sergeant.

And he was. As soon as McBohin stopped his car, Hergenhan ordered him to remove the tape.

"No," said McBohin slowly, trying to remember the lines we'd painstakingly schooled him in. "No, I will not. I paid twelve-fifty for them plates and nobody gave me no compensation for the advertising thereon, which advertises the Fair, and the state ain't got no right to make me carry around an ad on

306

my car for something that is a commercial enterprise. With me, it's a matter of principle."

Hergenhan dutifully jotted down all of these heretical remarks in his notebook and next day, when swarms of reporters descended, he was able to serve them up, word for word. Meanwhile, he had handed McBohin a ticket for violating the State Motor Vehicle Law.

I wrote a magnificent story that night all about the brave ex-Marine sergeant who was down on his luck but who was patriotic enough to stand up for his Constitutional rights and who was striking a blow for every American who hated the steel-shod foot of tyranny upon his neck

We splashed the story all over page one of the first edition of the *Reporter*. It was a lovely thing. Eight-column streamer, the main story with a three-column lead, a huge picture of Mc-Bohin affixing the tape, a color story on McBohin himself, telling of his Belleau Wood exploits, close-ups of McBohin and Sergeant Hergenhan, and a side-bar telling how he might have to pay for his independence by going to jail.

McBohin was very pleased with the layout and he strutted about the office in a state of elation. He was quite shocked, however, when he read the story that said he might be forced to go to jail, but we calmed him down by telling him that our lawyers never would permit it.

It was then that Bill and I remembered that we had not yet acquired legal counsel for our little lawbreaker. Once again I turned to a friend. He was Thomas J. O'Connor, a flamboyant, white-haired criminal attorney, who often said he was a descendant of one of the last kings of Ireland, and who had a majestic flair for oratory.

O'Connor was happy to take the case and within minutes after his appointment, he was sounding off at a press conference attended by nearly 20 reporters representing all the New York newspapers, Westchester County publications and radio stations.

"My client," thundered O'Connor, "is a brave American. A

man willing to risk his very liberty to stand up for principle." McBohin, on the outskirts of the crowd, shivered a bit.

"My client is striking a mighty blow for freedom," cried Tom O'Connor. "His Constitutional rights—OUR Constitutional rights—are in grave jeopardy, and this brave little man stands ready, as he stood courageously in Belleau Wood, to fight off the aggressor, to uphold the American way of life, and to put down oppression wherever and whenever it might spring up.

"The state should be prevented from establishing a precedent like this. If it is allowed to compel motorists to propagandize the Fair this year, it may compel them in future years to carry advertisements for some kind of non-skid tires or mustard or liver pills."

"Or corn flakes," said McBohin. But nobody paid any attention to him. They were transfixed by O'Connor's eloquence and electric histrionics.

"The Senate and the Assembly," thundered O'Connor, "were guilty of passing class legislation when they authorized this advertisement. Moreover, the inscription has made it necessary to print the important numerals and letters on the plates so small that they cannot be read easily."

Sergeant Hergenhan also held a press conference and recited the section of the motor vehicle law which reads: "Number plates shall be kept clean and in a condition so as to be easily readable, and the view thereof shall not be obstructed by any part of the vehicle or by anything carried thereon."

Then he pointed out the section in Chapter 16 of the state laws of 1937 that read: "The number plates assigned to all motor vehicles and trailers for the years 1938 and 1939 shall also contain the inscription 'New York World's Fair 1939' in such form and design as the Commissioner shall prescribe."

Well, as you can imagine, this whole business touched off quite a hullabaloo. The New York papers carried column after column on the case, including interviews with and pictures of McBohin. The Associated Press, United Press and International New Service sent out stories to thousands of newspapers and radio stations all over the country, and the newsreels descended and shot thousands of feet of McBohin—smiling, grinning, shaking his head in anger, raising his fist, crying for freedom and the elimination of oppression, driving in his car, pointing to the taped-out inscription and even with head bowed in prayer, asking for strength to continue his fight.

He told over and over how he'd fought at Belleau Wood, he reenacted in the Barrymore manner his historical encounter with Sergeant Hergenhan, and he made ringing statements about life, liberty and the pursuit of happiness.

He became such a hero, such a sought-after figure, that Bill and I had to sneak him out of his apartment and lock him up in another one we'd leased. We did this because he was giving so many stories to the New York papers and wire services that very little was left for the *Reporter*.

A few days after his arrest, McBohin was due to appear in police court in Armonk before Justice of the Peace Julius A. Raven. And, as you can imagine, we prepared for the trial very carefully. We were absolutely sure that McBohin would be found guilty—it was apparent on the face of it, to us, that he had violated the motor vehicle law—but, of course, the main question was whether that law itself was not a violation of Constitutional rights.

So Bill O'Donovan and I drafted key statements which would be voiced in court by O'Connor to get our position into the record, a record which would be referred to time and again as our appeal went up through the courts to the highest tribunal.

Tom did his homework very well and he daily let newspaper reporters get a few hundred hints of what he was going to say. This fanned interest in the case, and in a little while it was announced that the North Castle town attorney James B. Stilson, who might have been expected to prosecute the case, was not going to be asked to appear in court.

It seems that Mr. Stilson had expressed himself as of the belief that "the defendant is right in this case." He went on to say that he felt no person could be asked to advertise against his will. So, the police let us know that no less a personage than Elbert T. Gallagher, chief assistant district attorney of West-chester County, would be the prosecutor.

Although Gallagher was one of the best legal minds in the county (he later became a state supreme court justice), Tom O'Connor wryly announced to the press that he felt the prose-cution should obtain the services of a more learned and expe-rienced counsel, possibly the Attorney General of the United States. This got Gallagher mad, but he politely refrained from saying what he thought of O'Connor.

Anyway, we went to trial on the night of January 11, 1938—one of the more important dates in American history.

The thing had been ballyhooed to such an extent that the tiny police court in the North Castle town hall in Armonk was crammed with people. There hardly was room for McBohin, Hergenhan, the two attorneys and their assistants, and the clerk of the court. More than 125 people were huddled in the court-room, which had been designed to hold 35 at most. Men and women opened the windows and sat and stood on the window-sills, and there were so many souls packed in the courtroom that the wintry blasts from the open windows weren't even felt.

Outside, in the cold, at least another 150 people huddled around the windows and the front door, waiting for snatches of information to be passed to them by those fortunate enough to be inside.

There were reporters from at least 25 newspapers and wire services. Newsreel lights illuminated the court like a movie premier, and the incessant flaring of photographers' flashbulbs gave the whole scene an eerie look.

The trial itself, unfortunately, was somewhat anticlimactic. McBohin wasn't called to testify—although he did manage to tell the newsreels that he thought the least the World's Fair could do would be to give him a pass—and Sergeant Hergen-han testified merely that he ticketed McBohin after he saw him driving with taped plates.

The two attorneys turned on as much steam as they could, but it was so hot in the room that the forensics were held to a minimum. Gallagher, who was assisted by Thomas F. Daley, an attorney representing the World's Fair corporation, made the point that the Fair was a public, or quasi-public, function and that therefore the state "is well within its rights in enforcing display of the World's Fair advertisement on license plates throughout the state." He also contended that the state attorney general had ruled that, even though motorists paid for them, license plates are state property.

He said that millions of dollars would accrue to the state from "fifty million visitors to the Fair," and he read from a memo prepared by Daley that said that the profits of the Fair would go to charity. (It later developed, of course, that there were no profits. Only deficits.)

"If you love the State of New York," cried Gallagher, "you'll support it in its Fair. Let us be good citizens of the State of New York."

A great cheer went up, and here and there, as people elbowed each other and fought for breathing space, two or three minor fights broke out. North Castle police shouldered through the sardine-packed assemblage and made threatening statements. Relative quiet prevailed.

Then O'Connor, a white gardenia in his buttonhole and his pinkish face lifted toward the ceiling, much in the manner of one of the last kings of Ireland, took over. We do not have sufficient space in this book to record even half of what O'Connor declaimed with a passion, a flow, a power and a persuasion never before heard in Armonk. Or since.

But I'd like to give you a line or two.

"Look at him sitting there," cried O'Connor, stabbing a finger in the direction of McBohin, who had slunk down behind the defense table, which, incidentally, was a folding card table that had been brought from the Hergenhan house just for the occasion.

"Look at him," thundered O'Connor. "A beaten, harried, persecuted man—hounded by the press, by the newsreels, by radio, by his neighbors, and *by the police,* merely because he expressed his Constitutional right, his God-given right, to prevent himself from becoming an unpaid sandwich man for the World's Fair.

"How can we countenance such a travesty of justice? How can we permit this monopoly, this dastardly commercial operation, this . . . ah . . . this money-grabbing maneuver [little did he know how wrong he was!] to take away this poor man's independence, his human franchise, his emancipation and his exemption from restraint?"

There was a good bit more, some of it most inflammatory yet glorious to listen to, but what with the heat, the shoving of the reporters and newsreel men, and the fact that my pencil was knocked out of my hand at least three times, I missed a lot of it.

However, I remember that O'Connor, turning to Judge Raven, spreading his hands and almost going down on one knee, cried, "We have no argument with the World's Fair and we do not say that we are against it. But if you carry this thing to its logical conclusion, what is to prevent the state from advertising the State Liquor Authority or similar subdivisions? What is to prevent the Alcoholic Beverage Control Board from printing on liquor licenses: 'Lush pills—Vitamin B. Escape the Jitters'?

"Prevent this, your honor. Prevent it and strike a blow for freedom. Preserve our inherent rights. Free this man. Find him not guilty. Let him return to his peaceful, normal way of life —free to walk among his fellow men with head held high, with no dastardly black mark on the escutcheon of his soul!"

O'Connor's plea was so impassioned that I was afraid he'd gone a step too far. I feared he might have won over the judge and that McBohin would be acquitted and then we'd have no case for the Supreme Court.

I needn't have worried, however. Judge Raven listened with his eyes half-closed and, at the last ringing O'Connor tone, he rapped his knuckles on his desk (he didn't have a gavel), and slowly intoned, "I find the defendant guilty and fine him five dollars."

Gallagher, the gallant, promptly leaped to his feet and recommended to the judge that the sentence be suspended. The judge agreed—and we didn't even have to put up the five bucks. Gallagher then congratulated Tom O'Connor on his spirited defense and Tom told Elbert he thought he'd done pretty well, too.

O'Donovan, O'Connor, McBohin and I fought our way through the crowd, drove to White Plains, and invaded the Court Grill where Bill and I bought the drinks. For nearly two hours we drank toast after toast and congratulated ourselves on losing our case.

The next day as O'Connor, with an ice pack on his head, was preparing our appeal to the Westchester County Supreme Court, where we expected to lose so we could appeal to the State Supreme Court, where we expected to lose so we could appeal to the U. S. Supreme Court—where we expected to win!—the first bombshell exploded.

A New York attorney came to see us. He said he represented a lady who claimed to be the wife of Martin McBohin—a wife whom he supposedly had deserted some years before. He wanted to serve McBohin with papers and he wanted us to give him McBohin's address. He said his client had seen McBohin in the newsreels and had positively identified him.

While we were discussing this, a second attorney appeared. He said he represented a woman in California who said that McBohin had married her some years before and had run off. He said she had identified him from pictures in the papers and from the newsreels.

And, in the next two or three days, we had other troubles. A third lady, claiming to be McBohin's wife, turned up in White Plains and got out a warrant for his arrest.

Then we received word from Immigration officials to the effect that they'd studied his pictures and felt pretty sure that he was a European who had jumped ship in New Orleans 10 years before and thus was in the country illegally.

Internal Revenue agents advised us that they had a feeling that there was a little matter of back taxes involving Mr. McBohin and could they see him, please? But, worst of all, the

American Legion came to us and told us that they had checked into McBohin's war record.

The Legion said that, just as he had claimed, there was evidence that he had, indeed, fought at Belleau Wood in World War I—but on the GERMAN side!

Well—to make a long story short, this sort of discouraged Bill and me. We called Tom O'Connor to the office and told him all about it.

"What are we going to do?" I asked him.

"I don't know what you're going to do," he replied, "but I'm going over to the Elks' Club and get drunk."

That night we gave McBohin some dough and put him on a train to nowhere. He denied all the charges, but he said he was happy to get the hell out of the whole case. He took off, and we've never heard from him since.

The appeal—our beautiful application to the United States Supreme Court—quietly died. And I've often wondered whether the Justices felt we let them down.

But the icing on the cake, as they say, came when O'Donovan and I told Walter Hogan what had happened.

"Well," he said, "you shouldn't have used McBohin in the first place! You should have used some beautiful girl!"

I must say, in all fairness, Hogan didn't dock us a week's wages, or anything like that, but he made it pretty clear in the succeeding months that he trusted our judgment less and less.

He got along with O'Donovan, but he indicated that he felt I'd been a bad influence on the city editor.

Hogan and I tangled over one thing and another. But the big whooperoo came when Tuller and Hogan decided to break with the Macy chain of newspapers. For some years there had been an agreement between the *Reporter* and the Macy chain which boiled down to this: Macy, which published papers in many other cities and towns in Westchester, would not publish in White Plains, where the *Reporter* was the only paper, if:

1, The *Reporter* continued to cover the news in White Plains, the county seat, for the Macy chain—in return for which, the chain would cover the rest of the county for the *Reporter*, and

2, The *Reporter* permitted the Macy chain to represent it insofar as the sale of national advertising was concerned.

Tuller and Hogan got the idea that the *Reporter* could do better in the sale of national advertising if it represented itself and so they told us they were breaking the deal with Macy.

Both O'Donovan and I tried to talk them out of it. We pointed out that Macy had sold a lot of national ads in deals which guaranteed publication in a White Plains paper. And, if the *Reporter* pulled out of the agreement, Macy virtually would be forced to establish a paper of its own in White Plains.

This, we argued, would be catastrophic because the Macy chain had many millions in back of it, and the *Reporter*, although prosperous, had no Fort Knox to rely on. Tuller and Hogan told us our thinking was negative, and they broke the agreement.

Within a matter of weeks the Macy chain opened a paper in White Plains called the *Dispatch*, and, in short order, ran the *Reporter* downhill to the point where it had to sell out. The current White Plains paper (which the Macy interests recently sold to the Gannett papers) is the *Reporter Dispatch*. Tuller died and Hogan now is the night city editor of the Staten Island *Advance*.

But, before this happened, things got pretty tense in the city room of the *Reporter*. Hogan, foregoing his almost daily visits to the racetrack, took personal but jittery command of the editorial operation. He made assignments, he edited copy, he dictated the size and number of pictures, and he hired and fired. It was this latter activity that plunged Hogan and me into dire conflict.

His dictum, it seemed to me, was that we best could save money and fight the rich Macy chain by firing some of the "high priced" reporters—fellows who were making $30, $35 and $40 a week—and replacing them with kids fresh out of high school who would work for anywhere from $15 to $20 a week.

I felt this was tragic, and I told him so. But one day he fired a fellow named Charlie Barnum, who was getting $37.50 a week, although he had assured me that Barnum's job was secure—and I got angry. I told Hogan just what I thought about this firing. He said nothing.

About three days later, however, Bill O'Donovan came to me, I'd never seen him so upset before, and he handed me an envelope and said, "Walter went out a little while ago and he gave me this to give to you. Gosh, Nort, I don't know how to say it—but I've never been so sorry in my life."

I opened the envelope and took out a check for a week's pay and a note of dismissal! I was through as of that moment!

I guess I'd never been so shocked. Sure, Hogan and I had had our differences, but all my sympathy, my loyalty, my greatest energy and endeavor had belonged to the White Plains *Reporter*. Whatever I'd said or done had been said and done in an attempt to save the paper from dying and being gobbled up by the Macy chain.

I felt that Hogan was certainly within his right to can me if he disagreed, but I didn't think I deserved to be brushed off with a back-of-the-hand note after the kind of work I'd put in.

So, I asked Bill when Hogan would be back and he told me that it would be sometime after 6 P.M. I waited. And when Hogan appeared about 6:30, I told him how shocked I was and I asked if he'd be willing to give me his reasons.

"Well," he said, "I'm on my way to a meeting. I haven't got time to talk about it now. But, look, nobody's been hired in your place. So I guess you could say you're not out of a job. Not yet, anyway. Why don't you come in tomorrow afternoon, and we'll talk about it?"

I said I would and I went out of the building, got into my car and drove home to Mount Kisco. It wasn't until I got home and found my mother stuffing an enormous turkey that I realized that the following day was Thanksgiving.

I said nothing about my firing that night nor did I mention it the next day. We had a delightful Thanksgiving dinner, with several guests, including my aunt and uncle, and then, after dinner, I told everybody that I had to go to White Plains to write something for the next day.

When I got to the office, I went upstairs to the city room and found myself alone with Walter Hogan. He was sitting at a typewriter in the main office, banging out critical memos to staff members, and he had his glasses pitched far forward on his nose.

He looked over them at me when I came in and then he pushed them closer to his eyes and returned to his typing. I stood there for a few moments until suddenly, with a flourish —he's a two-finger, hunt-and-peck typist—he stopped. He pulled the paper out of the machine and said, "There. That oughta hold 'em tomorrow."

I then asked him why I'd been fired, and, without motioning me to sit down, he said, "Well, you were against Tuller and me pulling out of the Macy agreement, you're always fighting for more pictures in the paper, you're trying to keep the high-priced guys on the payroll, and you wrote a lousy review of the last show the Wayside Players did."

I stared at him in amazement.

Nothing he had said made any sense to me.

"But," he went on, "none of those is the main reason. The main reason is this—"

He leaned forward, the glasses slid forward on his nose, and he fixed me with a cold stare above them.

"The main reason is, Mockridge, you're slipping—and you've been slipping for a long time!"

I couldn't believe I'd heard correctly.

"But," I said, "you asked me to come down here today, all the way from Mount Kisco to White Plains, because you said you hadn't replaced me—that the job was still open."

"Yeah," he said. "I said that. But I thought about it later. I tell you, Mockridge, you're slipping. I don't want any guy on my staff who's slipping. You're through!"

Well, as I told you before, I resisted the urge to punch him through the window and merely gave him what-for, verbally.

But as I walked out of the building for the last time, I looked back and, I think, I had tears in my eyes.

I was slipping. I was out of a job. I was a has-been.

And I was only twenty-five years old!

Epilogue

I T'S funny how you look at situations differently after a bit
of time has passed.

On that Thanksgiving Day in 1940 I could have killed Walter
V. Hogan and written if off as justifiable homicide. But today,
looking back on that black holiday, I'm filled with gratitude. I
could kiss Hogan on top of his fuzzy bald head and thank him
for what he did for me. I have nothing but the fondest feeling

for him and, in fact, we often have friendly chats on the phone.

I feel that if Hogan hadn't fired me—no matter how nutty I considered his reasoning—I might still be in White Plains, working for a helluva lot less than I make now and hating myself and the world because of it.

You see, soon after I was canned by Hogan, Bo McAnney, city editor of the New York *World-Telegram*, hired me as a reporter and I spent twenty-six happy years there during which time I served as a feature writer, rewrite man, drama and film critic, departmental editor, Saturday editor and finally, for nearly eight years, as city editor. I was fortunate enough to preside over a staff that won 70 major awards, including a Pulitzer Prize, for journalistic excellence and outstanding achievement.

Four years ago, I resigned as city editor and did something I'd wanted to do for a long time—write a daily column about the funny, interesting, crazy and exciting things that happen to people in ordinary, everyday life. Fortunately, the then-editor of the *World-Telegram*, Richard D. Peters, encouraged me and started publishing the column every day in the *Telly*.

I had the support, too, of Jack R. Howard, president of the Scripps-Howard Newspapers, who, from his lofty perch, even went so far as to provide me with some items in the early days of the column. (He seldom gives me any nowadays, probably because I refused to pay him space rates!) But anyway, the column caught on, I'm happy to say, and it appeared in the *Telly*'s successor, the New York *World Journal Tribune,* and now is syndicated by United Feature Syndicate to 65 other newspapers all over the country.

In the intervening years, I've written six books, two in collaboration with my buddy, Robert H. Prall, and more than a hundred magazine articles. I lecture under the auspices of the Keedick Lecture Bureau. I've had my own radio shows, the most noteworthy of which was on WCBS in New York for a year. And currently it's possible to hear me every weekend on 280 stations from coast to coast on the CBS network's "Weekend Dimension" series.

I'm happy with what's happened, and I think I owe it all to Walter Hogan.

I'd never have got anywhere, if he hadn't noticed I was slipping!

Index

324